The Unbeaten Lions

The Unbeaten Lions

THE 1974 BRITISH ISLES RUGBY UNION TOUR OF SOUTH AFRICA

By

John Reason

RUGBY BOOKS, LONDON

First published in Great Britain by
Rugby Books
56 Lonsdale Road
London, S.W. 13.9JS

Printed in the United Kingdom by
W. & G. Baird, Ltd., Antrim

October 1974

ISB No. 0 903194 02 3

Contents

to William

Proceeds of this book will be given to

The Leukaemia Research Fund
61 Great Ormond Street
London, W.C.1

Illustrations

Illustrations appear between pages
74–75 and 170–171.

CHAPTER 1

'There will be a Lot of Kicking'

SYD MILLAR, the coach of the British Lions team to tour South Africa in 1974, had his attitude to the tour conditioned by his experience in that country as a player. He had toured South Africa as a Lion in 1962 and 1968 and he had toured New Zealand as a Lion in 1959. The Lions teams in 1962 and 1968 were not so well endowed with playing talent as the one in 1959 but the bumps and bruises from South Africa and his own physical contact with the game in the front row were still fresh in Millar's memory and they shaped his thinking.

Talking about the 1974 tour a month before the team was picked, he said, 'Winning a series in South Africa is much more difficult than winning a series in New Zealand. The All Blacks beat us 2-1 in New Zealand in 1959, with another match drawn, but only because we scored four tries to nil in one match and lost it when Don Clarke kicked six penalty goals.

'We have never come as close as that in my experience in South Africa, and I played there with the Irish team on a short tour in 1961 as well.

'The point is that the conditions are so different. In New Zealand, the conditions are the same. The grounds are the same. The grass is the same. The mud is the same. The wind is the same. The rain is the same. The matches are all played at sea level. A New Zealand winter is like a mild winter in Britain.

'Once you become used to the time change, you might just as well be playing in Britain. The ball does the same things. It bounces the same way. It kicks the same. It passes the same. Tackles feel the same.

'But not in South Africa. The whole set-up is different. The sun shines. The grounds are hard. The grass is different; it's more wiry. The air is thinner and drier. The ball travels farther and faster. It behaves differently. It bounces more. It does not sit still for the ruck. And just as the grounds are harder, the games are harder from the point of view of injuries and recovery time. A team tends to have more major injuries in South Africa and there are more skin abrasions. Tacklers hit you harder because they can get a more secure foothold and so drive in harder. Line kicking is different. Place kicking is different. Tactical kicking is different. The ball moves in the air differently when one man goes to pass it to another. The hand ruck becomes more important than the ground ruck. And of course, there is the over-riding problem of altitude. It's a different game.

'I agree that provincial Rugby in New Zealand must now be of a higher standard than it is in South Africa, but this only serves to emphasise the difference between a test match and the rest of the tour. In New Zealand, in a way, they condition you for the tests by knocking seven bells out of you in the provinces. The atmosphere of a test still surprises you, but it does not take your breath away as it does in South Africa. The All Blacks found in 1970 that winning your provincial matches by a street does not provide a good conditioning for test matches.

'The test series and the provincial tour have to be treated as two entirely separate and different matters. The sort of football you have to play in the tests will probably be entirely different from the sort of football you play against the provinces.

'I have always had a great respect for South African Rugby. They base their thinking on sound principles. They know what they want from their players—or they did when I played them—and they pick men to do a specific job. They bank on experience, no matter how far back they have to go to get it, and they have been proved right. They work on the principle that once a player has established himself as a Springbok of genuine test class, then he will have that ability long after most people are prepared to write him off.

'Look what they did in 1970, when they brought in Lofty Nel and the others against the All Blacks. And they were right. There is no substitute for experience.

'I remember trying to tell other players this after my first tour. I told them that Wales versus England at Cardiff Arms Park was one thing, but a test series in South Africa and New Zealand was far harder. Maybe it is because test series do not occur so frequently, and so Springboks and All Blacks gear themselves up that much higher. But the pressures of a test series are far more intense than the international championship in Europe.

'In this respect, the Lions are fortunate. We now have a very strong nucleus of players who have had experience of playing in one, two or sometimes three test series, and so they know what it is all about. Mike Gibson played in New Zealand in 1966. Some more played in South Africa in 1968. A lot of them played in New Zealand in 1971. This gives us something of an advantage to offset all the other local advantages enjoyed by the home team. To that extent, the situation has changed.

'When I played in South Africa in 1962, the Springboks still had 80 per cent. of the team that toured Britain the previous year. The result was that they were much more of a team than we were. Again, when I played in South Africa in 1968, they still had the nucleus of the side that had been built up through the mid-'sixties, the last one to play in New Zealand. So they were still in that process of evolution which used to give them such an enormous advantage over us. They stayed together as a team, home and away. The Lions played for three months as a team, and then went back home and for the next three or four years, they played as England, Scotland, Ireland and Wales. We had no continuity at all.

'Now the Springboks have lost that continuity, and it must be giving them cause for concern. They may think that they know where their playing strength is, but they cannot be absolutely sure, because it has not been sorted out on tour. Consequently, they will probably have to do far more adjusting in the course of the series than they would like. As I said, there is no substitute for experience at test match level, and I have no doubt that the Springboks will pull together all the experience they can muster, but obviously, this is now a problem for them and it is becoming progressively more difficult. They have not played a major series for four years. A lot of water has gone under the bridge since then.

'In that time, they have been beaten by England. By all accounts, they were at sixes and sevens in that match. I am not surprised. Their continuity has been disturbed. Ours hasn't. That match cannot have helped their self-confidence. They will also have seen what the Lions did in New Zealand and what England did there last season. They will know that they are in for a hard series. They may even suspect that we are now better than they are. But that won't stop them playing their guts out for South Africa.

'Of course, this game is very much one of organisation now. We have come a long way in Europe in the last eight years. I think Avril Malan and the side he coached were the first ones to feel the improvement when they toured Britain in 1969-70—and that was only our beginning. I think we understand organisation now. And I know we understand forward play.

'This used to be the greatest single advantage that the All Blacks and the Springboks had over us. We could produce great individual backs, but we could never match their forward play. As soon as we did—in New Zealand in 1971—we beat them. England had showed that it is possible for the Lions to beat the Springboks in 1974. We have got some players who know what it feels like to win in New Zealand and in South Africa. That must help.'

At the end of the Lions tour of South Africa in 1968, Millar had said that he did not feel that the pressure from the Springbok pack of 1968 was as great as the pressure exerted by the Springboks in 1961 and 1962 but that he felt that it was still strong enough to be the essence of their game. Paul Roos had sent a telegram to the 1937 Springboks in New Zealand which simply said, 'Skrum, skrum, skrum.' It summed up, as nothing has before or since, the whole of South Africa's philosophy about Rugby football, even down to the domination of the game by the Afrikaaner forwards and hence the use of the letter 'k' in the word 'skrum.'

Even before he was appointed coach of the 1974 Lions, Syd Millar had adopted the same approach. 'I admit that my attitude to the game is the same as the Springboks. They have always based their philosophy on the importance of the scrum. That is what I feel about the game, too. Maybe it is because I was a prop . . . But I know that you cannot play Rugby unless you have a competitive scrum.

'I remember preaching this at my club back in the mid-'sixties. I told them that it meant a lot of hard work, but that it would be repaid. It was. We paralysed everybody for nearly three years. The point is that if you have a competitive scrum, all things are possible. Your half-backs can play. Your loose forwards can play. Your backs can play. Your wingers can run. You can do your miss moves and your scissors and the rest. All because you are going forward.

'Equally, if you are going forward, the opposition has to be going backwards. So their half-backs are under pressure. Their loose forwards can do nothing. Their backs are busy clearing up the mess. All they can do is defend. They are depressed psychologically, too.

'This is where the All Blacks went wrong after that French tour of New Zealand in the early 'sixties. All the New Zealand forwards wanted to run with the ball. No one wanted to work. Scrummage technique went out of the window. For a time, they got by on sheer bulk, sheer physique, and in 1967, they were tremendous. They had a great coach in Fred Allen at that time, and they were at their peak.

'By the time they went to South Africa in 1970, they had gone off the boil a bit, and they did not understand the difference between test Rugby and provincial Rugby in South Africa. But even worse than that, they had no scrummage technique coming through from below back home, so when the Lions went there in 1971, with some very good scrummagers indeed, the New Zealand forwards were destroyed in the scrums at both provincial and test level. The Springboks won't make that mistake. Neither shall we. We shall go to South Africa with the two most competitive scrummages we can select. We shall have big flankers, too. On every tour I've been on, we ended up putting locks in the back row, either on the flank or at number eight.

'Unfortunately, the lineout is a different matter. The changes in the law have not worked. It just is not natural for a player to stand still after the ball has been thrown. It is against all his instincts. His natural movement is towards the ball. This is an area where there may be changes in the law, to tighten things up, or where there may be differences in interpretation by referees. At the moment, scrum-halves are in a very difficult situation. They cannot be protected and they are entitled to protection. Bad as the old lineout was, at least it tied up the forwards in a private battle for a few seconds and let the backs have some of the play. We saw our best Rugby then. There is not so much movement in Rugby now. The field is too cluttered with players. There is more kicking. There is not as much innovation among the backs.

'I am sorry that this has happened. I think that the game has lost a lot. The changes in the lineout laws were well-intentioned, but they have not worked because they have not succeeded in their first object, which was to reintroduce two-handed catching without all the illegalities in the lineout. Forwards are not being made to stand still and so catchers do not have the time they need and they are not free of interference. Still, this is a fact of life, and we shall have to adjust to things as we find them in South Africa. We shall also have to prepare ourselves for injuries and to make ourselves as flexible as possible.

'In 1962, we lost Richard Sharp with a broken jaw. In 1968, we lost Barry John with a broken collarbone. In 1970, the All Blacks lost Colin Meads with a broken arm. They are all key players. The Lions in 1971 were fortunate. Their only serious injuries were to two props, and fortunately their reserve strength in that area was sufficient to cover them and win the series.

'We now have more depth than ever before, in all positions, and I am absolutely sure that we shall need it. On every tour I have been on, injuries forced us into the situation at some stage where we had to play players out of position. This is part of what I mean when I say that a tour of South Africa is physically so hard. It is the most difficult place in the world to win a test series.'

Until the year 1970, there is no doubt that Millar's assessment would have been an accurate appreciation of the difficulties facing a touring team in South Africa. However, as he said himself, a lot of water had gone under the bridge since then. South Africa had lost their continuity of team-building, most of their leading players had retired and England had toured South Africa and had won convincingly. In a little over three weeks, England had played a third of a Lions' tour, with matches against leading provinces like Natal, Western Province and Northern Transvaal, as well as a test against South Africa at Ellis Park. England had completed their tour unbeaten, and had won with something to spare against the Springboks at Ellis Park.

Dr. Danie Craven, the president of the South African Rugby Board, said dolefully, 'This is the first time that a British team has beaten us in our own country this century, and naturally we are sad.'

The shock to South Africa's Rugby pride was increased by the knowledge that in the international season before they toured South Africa, England had lost all their matches. However, even though they were hurt and bewildered, it never seemed to occur to South Africans that England's tour might have revealed the true state of the game in the republic. They preferred to think that it was 'just one of those things' that could never happen again.

There were people in South Africa who did not think that England's success was 'just one of those things.' People like Avril Malan, who coached the Springbok team which toured Britain in 1969-70, and Tommy Bedford, who had been one of the senior players on that tour. They had seen enough then to convince them that British Rugby was organising itself in such a way that it would soon stride far ahead of South Africa, and they had said so, but no one in South Africa wanted to listen to Avril Malan and Tommy Bedford.

They preferred to think that Syd Millar's assessment of their Rugby was still the reality and that the task facing the Lions was as hard as he anticipated it would be. They would have done better to take notice of what he had said about the way the 1974 British Lions would play the game. His statement of objects could not have been clearer. As an exposition, it was just as precise as that telegram from Paul Roos to the 1937 Springboks. 'Skrum, skrum, skrum.'

Millar did add one rather defensive qualification.

'There will be a lot of kicking,' he said.

CHAPTER 2

The Management

THE manager and the coach of the 1974 Lions had been appointed by the committee of the Four Home Unions the previous summer in circumstances which were somewhat unusual.

Normally, the committee asks for nominations for the posts of manager and assistant manager from each of the Four Home Unions and then it meets at the East India and Sports Club in James' Square to interview the candidates and to make the appointments. In days gone by, these appointments were made only a few weeks before the beginning of the tour, but in 1968 the Four Home Unions established the successful precedent of appointing the manager and his assistant the previous summer so that they could have the whole of a home season to work with their selection committee in choosing the team. They did the same thing for the subsequent tour of New Zealand.

This was a distinct advance, but by 1971 it was apparent that the procedure was invidious in that the various candidates had to approach their employers for permission to take time off for the tour even though they were far from certain of being appointed. It was felt, quite rightly, that it was unfair to ask men established in business or in a profession to make an approach of this sort to their employers, particularly as after the appointments had been made, all except two of the candidates then had to go back to their employers and say, 'Sorry, they don't want me after all.'

The obvious solution was to make the appointments by invitation, and it was surprising that this method was not adopted, because the 1972-3 season of the Four Home Unions was eminently suited to the task of assessing managerial candidates.

In that season, the New Zealand All Blacks toured Britain and France and so all the domestic teams were making a maximum effort to produce their best combinations of players and their most effective selections as coaches. All the candidates with any pretensions to the job of coaching the 1974 British Lions were heavily engaged in coaching teams to play the All Blacks, both at provincial and at national level, and their success or their failure was there for all to see.

Carwyn James, for instance, the brilliantly successful coach of the 1971 Lions team in New Zealand, thought that the experience gained by John Elders on England's unbeaten tour of South Africa in 1972 ought to qualify him as the logical choice as coach. He also thought that Alec Lewis, who had managed England on the same tour, ought to be one of the candidates as manager. John Elders, however, decided not to accept nomination as a candidate, and Alec Lewis made the same decision.

Apart from Carwyn James himself, the two most obviously successful coaches of the British teams which played the 1972-73 All Blacks were John Burgess and Jim Greenwood. Burgess coached the North West Counties team which won so well at Workington and Greenwood coached the Midland Counties team which beat the All Blacks at Moseley. Burgess had coached the England team on its tour of Japan and the Far East in 1971 and Greenwood, apart from specialising in physical education at Loughborough Colleges, had toured South Africa as a member of the British Lions team in 1955.

Traditionally, the Four Home Unions have always liked to make these appointments in secret rather like MI5, but even if the committee itself is not prepared to admit it, the candidates themselves know that secrecy is no longer possible, and some of them are not prepared to expose themselves to the embarrassment of failure. In the nature of things, it follows that some of the best candidates are lost because of this. There is no doubt that some of the best candidates for the 1974 tour *were* lost.

The task was not made easier by the fact that the individual Unions were so haphazard about making nominations at all that until the very last moment, only Wales had even bothered to submit any candidates for the post of manager. This caused more embarrassment and one can only admire the good nature of the two English nominees who allowed their names to go forward in what they must have known was a hopeless cause. They were Vic Roberts and Bill Patterson. It put them in a difficult position, and it ought to have ensured that nothing like it ever happens again.

Another weakness of the system is that the individual Home Unions do not all appear to attach the same importance to the task of selecting managerial candidates. The Welsh Rugby Union, for instance, seem to do far more homework than anybody else. As in 1971, their list of candidates was better prepared than those from the other countries.

Wales put up two nominations for the post of manager of the 1974 Lions, Alun Thomas and Handel Rogers. They put up one nomination for the post of coach, Clive Rowlands. All three had valid qualifications.

Alun Thomas had toured South Africa in 1955 as a British

Lion and he had been assistant manager of the Welsh team on their tour of South Africa in 1964. Handel Rogers had managed the Welsh team in New Zealand in 1969 and had been actively involved in liaison work with touring sides in Britain for years. Clive Rowlands was coach of a Welsh team which had been one of the most successful in history and which had provided the basis for the winning Lions team in New Zealand in 1971.

Rowlands had easily the best record of the four coaches nominated, but he was engagingly pessimistic about his chances of being appointed. 'I've too many enemies,' he said cheerfully. Whatever the truth of that, his prospects were not improved by the almost total shortage of candidates nominated for the position of manager by England, Scotland and Ireland. The Four Home Unions have not yet appointed a Lions manager and coach of the same nationality and although it is unfair, it is nevertheless true that a coach's chance of being appointed to a Lions team is directly related to the quality of the nominations for the position of manager from the other three countries. On that basis alone, Rowlands' chances were minimal, because Alun Thomas and Handel Rogers were the best qualified of the four candidates nominated as manager.

The committee of the Four Home Unions met at the East India and Sports Club in June, 1973, and admitted rather guardedly that it had, 'interviewed some candidates.'

Normally, the committee interviews the candidates over two days at the weekend and announces the appointments early the following week, but on this occasion, Albert Agar, the secretary of the Four Home Unions, caused something of a surprise by saying that he did not expect the appointments to be announced until the following month.

Inevitably, it was concluded that the committee was disappointed by its choice of candidates and that it proposed to explore the possibilities of going outside the official list of nominations and making at least one of the appointments by invitation.

It was believed that the post which was causing most concern was that of coach. If Alun Thomas was to manage the side—and his chief rival, Handel Rogers, was certain that Thomas would be chosen—then Clive Rowlands was eliminated as a possibility as coach simply because he was a Welshman. That left Bill Dickinson, the coach of Scotland, and Syd Millar and Roly Meates of Ireland. Millar had just completed his first season as coach of the Irish national team. It was argued, quite wrongly and quite unfairly, that Bill Dickinson was too old to coach a Lions team on tour and it was felt that both the Irish coaches were short of representative experience.

The theory that the coaching appointment was the one which was giving the Four Home Unions most difficulty gained substance when it was discovered that the committee had approached John Burgess and asked him if he would like to do the job. Burgess is not a man who believes in playing hard to get when he really wants to do something. 'I would give my right arm to do it,' he said, 'but I just can't get the time off.'

John Tallent and the rest of the Four Home Unions committee digested this and eventually came back and asked if Burgess would mind if they approached his chairman. 'Not at all,' he said. 'I would love to coach the Lions, but at the same time, I can see my chairman's point of view.'

A delegation from the committee then spoke to Burgess' chairman, but apparently, the answer was still the same and so the Four Home Unions accepted that it would not be possible to add the name of John Burgess to their list of candidates for the post of assistant manager and coach. It is hard to believe that Burgess would not have been appointed if his firm had been able to agree to release him. The pity of it was that the two management appointments had not been filled by invitation in the first place.

As it was, the Four Home Unions announced in the middle of July, 1973, that the manager of the 1974 British Lions would be Alun Thomas, and that the assistant manager and coach would be Syd Millar.

Alun Thomas had won 13 caps for Wales as a centre, wing and outside-half between 1952 and 1955, when he had toured South Africa as a British Lion. It was his misfortune that his tour as a player was interrupted by an attack of jaundice.

Syd Millar had won 37 caps for Ireland as a prop between 1958 and 1970. He had toured New Zealand with the British Lions in 1959 and had toured South Africa with the Lions in 1962 and 1968.

It was argued at the time that it took a good deal of courage for anyone to allow his name to go forward as a candidate for the management of the 1974 tour, because Dr. Doug Smith and Carwyn James, the manager and coach of the 1971 Lions team in New Zealand, had made such an outstanding success of their respective jobs that comparisons were almost bound to be odious. When Syd Millar said that winning a series in South Africa was harder than winning a series in New Zealand, he could not have been further from the truth, but he was taking out a sensible insurance policy.

CHAPTER 3

Team Selection

THE committee of the Four Home Unions did adopt a new procedure in choosing the selectors who would work with Alun Thomas and Syd Millar before picking the Lions team. Each of the four home countries was asked to submit two nominations as selectors and the committee then chose one. This was done so that the selection committee could ensure that it would achieve the right balance of playing interests and avoid the situation where it might contain three scrum-halves and one hooker. This injection of equity was nicely illustrated by the Welsh nominations. The two names submitted by Wales were Cliff Jones and Clive Rowlands, but even though Cliff Jones was much the senior of the two, with experience of the game stretching back to before the war, Rowlands was chosen as the selector because it was decided that his particular positional interest at scrum-half would be of most value to the selection committee.

Syd Millar, the Lions' coach, never made any secret of the fact that he thought the selection of the team should start with the scrummage, and there is not much doubt, either, that he anticipated that Ireland's tight forwards would prove themselves to be strong enough to be the basis of the Lions' scrum. Millar's estimates were given support by Dr. Doug Smith, who had managed the Lions' team in New Zealand in 1971. Doug Smith recommended that Ireland's Bill McBride should be captain of the 1974 British Lions in South Africa.

The captains of the four home countries in the 1973-74 season preceding the Lions tour were Ian McLauchlan of Scotland, Gareth Edwards of Wales, John Pullin of England and Bill McBride of Ireland. All had been British Lions in New Zealand in 1971.

Since that time, John Pullin had captained England to victory in South Africa and at the beginning of the 1973-74 season, he captained England when they beat the All Blacks at Auckland on their short tour of Fiji and New Zealand. It was an impressive record, but even then, it was apparent that Rugby in the southern hemisphere was in decline and Pullin knew better than anyone that England would have to make a good showing in the international championship at home before they would be accepted as a good team.

Not that Pullin thought that he would be asked to captain the 1974 Lions. In common with the majority of the Lions from the 1971 team, he thought that Mike Gibson should be captain of the team in South Africa in 1974, particularly as Syd Millar had already been appointed as coach. Gibson was easily the most senior of the backs, and as the most obvious midfield general, he was the player best qualified to provide the necessary balance with the forwards by giving the backs a powerful voice in the discussion of selection and of playing approach. Pullin did not share Doug Smith's view that the captaincy "would destroy" Gibson, and he did not share the assumption that Gibson would necessarily still be available for the tour if he was not captain. Neither did a lot of other people.

Paradoxically, there is not much doubt that Gibson's chances of being appointed captain would have been much stronger if the Lions' coach had been either an Englishman, a Scotsman or a Welshman. His skills have always been appreciated more outside his own country than within it, and it is significant that they did not really come to fruition until 1971 when he went on tour in New Zealand with a coach and a captain who were both Welshmen and both midfield backs. Indeed, it is not difficult to detect something of an anti-Gibson feeling at that level of Irish rugby where team-policy decisions are made. Tony O'Reilly once laughed off persistent local denigration of his own extraordinary ability by saying that Dublin is "the back-biting capital of the world", but it is sad that his own country has not afforded Gibson more opportunity of expressing his talent.

By then, it was not difficult to see that the Lions were well on the way to appointing Bill McBride as captain, even though he was rising 34. He and Syd Millar belonged to the same club and the Lions' coach had already indicated that the style of football which Ballymena played was the one he wanted the British Lions to adopt in South Africa.

McBride himself had told Alun Thomas that he would not wish to be considered for the tour if he felt that the international championship showed that he was not worth his place in the Lions' test team. He had already made four Lions' tours; to South Africa in 1962 and 1968, and to New Zealand in 1966 and 1971.

All this seemed to indicate that even though Syd Millar put a high premium on test experience, the selection of the 1974 British Lions team might not turn out to be quite as straightforward as expected, considering that 19 players of the successful 1971 team were still playing international Rugby or were still being considered for it. These suspicions proved to be well-founded, but it still came as a considerable shock when only eight of the 1971 Lions survived to be chosen for the 1974 tour.

Those who fell by the wayside were Gerald Davies, David Duckham, Mike Gibson, Alastair Biggar, John Pullin, Derek Quinnell, Delme Thomas, "Stack" Stevens, Ray McLoughlin, Sean Lynch and Peter Dixon. Some were not available, one or two may not have been considered and the others were dropped. All would have been first choice for the Springboks if they had been born South Africans.

Some of the matches played in the international championship had far more influence on the selection of the team than they should have done when you bear in mind that the Lions were starting with the enormous advantage of a winning team built in New Zealand in 1971. From a platform as secure as that, the 1974 selection ought to have been simply a question of filling in a gap here and there, but it did not work out like that at all. Not only was the style of play developed by the 1971 Lions abandoned completely, but even the selection went back a long way towards the age-old British hotch-potch of a hand to mouth exercise.

Perhaps the most significant result of the season, and the one which had most bearing on the eventual selection of the Lions team, occurred in the game between Scotland and England at Murrayfield. The England forwards, having their first game since beating New Zealand, recovered from a sluggish start to dominate the second half so completely that the Scottish forwards wondered if they were ever going to win another ball. In that time, England made up the deficit of nine points they had conceded at the beginning of the match and their forwards won enough possession to have put the issue beyond doubt.

Admittedly, England made such poor use of the ball that they only established a slender lead, but their forwards were so much in command that their backs had only to avoid mistakes in the last five minutes to win. That seemed a simple enough condition at the time but England had shown themselves prone to miss similar opportunities for many years and they did so again.

The first and most crucial mistake came when fly-half Alan Old missed touch after his forwards had won the ball from three mauls in succession. At that stage, the referee had already looked at his watch three times and there is not much doubt that he would have ended the match as soon as the ball had gone into touch. Even if he had not done so, England would still have had every justification to feel sanguine because they had dominated the lineout as completely as their back row had dominated the loose.

However, Old missed touch and Drew Gill, the Scottish right wing, put up a high kick. The Scottish forwards fell on it in desperation and won the maul and as the ball came out to the right, David Duckham was caught offside on the England left wing. It was a ghastly aberration on Duckham's part which contributed considerably to the depression he felt toward the end of the season because it gave Andy Irvine, the young Scottish full-back, the chance to kick a very difficult penalty goal from 45 yards to win the match. Irvine duly kicked the goal and won the match for Scotland. This deprived England of at least a share of the international championship and almost certainly cost John Pullin the chance of making his third Lions' tour.

The other crucial game in the championship was the one in which Ireland beat Scotland 9-6 at the end of the season. Ireland scored a try between the posts from a lineout throw by Ken Kennedy which was so crooked as the ball slipped out of his hands that neither side could believe it when the referee allowed play to continue.

More than that, the Irish forwards, who were the basis of Syd Millar's pre-season estimates of the Lions' scrummage, were comprehensively outplayed by Scotland. They were pushed off their own ball five times and left in a complete wreck on three occasions by a Scottish pack which supposedly contained a lock who was a doubtful quantity as a scrummager. The lock in question was Alastair McHarg who not only did all that was asked of him in the tight, but also helped Gordon Brown to win the lineouts by one of the biggest margins in the championship season. McHarg was a king that day and he went on to reign supreme in Scotland's match against France as well. He seemed to be involved in everything that was going on from start to finish.

Apart from the six points they scored from the crooked lineout throw, Ireland owed their victory over Scotland as much to Mike Gibson as anyone. He played so superbly that he seemed to have his finger stuck in every hole in the dyke. Ian McLauchlan, Scotland's captain, shook his head ruefully afterwards and said, "For most of the second half, it was fifteen of us versus Mike Gibson, and he won.'

Ironically, Gibson's success in saving the game against Scotland ended whatever faint hopes he may have had of captaining the Lions in South Africa because it gave Ireland the chance of finishing at the top of the championship instead of at the bottom. That in turn meant that the Lions' selectors could follow Doug Smith's recommendation and appoint Bill McBride as captain.

What made the situation even more ironic was the fact that Gibson himself was unlikely to be available for the tour as a player. He was the senior partner in a firm of solicitors and his wife was expecting their second child. Had he been offered the honour of the Lions' captaincy, there is not much doubt that he would have felt persuaded to set these things aside but he had already made three Lions tours as a player and obviously had to consider his family priorities.

It is possible that Gibson was also influenced to some extent by the feelings of Gerald Davies and David Duckham, both of whom had doubts about whether they would be available to tour. The Lions' backs in New Zealand in 1971 became a close-knit group of players with similar interests and a profound respect for each other's extraordinary ability. It was the sort of exclusive club born of pride of performance to which All Black forwards used to belong. When they returned from New Zealand, it was noticeable that the 1971 Lions' backs tended to act as one. If they were asked to play in a special game, they agreed among themselves beforehand whether they would be available. If one played, they all played. They inspired each other on the field, too. Their clubs noticed that they never produced a workaday performance in each other's company. Those performances only seemed to occur in the company of lesser mortals.

This identity of interests might have been used to ensure their presence on the 1974 tour. With five of the 1971 test backs still playing at the peak of their powers, it was obviously important that Mike Gibson, Gerald Davies and David Duckham should join Gareth Edwards and J. P. R. Williams on tour in South Africa if the 1974 Lions were to reach the unparalleled peaks of playing performance of which British Rugby had shown itself capable when the Barbarians crushed the All Blacks at Cardiff Arms Park in 1973.

Whether Syd Millar's ambitions ever ran as high as that is another matter. Back play of that order and at that level is supremely ambitious and Millar had already said that he doubted whether it would be possible in South Africa. He preferred to rely on the game he had helped to develop at Ballymena, a game which was based on scrummaging and kicking and on keeping the ball in front of the forwards.

That style of play would have held no appeal for Gerald Davies. Certainly, it would not have tempted him to reorganise his professional and family life to make the tour. He was a thoroughbred who was not in the least bit interested in anything mundane. He responded best to the grandest of visions.

It is interesting to speculate what would have happened if Mike Gibson had been made captain of the British Lions on the understanding that his first priority was to make sure that Gerald Davies and David Duckham made themselves available for the tour. Gibson is a persuasive fellow and he might well have convinced both the players and their wives and their employers that this one last sacrifice was one which was well worth making. Probably Gerald Davies would have turned out to be more susceptible to persuasion, but in the end, he decided that as he was changing jobs, he could not ask his employers to grant him three months' leave just as he was on the point of going to work somewhere else.

David Duckham had no difficulty in that respect. He had just changed his job but his employers were quite prepared to give him leave. His problem was chiefly that he felt himself to be 'saturated with Rugby.' This was always the danger after the Rugby Union had cancelled their tour of the Argentine the previous year and had replaced it with a tour of Fiji and New Zealand. A semi-social tour of Buenos Aires with a few hours of time-change was one thing; a high-pressure tour of a country like New Zealand was something entirely different. To start with, the time change in New Zealand is a total reversal between day and night and the physical exhaustion of getting there and back is only matched by the stridency and the competitiveness of the standard of play in the country itself.

Duckham had every justification for feeling jaded, but it is significant that he has never played in South Africa since the Barbarians' tour of that country in 1969. He had such a bad time when he played centre-threequarter in a match at Port Elizabeth at the beginning of that tour that he has never forgotten it. It is as if the experience has created a mental block about South Africa for him Duckham did not make himself available for England's tour of South Africa in 1972, either.

Whatever the truth of the matter, the fact is that one after another, David Duckham, Gerald Davies and Mike Gibson announced that they would not be available for the 1974 British Lions tour of South Africa, and the vision of what they could have achieved departed with them. Gibson was the last to withdraw from consideration. By then, he knew that the selectors proposed to ignore the difficulties experienced by the Irish tight forwards in the second half of the championship and make McBride captain.

Some of the forwards had nearly as much difficulty as the backs in making themselves available for the tour. For months, it seemed as if Gordon Brown would not be able to arrange leave and Sandy Carmichael was equally doubtful.

The movements and committments of Ray McLoughlin, the Irish prop, were as diverse and as far-reaching as his interests, as he seemed well on the way to becoming another tycoon like Tony O'Reilly, it was obviously doubtful whether he would be able to take three months out of his crowded schedule. 'Stack' Stevens, the England loose-head prop and an almost equally accomplished forward, was negotiating to add more land to his farm and if the negotiations proved successful, he felt that he would be unable to leave his father to do the work. The value of McLoughlin and Stevens, apart from their technical excellence as props, was that they were both loose heads who could play equally effectively on the other side of the scrum. In the end, both decided that they could not spare the time to make the tour, which opened he way for Mike Burton.

Gordon Brown, meanwhile, was still stuck on the cliff-face but he showed no signs of coming down without a struggle and eventually his persistence was rewarded. With the clock about to strike the witching hour, his firm agreed to release him and Sandy Carmichael's employers did the same.

The last act of the selection drama occurred on the day before the Lions team was chosen. That was the day that England played Wales at Twickenham, and beat them for the first time in 14 years.

John Pullin went into that game knowing that the Lions' selectors had no thought of making either him or Ian McLauchlan captain, as many people thought they should, but he must have had every expectation of being chosen as one of the Lions' hookers. After all, he was the most experienced test hooker then playing Rugby in the world and he had been a most successful captain of England.

England won the match, and Pullin took the most important strike against the head in the game, but the England forwards kicked a couple of balls into the Welsh scrum and they also lost another ball when the referee first gave the scrum to Wales and then changed his mind and gave it to England. Pullin bound into the scrum, expecting the ball to be put in from his right, and had no idea that the referee had changed his decision and that the England scrum-half Jan Webster was about to put the ball in on the left. Webster also failed to pass on the message as clearly as he should have done, so that Pullin suddenly found the ball coming in from the left when he was bound into the scrum and his feet were positioned to challenge for it from the right. Bobby Windsor took the ball against the head and with the two balls kicked through, Wales were able to take the ball against the head 5-3.

Even then, few people imagined that Pullin would be left out of the Lions' team. Syd Millar himself had expounded the value of test experience and no hooker had a greater stock of that than Pullin. Not that anyone expected Windsor to be left out, either. He seemed the obvious choice to go on tour as support hooker for Pullin, unless the selectors were prepared to recognise the precocious ability that the England reserve hooker Peter Wheeler had shown in the previous season.

When the team came to be announced the following week, however, Pullin was not in it. Many of the selections and the omissions created a surprise, but none created a bigger surprise than that. The hookers chosen were Windsor and Ken Kennedy, who had last hooked for the Lions in 1966. The only thing they seemed to have in common was that both were hookers who could throw the ball in from touch, whereas Pullin never made any secret of the fact that he disliked the chore. Otherwise, Windsor was principally a scrummager and a tight player, and Kennedy was principally a striker and a loose player. They had almost nothing in common as Rugby players, and neither could approach Pullin's experience of test Rugby.

Pullin was not the only forward with valuable experience of test Rugby who was left out of the touring party. Derek Quinnell and Peter Dixon were other key forwards who had played in the tests in New Zealand in 1971 and who had played well. It is hard to imagine the Springboks or the All Blacks ever dropping players like those. The All Blacks, indeed, would have regarded the omission of Quinnell as sheer lunacy, because they thought he was the best forward in the world after their tour of Britain and France the previous year. Of all the forwards in the British Isles, Quinnell had shown himself capable of raising his game to a level of competitiveness unmatched anywhere. It is true that with the domestic upset of changing jobs, he had not achieved the peak of fitness necessary to produce his best form in the international championship, but fitness was never going to be a problem in South Africa and Quinnell was of an age and of a character to respond to the challenge. In any case, once a young man has climbed Everest, you ought to know his ability. As Syd Millar said, the Springboks of former times always did so well because, 'they bank on experience, no matter how far back they have to go to get it, and they have been proved right.'

The same arguments applied to Peter Dixon. He was one of the most intelligent forwards in the British game, with exactly the physical presence that Syd Millar said the Lions were looking for on the flank, and the greatest strength of his play was his technique in the maul. This had been established long since as the most important asset for any loose forward in South Africa.

What made the omission of Quinnell and Dixon even harder to understand was that Stewart McKinney and Tony Neary were preferred to them. Both were far from being the 'big flankers' that Syd Millar regarded as being essential to the exercise, and neither had played test Rugby for the Lions. McKinney had not even been a regular member of the Irish team. Neary had made out a strong case for inclusion because he had played in the England teams which beat South Africa and New Zealand at Ellis Park and Auckland, but even his selection was hard to justify at the expense of Quinnell and Dixon.

If the form displayed in the international championship was to be the criterion, then one of the first choices among the locks ought to have been Alastair McHarg. He showed better form than Gordon Brown, who went on to have as good a tour as any of the forwards, and the two contributed notably to the destruction of the Irish pack. Apart from Scotland's success in the scrummage, they obliterated McBride at the front of the lineout, just as England had done at Twickenham. In those two games, McBride succeeded in making only one lineout ball available to his scrum-half.

All his life, McHarg has taken a mischievous delight in confounding those critics who say that his style of play is too loose for an international lock, and it must have given him great pleasure to do what he did to Ireland, even though he knew that the Lions had already committed themselves to McBride as captain and that therefore the chances were that he himself would be excluded.

In the event, of course, the Springboks turned out to be so poor that it did not much matter who the Lions chose as captain or who they chose in their team. British Rugby could have won the series with any one of three or four teams. The only issue at stake in the selection of the 1974 Lions was the fundamental one of producing the best team available and therefore of doing justice to Britain's best players. That justice was not done.

CHAPTER 4

Assembly, Departure, Arrival

THE weeks before the tour had been punctuated by the usual spate of denunciations and vague threats by left wing politicians. Mr. Dennis Howell, the Minister for Sport, 'made his views known,' Mr. Peter Hain fulminated away (though as middle age approaches, he seems to be losing something of his former zeal,) and various local education authorities in Wales said with that unctuous self-righteousness which they have made their special preserve, 'If so-and-so goes on the tour, we certainly shall not pay his wages.'

No Lions tour of South Africa would be complete without these little trappings, and it really is surprising that so many people in so many places should take them seriously. For instance, it seemed quite impossible for South Africans and their newspapers to accept that once the British Lions had said they would come, then all they had to do in South Africa was sit down and wait for them to arrive. A seemingly endless stream of telephone calls from Johannesburg of various degrees of agitation flew a succession of journalistic scare stories, each one more ridiculous than the last. Unfortunately, South Africans have this masochistic obsession about what the world thinks of them. They have to lash themselves to despair with stories about tours being cancelled or tours being threatened until the whole country is positively twitching with nervous tensions. Sometimes, this even creates a problem where originally none existed.

Even worse, this unfounded agitation rubs off on other people. By the time the Four Unions have had their 93rd telephone call from a heavily accented South African fearing that the end of the tour (and therefore, the world) is at hand, they are beginning to believe it themselves, with the result that even a man as equable as Albert Agar starts to get snappish. He was the secretary of the Four Home Unions, and when the B.B.C. approached him with a perfectly reasonable request to do some interviews with the management and players for a Rugby Special television programme they were preparing for the start of the tour, he reacted as if he had been asked by Peter Hain himself. This was like Horatius getting stroppy with his two companions.

There was no need for this at all. The position of the Four

Home Unions had been nicely enunciated by Albert Agar himself. Commenting on his discussions with Dennis Howell, Mr. Agar said, 'There are two views on this subject, but we believe that by maintaining sporting contact with South Africa, more progress will be achieved than by abolishing that contact.' It was a perfectly viable position, and the Lions had a fixture list to prove it, because instead of sitting on their backsides muttering about the isolation of the coloured and African communities in South Africa, they were actually going out there to play them. The Four Home Unions had no need to be defensive about this at all. Just the opposite.

Unfortunately, too, some of this defensiveness rubbed off on Alun Thomas, the Lions' manager. An important part of the exercise in managing a British Lions tour of South Africa is concerned with public relations and the manager has to be sufficiently confident and sufficiently well prepared on the political issue above all others to be endlessly patient and co-operative with the various South African newspapers. From the moment he landed at Jan Smuts airport at Johannesburg, Alun Thomas sounded both apprehensive and defensive. He knew that one of the provincial Unions in South Africa had proposed that the 1968 Lions be sent home because of their bad behaviour, and he would not be drawn on either the political or the social issues. He spent a fair part of the training week at Stilfontein avoiding the various newspaper correspondents who wanted to talk about these matters as well as about his team. The result was that the Press relations got off on the wrong foot and they never really recovered. Perhaps Peter Hain would count that as a victory.

Mr. Hain did not have much luck elsewhere, because although he almost set up camp outside the Britannia Hotel in Grosvenor Square when the Lions assembled for the tour, he did not manage either to detect or to disrupt the proceedings when the Lions twice went off quietly for training sessions at Rosslyn Park over the weekend.

On previous tours, the Lions had always assembled at Eastbourne for a week's training, but after the 1971 tour, Dr. Doug Smith and Carwyn James, the manager and coach, had recommended that instead of training in Britain, the Lions would be able to use their time more profitably if they did their training in the country where they were due to tour. This suited the Four Home Unions admirably in 1974 because it enabled them to avoid the political demonstrations which might have been made.

The new arrangement had much to commend it, but it did

have one snag that was not foreseen when it was made. By dashing straight off to South Africa, the players did not have to undergo the fitness tests which used to be an important feature of the training week before a Lions tour. In recent years these tests have resulted in players like Bryan West and Chris Wardlow being left behind and replaced.

Some of the Lions were very glad of the new dispensation, because four or five of them had injuries which might have made it difficult for them to persuade the authorities that they were fit to play at the start of the tour. That always used to be the criterion, and the treatment room at Stilfontein was full of relieved young men who knew that they would have had very little chance of meeting the old fitness requirements.

The Lions did even further damage to themselves at Roehampton. Stewart McKinney was doing squats with a player on his shoulders and injured his back so seriously that he could not play until the fourth match at Port Elizabeth.

The last of the scare stories from Johannesburg came whistling over the wires as the Lions assembled in London on the Friday before flying out on the Monday. This averred on the usual 'very good authority' that the Lions would be flying out early to Johannesburg and that they would be leaving that Friday evening instead of on the Monday. Checks at London Airport and the Britannia Hotel revealed that the Lions had not changed their flight booking, that it was still arranged for Monday and that it was still public knowledge. Even more to the point, the Lions were still ensconced in the Britannia Hotel, listening to various gentlemen telling them about the perils of South African refereeing and of going to bed with a coloured girl. The Lions left on Monday according to schedule.

When they arrived in Johannesburg, Bobby Windsor was found to be suffering from gastro-enteritis. As this is infectious, he was taken off to hospital while the Lions were welcomed by Dr. Danie Craven, the president of the South African Rugby Board, and by Dr. Piet Koornhof, the South African Minister for Sport. The Lions met their liaison officer, Chute Visser, and after Alun Thomas had given a rather edgy Press conference which was not the happiest of auguries for a successful relationship with the media, the touring party drove off to the Three Fountains Hotel at Stilfontein 100 miles away.

Stilfontein is a rural community, very small and very quiet, and the Lions were due to stay there for ten days before their first match against Western Transvaal at Potchefstroom. The prospect of this was so discouraging for some of the older hands at touring

South Africa that it made them pause for at least two seconds to wonder whether it was all worth it. The training facilities at Stilfontein are excellent, but unfortunately, once you have seen the local golf course and been down the nearest gold mine, you have seen it all, and the Lions did not even go down the gold mine. The quiet is of the grave, and although a touring team does not want bright lights and night clubs in its training week, it does want something to see and something to do. Stilfontein could provide neither.

Even so, South African journalists were somewhat startled when the Lions went out for their first training session. The players just had a little jog and did some deep breathing exercises. These involved the use of the arms and were designed to open up the lungs fully.

"These are what you will do," said Millar and the Lions did them faithfully throughout the tour. They adhered just as faithfully to Syd Millar's instruction that no one, but no one, was to start kicking a ball in practice until he had warmed up. If any hamstrings were going to be pulled, Millar wanted them pulled after everything had been done to avoid an injury of that kind.

The Lions' coach was also much concerned to work up gradually to fitness. He did not want to run his players into the ground, as the All Black coach Ivan Vodanovich had done on the New Zealand tour of South Africa in 1970. We had all read with much amusement of 'Jazz' Muller's rueful estimate that he would need at least a couple of months to get fit for the All Black training runs, and Syd Millar did not intend to make the same mistake.

He went along slowly, adding trunk strengthening exercises and pyramids of threequarter pace and sprint running, and he started work on the scrummaging, which he had already announced would be the basis of his approach to the tour. The scrummaging increased in intensity until the forwards were doing forty scrums in a session. The dry ground enabled the Lions to alter their foot-placings and scrummage much lower than is possible in Europe.

Welsh had been so much the prevailing accent on the 1971 tour of New Zealand that training sessions had sounded like a Welsh revivalist meeting, but in 1974 the distinctive accent of Ulster was so predominant that it sounded like an extension of the nightly television offerings of the Rev. Ian Paisley and Mr. William Craig.

'Ai am going to mehk yue sick of the soornd of the worrd scrom,' said Millar. 'Yue will scrommage and scrommage until yue are fed op with it, and then yue will scrommage some more.'

The Lions had their casualties in training. The most serious was Mike Burton, who fell and injured a knee so badly that it swelled up to a grotesque size and convinced him that there was every chance that his tour had come to an end before it had even started. He was operated on by Dr. K. W. Kennedy, and the sight of Kennedy in a mask, scrubbing up and lifting his hands to have his surgeon's gloves put on provided one of the most remarkable moments in the history of Lions' tours.

Burton had to hobble around on crutches after the operation and he took his place in the queue of players receiving treatment. Roger Uttley had a shoulder injury, Andy Ripley had trouble with an old back injury, Alan Old was having treatment for the hamstring injury he had received in the match against France, Fergus Slattery had a stud wound received in a game in Ireland at the end of the season, Tom Grace had an ankle injury, John Moloney was also having treatment, Stewart McKinney had a bad back and then Geoff Evans and Clive Rees went down with influenza.

From the beginning of their training, the Lions took the salt pills first used in British Rugby by the England team touring the Far East in 1971. Dr. Tommy Kemp, then President of the Rugby Union, used to go round three times a day in various exotic places in the Orient shaking his tin of pills like Edmundo Ros. He became known as 'slow sodium', which is how this slow-acting variety of salt pill is described by the athletes for whom it was developed originally. England found them very successful and used them again in South Africa in 1972.

The Lions took two of these pills three times a day for most of the tour, though the forwards found that the pills tended to make them sweat inordinately and towards the end of the tour, a few of the players like Mike Burton and Andy Ripley stopped taking them. This caused something of an altercation with Dave Goddess, who was known to the Lions as 'The Weasel' and who was attached to the team as masseur.

Bobby Windsor rejoined the Lions in Stilfontein when he had recovered from his attack of gastro-enteritis. Windsor had acquired something of the gift of expression with which Ray Prosser, his coach at Pontypool, used to enrich the 1959 Lions tour of New Zealand. Prosser, a steelworker, once said of David Marques, of Cambridge University, the Harlequins, England and the City of London that, 'He's a bewtiful jumper, but he will keep on using long words like corrugated iron and marmalade.'

Those who watch the television comedy in Britain called 'It Ain't 'Arf 'Ot, Mum,' will know from the sergeant-major at the centre of the story exactly the rasping East Welsh accent in which these lines were delivered. Windsor spoke in the same way. He had already caused amusement by saying that his stomach upset had been caused by having a drop too much to eat, which sounded pure Prosser, and he brought a wayside restaurant between Johannesburg and Stilfontein to a halt when the party fetching him from hospital stopped for a meal.

Windsor was asked what he wanted to eat, and after examining the menu for some while, he said he would have an omelette.

'What sort?' asked the waiter.

Windsor looked up in surprise. 'One o' them egg ones, o' course,' he said.

It was while the Lions were in Stilfontein that the entire population of middle-aged and elderly ladies in South Africa decided that Andrew Ripley must be a really nice young man.

The Lions went to a reception one evening, and as they were going into the building, Ripley noticed what he thought was a white glove lying in the dark gardens outside. He went across to pick it up, and saw that it was a little white kitten which was so desperately ill that it was only just alive.

Ripley took it back to his room with him and tried to feed it some milk. Then he settled it as comfortably as he could in some playing kit and left the saucer of milk beside it while he went to sleep. He fully expected the kitten to be dead when he woke up in the morning.

To his surprise, though, the kitten was alive and it was just about strong enough to take some nourishment. Ripley went on nursing it for several days but when it had recovered enough to walk and to play games he could tell that it was blind, so he went out to a chemist's shop to buy some anti-biotics. The man and his wife who owned the shop were immensely helpful and Ripley dutifully dropped the drops of anti-biotic into the kitten's eyes in the hope that the animal would recover its sight.

Unfortunately, the treatment did not have the desired effect, but the kitten did recover its health and strength in all other respects. Ripley then had to decide what to do with it, because the tour was just about to go on the road, so he had himself photographed with the kitten in the hope that one of the newspaper readers would provide a home for it. He was inundated with offers, and in the end, a couple drove down from Pretoria to take the animal home and to care for it.

The Lions insisted that Andy Ripley was often in danger of acquiring a menagerie afterwards. He modestly denied such claims as being exaggerated but he did admit that he nearly acquired a stray dog in East London.

CHAPTER 5

Western Transvaal

IN the past, one of the most persistently disturbing problems for a team touring South Africa had been the question of refereeing interpretations. In 1968, for instance, the Lions were still trying to discover just what South African referees would allow in the lineout and what they would not allow when they were preparing for the third test. By that time, very little of the tour remained and their chances of saving the series had almost disappeared.

Nothing seemed to alleviate this problem. Ronnie Dawson, who was the coach in 1968, was the most methodical and conscientious of men, and he went to great trouble to discuss interpretation both with active referees and with officials of the South African Referees' Society, but to no great profit. His players still came off the field either dissatisfied or sometimes even convinced that they had been cheated.

The Lions had discussions with a representative of the South African referees while they were in Stilfontein. He confirmed that players were allowed to bind on to jumpers in the lineout and hold them in the air providing they did not do it before the ball had been played. He also confirmed that as in 1968, South African referees still regarded the ball as dead while it was in the scrum-half's hands before being put into a scrum. This meant that hookers could wave their feet about as much as they liked as long as those feet were in the proper position at the moment the ball was put into the scrum.

South African referees had just been told very clearly by the South African Rugby Board that they must tighten up their refereeing. Specific points mentioned in putting the ball into the scrum were putting it in straight, putting it in quickly and putting it in along the middle line of the scrummage. In the lineout referees were instructed not to let forwards move before the ball had been touched. 'Referees are even penalising players for lifting,' said the Board. 'This is ridiculous, if referees insist on players remaining in their positions according to the requirements of the law.' Referees were also told to stop jumpers deliberately bumping their opponents out of the way, and they were told to give a penalty kick for a deliberate knock-on when one jumper knocked the ball out of the hands of another.

The Board was just as explicit about the infringements in the loose, particularly about joining a maul in front of the ball and falling over the ball to kill the ruck.

All the points made by the South African Board would have brought their game into line with that being played in Europe, but as the tour went on, it became more and more obvious that South African referees were not taking the slightest notice of what they had been told to do. The ball was put into the scrum so far from straight that the Lions decided that for most of the time, they would only strike on their own ball and would concentrate on an eight man shove or a wheel when the opposition were putting in the ball.

This helped to expose the deterioration in the standard of South African scrummaging and it also removed most of the opportunities for South African referees to penalise the Lions for infringements in the front row. In the past, these had proved to be very expensive for the Lions, and they had constituted a fruitful source of points for most of their opponents.

What is more, as soon as the Lions discovered that their scrummaging was better than the South Africans', they delayed putting in the ball for as long as they could while their tight forwards worked on the opposition. They bumped their opponents out of the lineout as well, and they got away with both of these things almost throughout the tour.

As for lifting in the lineout, this was done so often and allowed by so many referees that it would have been more to the point if instead of saying that it was 'ridiculous' to penalise lifting, the South African Board had said that it was 'ridiculous' that the offence was being detected and penalised so infrequently.

At that stage, though, this was all in the future. The Lions had done what they could to insure themselves against the slings and arrows of outrageous refereeing in the scrums, and in the lineout, they resolved to test the water gently by seeing how things went.

The only way they could discover that was in match play, and in their first game, they were due to play Western Transvaal, a team which had won both its easy matches in the Currie Cup the year before and had lost both its difficult matches. The expectations were, therefore, that the Lions would win fairly comfortably.

For the two days before the game, the Lions went over to train at the stadium at Potchefstroom where the match was to be played. Potch had not changed much since the Lions and the Barbarians had played there in 1968 and 1969. It was still the arid, uncompromising place it had been ever since the British rooineks had set up an ill-fated prison camp there for the wives and the children of their enemies in the Boer War. Those camps had been decimated by epidemics and the attitudes formed by the experience were still in the eyes of the people.

The Lions were not quite decimated themselves, but the selection of their team to play Western Transvaal was simplified to some extent by the various illnesses and injuries. Syd Millar had said that he would not choose any player who was not fit, either medically or athletically, and so the list of the possible starters for the first game was reduced to not much more than the team and the panel of six substitutes.

As it happened, the Lions were able to choose what they clearly judged then to be their strongest pack, because four of the five tight forwards had been Lions in New Zealand in 1971 and the other four forwards were favoured as the form selections from the British international season which had just ended. Behind the scrum, too, the Lions were able to choose both Roy Bergiers and Ian McGeechan in the centre, to give them the aggressive defence they were looking for, with Phil Bennett to set things up and kick the goals at fly-half and J. P. R. Williams to do whatever else was required at full-back.

The combination proved to be more than ample for the job, because in mercifully overcast weather, the Lions won by 59 points to 13. This was the highest score ever achieved by a Lions team in South Africa, and it remained so for a fortnight. The Lions were opposed by a heavy pack, which, thanks to Johnny Burger, managed to achieve something like parity in the tight and which even won the strikes against the head, but the shortcomings of Western Transvaal in both fitness and in defensive strength were exposed unkindly late in the game when the Lions added nearly 30 points. The Lions scored nine tries and Bennett converted seven of them as well as kicking three penalty goals.

The first try of the tour was scored by Gordon Brown which, in view of the great success he enjoyed subsequently, could not have been more fitting. A determined effort by the Lions' forwards in a scrum had Western Transvaal struggling to pass under pressure and a reverberating tackle by Bergiers created a loose ball for his back row. The moustachioed David smashed forward with the ball in that flashing-eyed piratical way of his and Brown dived over the line like a hulking, 100 yard swimmer starting a race.

Neary whipped the ball across for Steele to score a try between the posts after another powerful tackle by Bergiers, and as Bennett converted that try, and also kicked a penalty goal, the Lions scored 13 points in little more than ten minutes. Inevitably, their progress for the rest of the half was a little slower, but after a lineout peel by McBride, Moloney went snapping in for a try behind another goliath of a run by David. Bennett converted that try and also kicked a penalty goal.

Western Transvaal had been playing some football of their own. Owen made ground from a short lineout and his No. 8 Stoffberg went on to score and then Schaap scored a try on the left wing after he had juggled with the ball for so long that the crowd caught its breath in anxiety. De Bruyn converted that try with a well-struck kick and also kicked a penalty goal.

Western Transvaal did not add to their score in the second half. The Lions did. They ran in six more tries, and Bennett converted five of them. He also kicked another penalty goal.

Most of these came in a rush of scoring at the end of the match, when the Lions decided they were safe to attack with their own set ball. Until well after half-time, they had used it only to kick or to set up second phase situations and they had scored only from loose ball or from mistakes made by the opposition.

Unfortunately, Moloney dislocated a shoulder early in the second half and had to be replaced by Edwards. As soon as Edwards arrived, he started fizzing all over the field and went straight through to score from a set move using a midfield pivot from a tapped penalty. It was a standard move in Europe but it baffled the Western Transvaal defence completely.

With J. P. R. Williams moving forward and Bennett probing with the occasional zig-zag run, Davies scored two tries, Edwards scored another and Rees and Ripley scored one each. J. P. R. Williams was not too pleased with himself, though. He dropped a catch, and fretted about it for weeks. 'I don't want to make excuses,' he said, 'but what with my injury at the end of the season back home, I haven't played for a long time. Still, I should have caught it.'

The Lions suffered two more injuries near the end of the game. Carmichael hurt a hip and was replaced by Cotton, so when Bergiers also left the field, with a damaged rib, the Lions had to finish with 14 men. They managed it quite comfortably.

Through it all, Bennett kicked with remarkable accuracy from most parts of the field. His seven conversions and three penalty goals gave him 23 points, which equalled the Lions record for an individual player set by Bob Hiller against Border in 1968.

CHAPTER 6

South West Africa

THE injury to John Moloney must have made the Lions think long and hard about whether they should replace him. They knew that most previous touring sides would have taken that decision without hesitation, because scrum-half is such a specialist position that the Lions would have been made to look ridiculous if Gareth Edwards had been injured in the time it took Moloney to recover. Even the most optimistic of opinions estimated that it would take Moloney at least a fortnight to recover, and for the whole of that time, Edwards would have to play in all the matches. The pressure on him would not only be constant, but it would also have a cumulative effect on him later in the tour. The Lions also knew that they would have to play at least four games and possibly more with a player as substitute at scrum-half who could have no pretentions in the position.

It was a risk the Lions decided to take, but as they made the long flight up to Windhoek, and to the heat of South West Africa, they must have remembered the damage Jan Ellis did to Barry John in 1968 when he broke his collarbone in the first test, and wondered whether they had made the right decision.

South West Africa was settled first by a splendid English family called Bassingthwaighte who were shipwrecked on the nearby Skeleton Coast. They little thought, as they trudged inland, that a king's ransom of diamonds lay under their feet. All they wanted to do was get away from that hellish coast and they succeeded so well that they set up a community inland which survived even the German colonisation of the territory. The Germans built castles and started brewing South Africa's most famous beer, but they could not suppress the Bassingthwaightes. One of them even played in the front row against the 1968 Lions.

Gareth Edwards played a memorable game against S.W. Africa on that tour. He scored two tries, and really took Jan Ellis apart.

Edwards had first played in Windhoek in 1967, on the Cardiff tour of South Africa. Edwards was then a boy, and it was the first game of Cardiff's tour. It was May and it was also hot. The next year, the Lions match in Windhoek was much later in South Africa's winter and the weather was altogether different. The nights were so cold that the hotel ran out of electric fires.

In 1974, the Lions' game in Windhoek was in May again and

the weather was just as hot as it had been when Cardiff had played there seven years earlier. Gareth Edwards was in the team again, too. The difference was that this time he returned as the captain of the British Lions team to play South West Africa, and as one of the two best scrum-halves in the world.

Tom Grace was still not fit to play, and neither was Stewart McKinney, and although Mike Burton was off his crutches and moving around in light training again, there was not much prospect of him being fit for another ten days. The result was that three players had to play their second full game in succession, Clive Rees on the wing, Ian McLauchlan at prop and Tom David in the back row. David was looking forward to playing against Jan Ellis. 'I'm dying to 'ave a go at him,' he said. Things had gone well for David at Potchefstroom.

In the season before the Lions went to South Africa, Syd Millar had been under the impression that Western Transvaal were a stronger team than S.W. Africa.

Unfortunately, this assessment of the relative strengths of Western Transvaal and S.W. Africa turned out to be some way adrift, because Jan Ellis and his team played with such determination that they argued that they had been very unlucky to lose.

They were particularly upset by a try scored by Edwards early in the game. Davies picked up the ball from the back of a scrum and passed to Edwards on the blind side. Edwards drove for the line and was brought down short of it. He wormed his way over the line and the referee said that he had got there on his own momentum. Ellis and his team were quite convinced that Edwards had crawled there. The referee gave Edwards a try. S.W. Africa thought that Mr. de Bruyn should have given them a penalty kick. This gave the Lions the lead at 7-3, because Karg had kicked a penalty goal for S.W. Africa and Old had kicked one for the Lions.

However, things were not going well for the Lions. In the extremes of heat and altitude, all the players found breathing so difficult that they thought they would either die of the heat or asphyxia. The forwards looked bereft and with Old looking sadly out of practice after his long lay-off at fly-half, their backs were unable to shake free of their opponents' determined tackling.

To make matters worse for the Lions, Irvine was hesitant at full-back. His fielding was erratic under the high ball and he missed a straightforward tackle which gave S.W. Africa the best try of the match. Prinsloo first took Rees by surprise by moving in off the wing and he ran straight through the middle. He then set himself rather obviously to beat Irvine on the outside and the

Lions watching from the stand sighed with relief. 'He will never be quick enough to do that,' they said. But he was and he scored a try without too much difficulty.

That try, and another penalty goal by Karg, put S.W. Africa ahead 16-14, because they had already scored a try, which Karg had converted, when Ellis had forced his way over from the back of a scrum. The position of that attacking scrum had also been made by Ellis, because he had kicked a high ball which Irvine had dropped near his line. It was the third time S.W. Africa had been in the lead, and they held it until ten minutes from the end, when their midfield defence lapsed at last and the Lions produced two thrusts to save the game.

The Lions threw the ball to the back of a lineout, where Davies tapped the ball down to Cotton running round on the peel. Cotton set up a maul in midfield, and when the Lions worked the ball back, Irvine came into the line to make an opening for Milliken to score. The conversion was far from easy, but Irvine kicked it and he finally crushed S.W. Africa's hopes by kicking a penalty goal. Irvine had kicked a penalty goal just before half-time, too, to give the Lions a 10-9 lead. Rees scored the Lions' other try from a kick ahead by Milliken.

It was not a convincing performance by the Lions and the management were the first to admit it. Syd Millar said, 'Obviously we are not satisfied. We knew that it would be a difficult match because of the heat and the altitude, but that is not an excuse. Still, it was not a bad thing to have met such strong opposition so early in the tour. Now the players know, as I found out on my three previous visits here, that there are no easy games in South Africa.'

Syd Millar was not really satisfied with that analysis, because he liked to have an explanation of success or failure. After thinking about the match at length, he decided that the Lions had faltered because they had not gone forward enough. It was just as well, too, that Alan Old did not have to substitute for Gareth Edwards at scrum-half, and Tom David was noticeably quiet about his contest with Jan Ellis.

When the Lions left, Gordon Brown was proudly carrying a springbok head. It had been presented to him by the pupils of Windhoek High School. At the same time, S.W. Africa were slightly disappointed that they had not won the lion mascot that Lions teams take abroad with them to present to the first team that beats them. The mascot became pretty tatty by the end of the tour, but in Windhoek it was still only slightly shop-soiled.

CHAPTER 7

Cape Town

THE first visit to Cape Town is always something special for any team touring South Africa, because like Hong Kong, the place is absolutely unique. The Lions do not have the pleasure now of steaming into Table Bay in an ocean-going liner and looking up at that extraordinary flat-topped mountain towering 3,000 feet above the city, but even through the opaque windows of an aircraft coming in from the north, the view can be breathtaking.

The pity is that so much of the old colonial city of Cape Town has been destroyed. Even to visitors going back there every other year, the place changes out of all recognition, and when the Lions went there in 1974, those beautifully balustraded buildings which used to stretch up from the water-front to the centre of the city had almost disappeared. In their place were huge perforated slabs of concrete, standing on their ends and blocking, like so many giant fingers of an outspread hand, the view to the wooded slopes of Table Mountain.

'Porky' Wells and the other Western Province officials who had met the team lost no time in arranging a trip for the players who wanted to take a cable car ride up the mountain.

This is one of the essential features of any visit to Cape Town, but for people with no great head for heights, it can be something of an ordeal. Even the drive up from the city to the cable car station at the foot of the mountain provides a marvellous view of Table Bay spread out below, but when you look the other way, and look up that vertical cliff of rock to the cable car station perched, as it seems, on the very edge of the mountain 2,000 feet higher still, then the whole operation begins to assume overtones of 'Where Eagles Dare'. One cablecar goes up the mountain as the other one comes down from the top, and as they pass in the middle, everyone on board is conscious of just how far it is to the rocky slopes below.

The worst part for the real sufferers is the last 200 feet as the car sways slowly up the vertical face of the cliff. Some strong men cannot even bear to look. They understand then something of the mentality of mountaineers who paste themselves to the North face of the Eiger and they shut their eyes in horror at the thought that anybody could be so mad.

Clive Rees was one of the Lions who found the experience alarming. The only trouble was that he wanted his photograph taken in the cable car with Cape Town spread out behind him. The fiendish Burton offered to take the picture for him, but made out that it would be impossible unless Rees was right by the side of the car. Rees inched sideways, taking care not to look down for all he was worth, and holding on to everything. 'Bit more. Bit more,' said Burton. Had it been possible, Burton would have persuaded Rees to hang over the edge, but when he had extracted every last drop of blood, he said, 'Smile.' There was a guffaw of laughter from the back of the car. Rees found it quite impossible to comply with the instruction. All he could do was show his teeth.

Down below, Tom Grace was prudently waiting for everyone else to reach the top before he ventured into a car. He was going to make sure that whatever else happened to him in the way of trouble and strife in South Africa, he was not going to be pushed out of a cable car going up Table Mountain, particularly as he had just about got himself fit to play.

This was as well, because the Lions' other three wingers were all injured. Clive Rees was feeling a slight hamstring injury, Billy Steele had a bruised calf and J. J. Williams had an injured knee. Williams eventually recovered sufficiently to play in the next match against Boland, but his training had to be interrupted for treatment.

The Lions had only just started to explore the delights of Cape Town when they learned that the British Government had forbidden their local Embassy officials to have any contact with the tourists while they were in South Africa. In the House of Commons, Miss Joan Lestor, a junior minister, had said in a written parliamentary reply, 'In view of the Government's known disapproval of the tour . . . it is natural and consistent that the Ambassador and his staff, while providing normal consular facilities, should not extend hospitality or attend matches or receptions for the team. This applies to all matches and social functions during the tour.'

The British Government had already announced that they had banned official Embassy entertainment for the Lions, so a Conservative member asked Miss Lestor if this ban extended to hospitality offered to the Lions by Embassy staff in their private homes. He was told that it did and that the Embassy officials would not even be allowed to watch the matches. It was the beginning of a rather tiresome episode in which both the main political parties in Britain sought to make political points out of the tour. This continued even after the tour was over.

The ban was certainly no hardship on the Lions. Touring teams regard cocktail parties and official receptions as part of the crashingly boring price they must pay for all the other pleasures associated with the trip, and the ban by the British Government simply meant two fewer occasions when the Lions would have to climb into their number one rig on a lovely warm evening and listen to the small talk of a selection of heavies (the players' term for bores of all ages.)

The only people who were in the least disappointed by the ban were those young ladies in the embassy and consular staffs who are normally roped in to provide conversational fodder, and perhaps even other sorts of fodder, for the Lions.

The game against Boland was to be played at Wellington, at the foot of the mountains twenty miles from Cape Town. For clear air, spectacular scenery, and all the health giving propensities of the simple life, it is hard to imagine a more invigorating place than Wellington, but sadly, the weakness of the flesh, and particularly the flesh of young or youngish Rugby players, is notoriously susceptible to the smog and the concrete canyons and all the perilous pitfalls of Cape Town. So the Lions stayed in Cape Town and they drove over by bus to Wellington on the day of the match.

In the past, Lions' matches against Boland had often been hard. Syd Millar himself had rueful memories of the game in 1968, when David van der Merwe had given him an uncomfortable afternoon. Millar did not lose any ball in that match but he did lose his place in the following test match, so he was unlikely to take any chances in 1974. He chose what was then regarded as the Lions' strongest pack, except for Ian McLauchlan, and must have been interested to see that van der Merwe was still playing for Boland.

The confrontations between tight forwards are always the most interesting aspect of a game to other tight forwards, and the Lions' coach was as interested as the other specialists in the outcome of the clash between van der Merwe and Fran Cotton. In the few minutes he had played against Western Transvaal, and in the match he had played against S.W. Africa, Cotton had played tight head. Against Boland, he had been chosen in his tour position as the reserve loose head. It was obviously going to be an important occasion for him.

Cotton found that van der Merwe (which he always pronounced in his rich Lancashire accent as van der Merwee, instead of fun der Murva) was a good prop, one of the best he met on tour. However, Cotton did well enough against him to protect the Lions' ball in the scrums and that in turn enabled the pack behind him to take command. Cotton managed quite nicely, thank you, and the elite of the Lions' tight forwards realised that another player was about to join them.

For a while, the Boland defence was stubborn, but the changes in the laws relating to touch-kicking make it much harder to shut up the game than it was, and in the boiling heat, the Lions' gradually worked themselves into a position from which they could launch a heavy assault without fear of retaliation. The Lions scored 23 points in the second half and again exposed the comparative lack of fitness of their opponents by scoring two tries near the end.

Both teams concentrated on kicking and spoiling in the first half. It was 20 minutes before Old passed the ball to his centres. Thiart, the Boland fly-half, did not pass it out at all. Boland were content to contain the Lions' attempts at lineout peels and to concentrate as much pressure as they could on Edwards. The only runs of any consequence were made by Brown and McGeechan. Brown once made a lot of ground before he was stopped and on another occasion, McGeechan cut through the middle so cleanly that the break was made to look all the more dramatic by its unexpectedness.

The Lions led 10-0 at half-time. Old kicked a penalty goal and Grace scored a try after David and Ripley had moved away from the blind side of a scrum. Old kicked another penalty goal when du Plessis ran offside in front of his posts. Du Plessis looked suitably chastened because until that moment, he had been the most effective of the tenacious Boland loose forwards.

Old kicked another penalty goal early in the second half and then put up a high kick which le Roux dropped. J. J. Williams followed up to take the ball and put in Milliken for a try which Old converted.

Wolmarans, the Boland scrum-half, managed to launch some sorties past David on the blind side, despite a poor heel from his forwards but Boland's only chances of scoring came from kicks at goal. Full-back Visser took the first two and missed them both. Eventually, du Toit, the Boland captain, called up his fly-half Thiart and he was immediately successful with the next two.

They were only gestures. Ripley took the ball from a lineout and gave it to David and when he was checked, the ball was moved out to the backs where Grace passed inside for Milliken to score. David pulled a hamstring in that attack and had to go off the field. For the last 20 minutes of the match, he was replaced by Uttley.

In that time, the Lions scored two more tries. Brown caught a bad kick by Boland in midfield and drove forward so hard and so far that when he was eventually stopped near the corner he was able to turn and give a scoring pass to McBride who was following up behind. Old converted that try. The last try was scored by Edwards. Boland managed to check a lineout peel by the Lions but they were not able to check Edwards when he picked up the loose ball.

David's hamstring injury was a nasty blow because with McKinney and Ripley suffering to various degrees with back injuries, and Slattery and Davies still to make their way, the Lions were being hampered by a series of niggling set-backs in their attempts to develop a worthwhile presence at loose forward. Most estimates before the tour had pointed to this as the area of South Africa's greatest strength, and the Lions had uncomfortable memories of the damage Jan Ellis had done at Windhoek four days before.

After the match against Boland, the Lions went to a reception at the town hall at Wellington. It was well on the way to being another formal and uneventful occasion when Mike Burton and Bobby Windsor decided to do something to liven it up.

Burton has a remarkable ear for accents, and he also has a considerable ability as a mimic. By the end of the tour, he could imitate the voices of his team-mates so well that it was hard to tell the difference. He caught perfectly the soft and rather gentle Lancashire voice of Fran Cotton saying, 'Ah'll tell you soomthing, Michael. Ah'm going to give that steak and chips soom-oompty tonight,' and to hear Burton doing a cross-talk act between Syd Millar and Bill McBride was just like listening to the real thing. He even had the curled forefinger of McBride as he pointed and said, 'Thur is no esceyep. We must goe arn.' Burton could imitate the different accents of Wales just as well, and what made the performance even funnier was that he could always remember the most characteristic remarks of the players he was imitating.

At Wellington, Burton and Windsor did a ventriloquist's act. Windsor sat on Burton's knee, and pulled his blazer off the top of his shoulders so that his arms flopped about and he jerked his head from side to side in a suitably wooden way.

'What sort of omelette would you like, sir?' asked Burton.

And through his clenched teeth, back came the reply in purest Pontypool, 'One o' them egg ones.'

The locals loved it.

CHAPTER 8

Eastern Province

THE Lions left the next morning for Port Elizabeth. This is always one of the places remembered with affection by Rugby teams touring South Africa, partly because of the ideal situation of the hotels along the beach and partly because Jimmy Ward and his liaison staff from the Eastern Province Union are so unfailingly helpful. Jimmy was there to meet the Lions when they arrived and to take them past the Boet Erasmus stadium and down the hill to the sea and along the coast road leading to the Marine Hotel.

The Marine was the best hotel visited by the Lions in 1968 but since then, it had seen hard times. It was hit pretty badly when the new Elizabeth Hotel was built in time for the All Blacks tour of 1970. In 1974, the Marine Hotel was on the way back up and in any case, the weather was so good and the prospect from the hotel so infinitely pleasing that the Lions were well content.

Syd Millar gave the team a stiff training session that day. Mike Burton and Stewart McKinney had been chosen to play their first games of the tour but Chris Ralston was held out and Gordon Brown chosen again at lock with Roger Uttley. With John Moloney still injured, the Lions had no choice but to pick Gareth Edwards at scrum-half again, even though they knew the risk of putting so much pressure on such a key player at that stage of the tour. To make matters worse, a scrum collapsed in practice and Ken Kennedy injured a shoulder and had to withdraw from the team. Bobby Windsor replaced him to make his third appearance in four matches.

Eastern Province had difficulties of their own. Their team had shown signs of improvement, and with the arrival of young players like Gavin Cowley, they were hoping that it would develop into a significant force in South African Rugby again.

However, not all their committee were enamoured of the idea of Hannes Marais as captain. Some of them said quite openly that the team went better when their number eight, George Barnard, was in charge. They also thought that Marais was much less effective than he had been as a prop because in the few months since he had started playing again, in response to what everyone believed was a request from the Springbok selectors, he had played a fair amount of his club football as a flanker. The feeling was that Marais had not been as fully involved as he should have been, either as a specialist prop or as a captain, to be really effective. There was a passive acceptance of the idea that Eastern Province should go along with Marais as captain, simply out of loyalty to South Africa, but the committee were not convinced that it would work out. They were further constrained by the fact that Ian Kirkpatrick, who had taken over as coach of Eastern Province, was also a national selector and was one of the joint coaches of the Springbok team.

Still, there was a niggle of protest in Port Elizabeth that Eastern Province were being used and that niggle swelled to a roar when Johan Claassen, the chairman of the Springbok selectors, went into the Eastern Province dressing room before their match against the Lions and talked to the players. According to several irate officials, Mr. Claassen told the Eastern Province players that the British did not have much appetite for the more physical aspects of Rugby football and he suggested that it might be no bad idea to try a little of what the New Zealanders call 'stoush', just to see how it worked.

If this was true, it betrayed a sadly outdated image of British Rugby, because the Lions had several forwards who were singularly well-equipped to deal with that sort of situation. They had travelled the world and they had fought many battles together and they had survived. One or two of them, indeed, enjoyed the battles at least as much as the Rugby so that they had no objection at all if the opposition wanted to start a fight.

What is more, they had even produced an organised team effort to deal with it. A lot of intelligent people in British Rugby do a lot of thinking about tours these days, and as part of their homework, the brains trust working on the 1974 tour of South Africa had noticed that at fairly predictable points of their journey round South Africa, there was a tendency for visiting teams to be confronted either by a thoroughly nasty match or by one in which one of their key players was injured. They remembered the injuries to Richard Sharp in the 1962 Lions, to Barry John in the 1968 Lions, and to Colin Meads in the 1970 All Blacks. Perhaps these injuries were simply an unfortunate coincidence. Perhaps not. Anyway, the 1974 Lions made up their minds to be at least as well prepared for an eventuality of that kind as they could be. With an Irish prop forward as coach, and an Irish lock forward as captain, it was the sort of precaution that might have been expected.

The Lions knew from long experience in New Zealand and

elsewhere, that if trouble did break out, it was best dealt with unanimously. Players fighting in isolation rarely achieve much and they tend to be penalised or even sent off the field, as John O'Shea had been at Springs in 1968, whereas players involved in a pitched fight can achieve much more in the way of deterrent activity and they tend to get away with it. They get away with it because the referee is put into the position where he has no thought of making an example of an individual player and is more than happy to settle for restoring law and order. Referees shrink from sending off players wholesale and they are just as reluctant to abandon a match, because both courses of action reflect on them as referees. After all, it is just as much of an honour for a referee to handle a game between the Lions and a provincial team in South Africa or New Zealand as it is for the players to play in the game. A match like that is not an everyday occurrence, and therefore the referee is just as anxious for it to be a good day for him as for the players.

Consequently, the Lions decided that if there was trouble of a really serious nature, the players in charge would shout the code-number 'Ninety-nine' and they would all go to war. It proved remarkably effective, because in the course of the tour, the Lions threw fifty times as many punches as John O'Shea, and none of their players ever looked like being sent off the field.

The referee could not be sure that this was a deliberate command to start fighting because the Lions used a combination of numbers as one of their alternative sets of lineout signals. Any number between one and four, for instance, would be a throw to the front of the lineout, any number between six and nine would be a throw to the middle of the lineout, number five would be a set move, and the numbers above ten would cover other moves. It is true that the number 99 represented a considerable escalation, but then, so did the activity envisaged.

This battle plan was first put to the test by Eastern Province, and at the end of the day, it looked as if they rather wished that they had not listened to Mr. Claassen. By the middle of the second half, Eastern Province had had enough.

The trouble started almost from the beginning of the game and it was fairly obvious that the prime target for Eastern Province was Gareth Edwards. The Lions certainly set Edwards up, because they knocked back uncontrolled ball from the lineout and Eastern Province poured through the gaps to descend on him. They descended on him whatever happened, whether legally or otherwise, and he took some fearful bumps.

One of the earliest raiders to break through was Basil de

Coning, the splendidly named Eastern Province hooker, and no sooner had Burton stopped up that gap than Parker went through. The next time, Burton left a larger gap, and as Parker took it, clearly suspecting something fishy about such a tempting offering, his suspicions were confirmed in a cloud of shooting stars.

The Eastern Province lock, van der Westhuizen, had also thumped Edwards, and Burton made up his mind to do something about that, too. On the first occasion that he tried, Burton had to suffer some small inconvenience himself, because van der Westhuizen was jumping for the ball and he brought up his knees sharply in Burton's face. He patted Burton on the head, and jeeringly called him 'Sonny', thinking that a little blood around the nose and mouth would dissuade Burton from exacting revenge for what had been done to Edwards. This turned out to be a fairly serious error of judgment, because when soon afterwards van der Westhuizen collapsed in a heap, even Windsor was moved to admiration. 'A blinking classic,' he said, and they have high standards in these matters in Pontypool.

A hurried conference among the Eastern Province forwards resulted in Parker changing lineout positions with Marais, and as the Eastern Province captain moved up to mark him, Burton thought that it would only be a question of time before he had a whiff of anaesthetic himself. In his part of the world, and in Wales, a change of lineout positions like that means only one thing.

To Burton's surprise, however, the anaesthetic was not forthcoming. Marais confined himself to wagging a reproving finger and saying, 'You'd better not do that to me.' Which was like saying to a rabbit, 'You mustn't eat the lettuce.'

Stewart McKinney also had some difficulty. He was pulled back as he went through a lineout and turned and hit the flanker who had pulled his arm. Obstruction in midfield led to more fighting until even the midfield backs were involved.

Some of the incidents were quite ugly, too. Marais kicked at Uttley's head when the Lions lock was trapped on the ground. It was a wonder the kick did not split open Uttley's head, and those on the nearby touch-line heard Brown, the other Lions' lock, call Marais a very uncomplimentary name. 'All you're any good at, Brownie, is swearing,' said Marais. By the end of the tour, that also looked a fairly serious error of judgment.

Gareth Edwards, as Lions captain for the day, asked Hannes Marais to tell his players to cut out the rough stuff quite early in the game. Nothing happened. So Edwards asked again. 'Look,' he said, 'you're an experienced player. Tell your boys to cut it out.'

Still nothing happened, so Edwards said grimly, 'Right. If that's the way you want it, that's the way you can bloody have it.'

And have it they did. The Lions wrought considerable carnage before the Eastern Province players saw that they were losing both the fight and the Rugby match and decided that they had had enough of both.

In view of Alun Thomas' apprehensions about the Press, Gareth Edwards would not normally have been so forthcoming about what had happened on the field as he was after this match, but he was concussed quite severely in the course of the game and on Monday morning, when his pointed comments were seen in print, he simply could not remember anything he had said. This was a case, though, as it so often is, where the frankness of their captain's remarks turned out to be of considerable value to the Lions. Every other team in South Africa saw that if that was the way they wanted it, that was the way they could bloody have it. It never pays to be worried about the Press, or to antagonise them. Better by far to use them and to enrol them as allies.

Edwards acquired his concussion from the bumps he took as he collected man and ball from the lineout. On one occasion he was knocked out and went off the field for a few seconds to recover. He was asked if he wanted to stay off because it was obvious that he was not fully in command of his senses. He shook his head and said that he would continue.

Some of the damage done to Edwards came from late tackles, but it has to be admitted that the rest came from perfectly legal challenges as Eastern Province poured through the gaps in the lineout to follow deflections by Brown. Whether by accident or not, the Lions played roughly to the laws of the lineout in this match. It was the last time they did it on tour. From that match on, they closed the one yard gaps in front of their scrum-half, they obstructed the opposition, they lifted their own jumper, they threw the ball crooked, they barged the opposition off the ball—in fact, they played exactly as they would have done if the new laws pertaining to the lineout had never been adopted. The game against Eastern Province proved that London Counties and Newport had been right when they came back from South Africa the year before and said that apart from starting with something of a gap between each player, the referees in that country seemed to allow everything in the lineout to go on just as it had before.

If they were to go on deflecting the ball instead of catching it in the lineout, the Lions had no option but to act as they did. With Moloney a doubtful quantity because of injury, they just could not afford to risk serious damage to Edwards with the first test only a fortnight away. He had to be protected, and from then on, he was.

It was in this match, too, that any doubts were dispelled about the playing tactics the Lions would use in matches which they thought might be difficult. They started with an emphatic measure of scrummage control and maintained it throughout, but Edwards did so much kicking for position that it was seven minutes before Bennett even touched the ball.

The Lions scored after only eight minutes when the Eastern Province fly-half, standing behind his own line, dropped a pass under pressure from a lineout. He tried to recover the ball and seemed to get his hands to it as it cannoned between himself, Slattery and Davies. The referee was not quite sure what had happened, and could be seen to be reflecting on his decision as he ran back. In the end, he gave the Lions a try, though neither Slattery nor Davies looked very sure who had scored it. Bennett could not convert.

The referee soon had another awkward moment at the other end of the field and again he looked as if he was uncertain what to do. Erasmus kicked ahead past Irvine after Eastern Province had switched the direction of an attack and raced for the ball with Bennett as it rolled deep into the Lions' in-goal area. There was enough bumping and boring for the stewards to raise an objection against either runner and when the players dived for the ball, the referee looked first as if he was about to turn away for a 25 drop-out. Then he raised his arm and signalled a try.

With the backs doing so much obstructing as they played this miserably barren game of kicking and chasing, they were soon as cross with each other as the forwards were and the match became thoroughly ill-tempered. The referee had no control of it at any stage and to make matters even worse, he went on making mistakes. There was a reverberating accidental offside as the Lions bumped into each other as Rees kicked ahead after Irvine had come into the line but the referee did not notice it and allowed Davies to score. With three notable exceptions, South African referees were not very good, but of all their many blind spots, this offence of accidental offside remained the one they most rarely saw. Bennett converted the try from well out on the left, and added a penalty goal from a lineout to one he had kicked after the first try.

Apart from some vehement fist fights, the players had to suffer the added nuisance of swarms of flies. An unusual spell of weather earlier in the year had provided exactly the right breeding conditions for these insects but at that time they were trying to settle into the kikuyu grass on the surface of the pitch. They were small flies, not much bigger than midges, and rose in an indignant cloud every time a player put his boot down or fell on the pitch. McLauchlan had difficulty in wiping one of the insects out of his eye.

McLauchlan did not have much difficulty elsewhere because he gave Marais a most uncomfortable afternoon as the Lions wheeled the scrums to suit their convenience. Watching their forwards under so much pressure in the scrums convinced Eastern Province officials that they were right to question the ability of Marais as a prop, and any lingering doubts were dispelled in the second half when McLauchlan caught him in a bad position and lifted him right out of the top of a scrum. It was an embarrassing predicament for South Africa's captain-designate.

The Lions played their best Rugby early in the second half. Bennett switched the direction of an attack after Uttley had peeled from a lineout off Davies and Steele scored on the right. It was an amusing try because three defenders, with their eyes sticking out like organ-stops, left no sinew unstrained as they rushed across the field. Steele saw them coming, and saw that they had lost all their positional organisation, so he beat them by a simple expedient of stopping and turning inside as they stampeded headlong into touch.

Bennett converted that try and kicked two more penalty goals, first when Irvine was tripped and then when the Lions caught their opponents offside at a scrum. Eastern Province showed a good profit when they tripped Irvine because he was running so dangerously through the middle of the field that there is not much doubt that the Lions would have scored another try if he had been able to continue.

With twenty minutes left, and the Eastern Province forwards out of contention, the Lions were in a position to thrash their opponents by forty or fifty points, but instead they relaxed, and lost their grip. It was as if they had said, 'We have won the match, and we have won the fight. What else is there to do?'

Eastern Province took advantage of the drop in the pressure to score two more tries, although the first of these was yet another gift from the referee. It started with a tapped penalty, which Eastern Province did not even kick, and it ended when the referee blew his whistle to stop the play but changed his mind and gave a try as Marais dived over the line past the stationary Lions' defenders.

Irvine had run with considerable spirit from full-back but the

Lions were clearly nervous about his fielding. Again this had been erratic, and by hanging back to cover possible mistakes the Lions lost their defensive formation to such an extent that they opened the middle of the field for Eastern Province to score. The open side wing went through the centre and passed to Campher who crawled over the line as he was tackled. Erasmus converted. It was the only time the Lions had three tries scored against them on tour and from that match onwards, Geoff Evans dropped out of contention for the Lions' test team.

Possibly the unhappiest man in Port Elizabeth that night was the referee, Fonnie van der Vyver. 'It is the worst game I have ever had in my life,' he said, and it happened on the day when obviously he wanted to have the best. The hopes and aspirations of referees are not much different from those of players and when he was chosen for one of the first four games of the Lions tour, Mr. van der Vyver must have known that if he did well, he would have been on the panel of four referees submitted to the Lions for consideration for the first test match. In one afternoon, he had seen all his hopes smashed to smithereens. He had tumbled from the position of being a possible test match referee to one in which he was not even considered for any more of the Lions' matches. It was hard not to feel sorry for him because although almost everything had gone wrong for him, at least he had been impartial.

Bill McBride, the Lions captain, said drily at the reception afterwards that it had been a hard-fought game, and Hannes Marais pleaded with the newspapermen not to make too much of the incidents that had taken place. Some hopes. The newspapers that evening and the next day were plastered with pictures of the fisticuffs. One of the favourites was the photograph of Gordon Brown on his back holding one of his opponents on top of him while he punched him repeatedly in the face. Brown had been enraged when his opponent had butted him deliberately in the face, and Brown went on discouraging him for so long that any photographer who might have missed the shot first time round had ample time to line up another. He would have even had enough time to run round from the other side of the field and change his film!

Rugby football did not present its best face in South Africa that weekend, because up in Springs, the French club Tarbes became involved in such a prolonged fight against Eastern Transvaal that the referee abandoned the match 20 minutes from the end. The result was that the newspapers had difficulty in deciding which Rugby fight picture to print biggest. In the end, they chose the match at Springs. At least that diverted some of the attention from the Lions' game, but it could have done nothing to persuade parents that Rugby football was a game for their children to play.

Roger Uttley had already decided that he had had enough for the day. He felt groggy after the kick on his head and he left the reception early. Gareth Edwards was also suffering from the effects of concussion though he did not realise to what extent until he read the newspapers on Monday.

In the meantime, Edwards had another unfortunate experience, and one which left his stomach feeling even worse than his head had felt on the Saturday afternoon. He loves fishing and on the Sunday, while one or two of the Lions went sailing, he and the others decided to relax by going out from Port Elizabeth in quite a big boat.

They went more than ten miles offshore, but before they had gone a quarter of a mile, Billy Steele was sick. As the shore line receded, and the swell grew bigger and bigger, more and more of the Lions succumbed, until in the end only Mervyn Davies and Mike Burton seemed completely unaffected. Some, like Phil Bennett and Ian McLauchlan, managed to hang on to their breakfast, but it was touch and go. Certainly, they had no thought of eating or drinking anything, which suited Burton and Davies admirably, because they had a crate of sandwiches and hard-boiled eggs, and they were able to eat them all themselves.

'Have a nice bit of fatty pork,' said Davies, hospitably. 'I've got a bit, thank you,' replied Burton, licking it as greasily as he could. The others just groaned and hung over the side. Burton and Davies had all the beer, too.

It was a debatable point whether Gareth Edwards was more ill than Roger Uttley, or whether Roger Uttley was more ill than Gareth Edwards. They both hung in the bows, with their false teeth in their hands, puking their hearts out. They took it in turns to lie in the most comfortable position. 'Please,' said Edwards to the skipper, 'I'm only asking you to take us back.'

Afterwards, he said, 'As soon as the boat stopped, and started to rock in that swell, I felt terrible. I've always loved life and living, and I've always thought that whatever else went wrong, at least I had that. But out on that boat, I wanted to die. I felt so bad that I really felt like throwing myself overboard and ending it all there and then.'

CHAPTER 9

Mossel Bay

THE Lions trained again at the Boet Erasmus stadium before they left for Mossel Bay on Monday. Bobby Windsor watched gloomily from the side of the pitch. He had injured his ankle in the last few minutes of the match against Eastern Province and an X-ray had revealed some damage to the bone. 'It might be a chipped bone, or even a hairline fracture,' he said. He was limping badly, and shaking his head at the thought that the injury might be serious enough for him to be sent home and replaced. At that moment, he would have been both astonished and delighted to know that after the game against S.W. Africa, he would turn out to be the only Lion to play in every Saturday match for the rest of the tour.

After warming up for a surprising time considering the heat of the sun, the Lions addressed themselves to a lineout practice. This was what we had been expecting to see. Syd Millar told the forwards that what had happened against Eastern Province could not be allowed to happen again. He was very explicit. 'Now we are going to do something about it,' he said, and threw them a ball. This area of the practice was effective. On the other side of the field, the backs were not nearly so good. They made so many errors in passing that the percentage of success in the moves they tried was unacceptably low. J. P. R. Williams tried to bring some order and consistency into the confusion around him but even though his own positioning and passing and watching of the ball were immaculate, very little of it rubbed off on the other backs.

When the Lions had finished training, they went up to the airport to fly in two DC 3's either to Oudtshoorn or to George, nobody seemed quite sure which, where they would look at an ostrich farm on their way to Mossel Bay. That particular flight down the coast is invariably bumpy as the air from the mountains rolls down over the sea, and when the aircraft turn inland to thread between the mountain passes, the view of the rocky, pine-clad slopes is a good bit too close for comfort for most people. What made it worse was that the aircraft went to the wrong place. Or at any rate, it went to the right place first and then went on to the other place, which meant that the Lions had to go all the way back in a bus. By the time they reached the ostrich farm, the degree to which they could be amused by three of the farm workers racing around on the backs of the ostriches was distinctly limited. Mike Burton climbed on the back of an ostrich, which managed to bear the weight without buckling at the knees, and Dr. J. P. R. Williams did a novel exploration for a possible tracheotomy by sticking his hand and arm all the way down the neck of one of the birds. He looked reasonably confident about it too, though one or two of the players watched closely to see if he would get both his hand and his arm back.

The Lions then had tea and set off on the long drive over the distant range of hills, with the protea growing wild by the roadside, and down the twenty mile sweep of empty land to the sea. The white lighthouse still stood high on the hill above Mossel Bay, just as it had in 1968, and the Santos Hotel was still tucked away in the shelter of the bay far below. The one-track railway line was still there, too, between the hotel and the sea, though trains seemed to run much less frequently. Perhaps the peach-canning factory further round the bay had cut production, or perhaps the shellfish had gone somewhere else. With the wall of the little harbour sticking out, Mossel Bay is an ideal place to go fishing and Tom David nursed his hamstring injury and consoled himself by hauling in the biggest fish of the tour.

It was at Mossel Bay, at the ground on top of the hill, that Syd Millar took it upon himself to instruct Andy Irvine in the arts of catching a high ball. As a coach of the scrummage, Millar had impressed all the tight forwards and had earned their respect, but it seemed something of a case of the halt leading the blind when he launched into the intricacies of basket catching and body flex and positioning sideways under the high ball in such a way as to avoid looking into the sun. In any case, it seemed extremely unlikely that S.W. Districts would be strong enough to test Irvine's capacity as a catcher. 'We shall be lucky to get any ball to kick,' said one of their officials gloomily.

S.W. Districts were not convinced that they ought to be playing the Lions at all. They were very much a minor union, and they had seen other small unions forego their right to play the tourists in exchange for the share of a gate at a bigger venue. N.E. Cape had learned against the All Blacks in 1970 that there was positively no point in a union such as theirs playing a major touring side. The All Blacks had scored 17 tries and had won 85-0.

This annihilation made South Africans begin to realise that they would have to reverse the policy which has led to the fragmentation of their provincial Rugby and which has caused so much damage to the quality of the game being played. Perhaps at one time it was politically expedient to dilute the power of the bigger battalions by creating smaller unions and giving them votes but by the time the Lions arrived in 1974 it had made so much of a mess of the playing structure of South African provincial Rugby that many of the games had become so one-sided as to be not worth playing.

There is now a move back towards a concentration of the playing resources of South Africa into fewer and more powerful provincial teams. This is bound to produce a badly needed improvement in South African Rugby and it will also suit the probable needs of tourists in the future for shorter tours of something like 16 matches.

The All Blacks provided the first healthy shove along this path with what they did to N.E. Cape in 1970 and the Lions gave the move further impetus with what they did to S.W. Districts in 1974. They won 97-0 and in the process they scored 15 goals, a try and a penalty goal. In the circumstances, it was a good job that they were fielding the bulk of their reserve team. The whole thing might have become quite embarrassing if they had been really trying.

J. J. Williams scored six tries, which broke the record of five scored by W. Wallace in South Africa in 1924. Alan Old scored 37 points from 15 conversions, a try and a penalty goal, which beat the British record of 23 points scored by Bob Hiller against Border in 1968 and by Phil Bennett against Western Transvaal in 1974. Old also broke the all-comers individual record established by Gerald Kember of the All Blacks in 1970, when he scored 34 points against N.E. Cape.

Old missed only one kick at goal all afternoon, and until the end of the match, when the Lions were strolling round to score by the posts, some of the kicks were far from easy. His achievement was so popular with the coloured community that they stormed on to the field at the end of the match and mobbed him with such enthusiasm that he must have wondered whether he would survive to celebrate. Old had already set the record for a British player in South Africa by scoring 24 points when playing for England against Griqualand West in 1972.

The 16 tries scored by the Lions against S.W. Districts also broke the British record of 13 established by the British Isles (no one had thought of calling them the Lions then) against Pietermaritzburg in 1891.

The highest number of tries scored in a match by a touring team in South Africa remains the 17 scored by the All Blacks against N.E. Cape in 1970 and but for the difference in scoring values, their win in that match would remain the biggest. As New Zealanders were quick to point out, the only true comparison between the two scores would have been either to add 17 points to the All Blacks' score, which would have given them victory by 102 points to nil, or to deduct 16 points from the Lions' score, which would have reduced their victory to a paltry 81-0. As Dr. Danie Craven said afterwards, all these records and the arguments about them were absolutely meaningless anyway, because a win by 97 points to nil does no good for anybody. All it did was prove how wrong S.W. Districts had been to hang on to their fixture against the touring sides for one more tour. I do not imagine that they will be allowed to do that again, which means that their name may be enshrined for all time as the province in South Africa that took the biggest beating ever from a touring team.

Some of the Lions, of course, might have argued that the exercise was worth-while. To a runner, a try is a try, and to J. J. Williams, his afternoon was worth that three times over. The six tries he scored equalled the six scored by David Duckham in rather sterner circumstances in New Zealand, and they represented a useful part of the healthy total he acquired by the end of the tour.

Not that the players would have stopped to think of what was at stake at the time. For instance, when J. P. R. Williams came on as substitute for the injured Tom Grace near the end and gave the scoring pass for J. J. Williams' sixth try, he could have scored himself. He saved that for later, producing the daintiest of side-steps to score between the posts. Later, he scored another.

One of the most interesting moments of the afternoon came in the second half when J. J. Williams kicked ahead from just outside the S.W. Districts 25 and was overhauled by Geoff Evans in the race for the try. Evans scored two other tries as well.

To Alan Old, too, those 37 points represented much more than a record. Inevitably, they coloured the immediate post-match thinking about the fly-half position at a vital time just before the first test match. Perhaps John Moloney, Gareth Edwards and Andy Irvine would have argued a case for S.W. Districts as well. The game may have looked like a semi-opposed practice session bit it gave Moloney a match after his injury and it gave Edwards a rest. Irvine caught everything, too.

Max Baise was also glad of the game. Most referees dislike processions. They prefer matches which present a challenge, but at least he had directed the procession along the right route and he had made his appearance at exactly the right time to take Fonnie van der Vyver's place on the panel of referees for the first test.

CHAPTER 10

Western Province

ON their way back to the airstrip at Oudtshoorn, the Lions were taken to see the Kango caves. These are huge underground caverns full of weird formations of stalactites and stalagmites. Some of these mineral growths, formed by the solids left from evaporating water, are so big that it is possible to calculate that the caves are more than half a million years old. They were formed originally by an underground river cascading through the mountain which cut the caves and then began to form the stalactites and stalagmites as the waters slowed to a trickle which dripped off the roofs. The caves were discovered by a farmer two hundred years ago when he shot and wounded a buck, and saw it disappear into the side of the mountain. The farmer was a humane man, and he went after it to put it out of its misery. He then found the caves and called his natives to bring him torches so that he could see them better.

The stalactites and stalagmites have formed themselves into shapes which look like works of sculpture and now they are all individually illuminated with coloured lights. The guide switches off the lights, to increase the dramatic effect, and then switches on the illuminations one at a time. One of the mineral formations is like the pipes of a huge organ. In 1968, John O'Shea had managed to creep across to it in the darkness and sit in front of it so that when the lights came up, he was able to mime to the recorded organ music which is played at the same time, as if he had just come up out of the pit in a theatre organ.

Syd Millar said then that the place had changed out of all recognition since he last visited it in 1962. The stalactites and the stalagmites had grown a hundredth of an inch. They had done it again in 1974. They are persistent things.

A visit to the caves involves a lot of walking along rocky ledges. It was not the sort of exercise to appeal to Bobby Windsor, who was still hobbling from his ankle injury. He was moving much better but remembering how he had felt on the Monday morning, it was still a considerable surprise to see that he had been chosen to play against Western Province in the next match.

The selection for the Western Province game at Newlands was the most significant of the tour to date. It was bound to be, because with the first test only a week away on the same ground, it was obvious that the Lions would choose the bulk of the team they expected to play against South Africa. The choice of Windsor, therefore, meant that he had been preferred to Kennedy, despite the injury to his ankle. The only conclusion to be drawn from that was that the Lions preferred Windsor's greater commitment in the loose and his solidity as a scrummager because neither hooker had been required to do much as a striker. Both had the pleasure of playing in a pack which went forward somewhere between a foot and five yards at every scrum, and as they were rarely required to strike on the opposition ball, neither of them had to do much more to win their own ball than stick their leg out. In Windsor's case, he sometimes went so low that he even headed it back!

Windsor's props were to be Ian McLauchlan and Sandy Carmichael. This was expected, because they were much the most experienced. They had played for the Lions in New Zealand in 1971 and since then had played so well for Scotland that they had persuaded a very influential body of opinion in Wales that they were the best in the game. The chance injury to Carmichael, however, gave Fran Cotton an opportunity which he had taken with such determination that he had made people think that perhaps he might turn out to be the better player after all. Once a player is saddled with the reputation of being not quite good enough in one department or another, it takes a lot of persistence and a lot of work and a lot of convincing performances to persuade the specialists that he has eradicated the weakness. Cotton had done that, which said as much for his character as it did for his ability.

At lock, the Lions had only to decide who should partner Bill McBride, and although Gordon Brown was better suited as a front jumper himself, the peremptory treatment of Chris Ralston after the game at Windhoek indicated that the selectors thought that he had not been fully fit for that match. Ralston did not play again before the unimportant match at Mossel Bay, and with Brown going from strength to strength, the issue was settled.

The selection at loose forward was more difficult. Andy Ripley, Tony Neary and Tom David had been fortunate enough to feature in the flying start against Western Transvaal and they played again in the convincing win over Boland. They were associated, therefore, with teams that had won well. The other loose forwards had been associated with the team that had struggled against S.W. Africa. In a sprint of matches as short as that before the first test, this was a considerable handicap. I had no doubt from the beginning that Fergus Slattery and Mervyn Davies should have been the front runners but at that time, the door in front of them looked firmly shut and it only opened when Tom David lost his place because of his hamstring injury. This was a cruel blow for him at the worst possible time. As Tony Neary prefers to play on the open side, Stewart McKinney was brought in as a blind side flanker to partner him.

From the beginning, Phil Bennett had been the obvious partner for Gareth Edwards in the test matches, and although Alan Old had strengthened his position at fly-half, the pattern of selection was bound to put Bennett in against Western Province. The only areas of doubt behind the scrum were in the centre and on the wing. In the centre, the Lions were looking for strength in the tackle and strength at committing a man and setting up a maul, and so they chose Roy Bergiers and Ian McGeechan. The choice on the wing was more difficult, or at any rate, the choice of left wing was more difficult. Billy Steele had done well enough on the right, but with three right wingers and one left winger in the party, the choice of left wing was either going to be limited or a makeshift. J. J. Williams was the only winger with international experience of playing on the left but the Lions seemed to think that Clive Rees might turn out to be the better bet.

The weather was still glorious when the Lions returned to Cape Town but Gerhard Vivier, one of the South African broadcasters with the party, sat in the shade outside the Arthur's Seat Hotel and shook his head pessimistically. 'This can't last,' he said. 'Not in Cape Town.'

I explained that in eight previous visits to the Cape in winter, I had never even seen a cloud in the sky. 'Then it is absolutely certain to rain this time,' he said with gloomy conviction. 'We're here for twelve days.' Gerhard must have had a built-in barometer. The weather broke that night and it rained so hard that the Lions had to train on an adjoining pitch when they went to Newlands the next day. For the next week, the sun struggled to hold its own with the rain but eventually it gave up an unequal struggle and went off to melt the roads in the Isle of Man while we looked round for a lifeboat.

For the first match at Newlands, though, the pitch was only soft. The Lions were due to play three of their next four matches there, as well as make their longest stay in one hotel in history, and it was then that the value of the work which had been done in improving the itinerary was appreciated. The first to recognise the importance of this were the South Africans themselves, and in particular, former Springboks like Dave Stewart who lived in Cape Town. He shook his head ruefully and said, 'The Lions will have trained and played at Newlands for ten days before the test.

It will be like a home ground to them. They will be far better acclimatised that the Springboks.'

However, this cosy prospect was given a nasty jolt by Western Province. They started the match as if they were going to lose by fifty points, but they pulled themselves together so well that by the middle of the second half, they were swarming all over the field and could have won. They only lost because of bad goal-kicking and because they failed to touch down a ball running loose in the Lions' in-goal.

Nothing looked less likely at the beginning. The game had barely started when Oosthuizen panicked so badly in defence in the Western Province centre that he sliced the ball right away from his forwards to Rees on the Lions' open side wing. Rees was standing there unmarked and all he had to do was catch the ball and run in and score. Bennett took the kick at goal but topped it so badly that it scuttled along the ground.

It seemed unimportant. Bennett kicked a penalty goal when McCallum was penalised for not putting the ball in straight, the Lions rolled forward in the scrums and Brown caught the ball so confidently in the lineout that Western Province looked little better than S.W. Districts at Mossel Bay.

This impression was heightened when du Plessis took a wild drop-out from his 25 and foolishly kicked the ball straight to J. P. R. Williams. The Lions' full-back caught it, and with his long hair flying under his headband, he surged straight through the middle of the field with such a combination of muscular power and shrewd little side-steps that he had reached the last of the defence before he was pulled down. The power of Williams' running was familiar, but the cleverness of it was something new. It looked as if it had been borrowed from Gerald Davies, and so did the way in which Williams made the ball available to his support. Instead of expiring head-on in a snort of effort against insuperable odds as he had done so often in the past, Williams made sure that he was able to make the ball available to his support. Brown was thundering up on his right and he took the pass to drive over the line and score. Again Bennett missed the conversion, which was not too difficult by his standards, and then had a spell when his place kicking went even further awry.

These failures gave Western Province some respite and then a spirited counter-attack launched by McDonald from his own 25 encouraged the whole team to sort themselves out. Immelman started to win a lot of ball at the front of the line-out and du Plessis did the same at the back. This enabled Western Province to launch the drives which the Lions had been using with such profit and it enabled their loose forwards to break round the tail of the line-out and into the midfield. This in turn enabled them to to set up some loose ball which they used to generate even more momentum. Coetzee was especially effective at close quarters and he and his scrum-half McCallum, who played equally well, were able to set up McDonald and du Plessis in the attacking game which they played best.

The Lions' loose forwards were made to look thoroughly anonymous. With their options in attack so drastically reduced, they were unable to tie in the opposing back row and their close tackling was not good enough to prevent Bennett being exposed to some very embarrassing moments in defence in midfield. Western Province just poured through and the Lions were fortunate that J. P. R. Williams and Edwards defended and resisted with such strength and such resource.

The Lions were also fortunate that Snyman's goalkicking was no better than Bennett's. He never even shaped as if he would kick a goal. Snyman missed two very easy kicks from in front of the posts before half-time and full-back Brink missed another.

Western Province also passed badly. On three occasions, they broke out of defence and either mistimed their passes or made them so poorly that they wasted overlaps. Oosthuizen especially had an unfortunate time. His strength was there for all to see but he either kicked when he should have passed or failed to work himself into the right position to set up the man outside him.

Even so, Western Province scored one try and should have had another. They forced a maul in midfield after a lineout on the right and McCallum went on towards his left wing where he made a try for Read. Snyman missed the conversion. Just after that, Steele came over to his left to cover a kick ahead but the ball squirmed away from him in goal and left Claxton, the Western Province prop, with nothing to do but fall on it to score. Somehow, he failed to do this properly and even though the referee Ian Gourley was criticised afterwards for his decision, there is no doubt that he was right when he said that Claxton had not grounded the ball.

The one contribution that the referee did make to the Lions' cause was his interpretation of the laws in the lineout, where he displayed such a light touch that he allowed the players to do almost what they wanted. He permitted the forwards to bind and to wedge and to widen and close gaps as they pleased. Above all, he allowed the throwers to throw the ball straight at the jumpers instead of down the line of touch. This enabled the Lions to win some ball that they would have been sorely pressed to win otherwise, because Ripley was so handicapped by an old back injury that he could not stretch himself to jump properly.

Still, the Lions were more than thankful to reach half-time leading 11-4 and in the second half, they were just as glad to see Edwards kicking so well from the back of the scrummage that he was able to preserve a precious positional safety margin against any further alarums and excursions.

There were quite a few of these but only one led to anything. McCallum broke to the open side from near his own 25 and du Plessis and McDonald went straight through the middle of the field before throwing a long pass out to Read on the left wing. Read took rather a long time to attach himself to the ball but he caught it at the third attempt and ran on to score his second try, which again was not converted.

The scrummage was the only part of the game where the Lions retained control. Cockrell hooked well for Western Province in exceptionally difficult circumstances, because his front row was short of weight and his scrum was retreating at a rate of knots, but at least the Lions were able to reduce the value of the Western Province ball, and on their own put-in, they were able to give Edwards the quality of possession he needed to make room for his kicks. These kept the game mostly in the Western Province half, however precariously, and put Bennett within range to kick penalty goals should the opportunities present themselves.

Two more did. The first increased the Lion's lead to 14-4 early in the second half, and the second, kicked from far out on the right touchline, closed the door firmly in Western Province's face right at the end of the match. The Lions might also have scored another try, but Rees had a moment of positional uncertainty and knocked on when he had the chance of picking up a loose ball and scoring in the corner.

Western Province went on doing the right thing even after the match was over. Morné du Plessis took his team into the Lions' dressing-room to congratulate them on their victory and at the reception afterwards he thanked them in one of the best speeches of the tour.

'As players, we have to work hard at this game,' he said, 'and sometimes we wonder whether it is all worth it. But then comes a day like this one. Everybody has been talking about it for weeks. When we got to the ground, there was this tremendous feeling of excitement. One of the boys sat in the dressing-room before the game and said, "This is a big day". He was right. This has been a big day, and we in South Africa have been short of big days. We must thank the Lions for coming here and making it possible.'

CHAPTER 11

Proteas

ONE or two of the Lions who had been watching from the stand felt like thanking Western Province for making other things possible, too, because the game had gone so badly for the projected test team that the whole selection had been thrown open again. All but one of the loose forwards who had not played against Western Province knew that their hopes of being chosen for the test team were much, much brighter and some of the backs also looked forward to the mid-week game against the Proteas with the keenness of men who saw that a chance was there for the taking.

The odd man out among the loose forwards was Tom David. He had not recovered sufficiently from his hamstring injury to be chosen for the Proteas' match, and therefore he knew that he would not be considered for the test.

The Lions were probably glad of the chance to experiment at loose forward in any case. The idea of playing Roger Uttley on the flank had been in their minds from the beginning of the tour. They chose Uttley and Fergus Slattery on the flanks, with Mervyn Davies at number eight. The only difference was that Slattery and Uttley were to play on the right and left of the scrum, rather than open and blind side as might have been expected. Uttley knew quite well that such an arrangement could expose his defensive limitations when he was on the open side, but he was prepared to go along with it and take the risk because Slattery much preferred to play on the right. Slattery was also chosen as captain.

With Gordon Brown and Chris Ralston in the second row, and Mike Burton and Fran Cotton propping Ken Kennedy, it looked a capable and productive pack and Uttley was put through a short course of instruction on his new duties when the team went to train at the Hamilton's ground at Green Point on the Monday.

That afternoon, the Lions visited the university for coloured students in Cape Town. In the evening, they were the chief guests of the coloured community at the opera. Lions teams had attended social functions of that sort on previous tours but they had never played a match against a representative coloured team and no one was in any doubt of the significance of the occasion.

The only fear was that the political significance would weigh more heavily with those responsible for the preparation of the Proteas team than the sporting significance. That was what had happened when England played the Proteas in 1972. The Proteas had gone on the field with the one object of achieving a better result than some of the White teams that had played England. They had not been concerned with the game as such. Perhaps this was understandable, and the Proteas certainly achieved their object because they had held England to a score of 11-6, but their anxiety to play a purely destructive game to keep the score down had led to a match in which the England players were buffetted and provoked by the most blatant late tackles and obstruction from persistently offside positions. The infringement of the laws in the mauls and the rucks was also done on such an uninhibited scale that it would have been comical if it had not been so dangerous physically.

England felt then that the problem had been aggravated by the fact that the match had been refereed by a coloured official whose lack of experience at that level had left him completely out of his depth. Even so, the England players had to exercise the utmost restraint to avoid a dangerous situation.

Everyone hoped that the decision of the South African Federation to invite a White referee to take charge of their fixture against the Lions in 1974 would make for a better game than the one they had played against England in 1972, but some of the England players still had their reservations about the whole operation.

One of them was Alan Old. He admitted that he was not looking forward to playing against the Proteas, even though he must have known that as things had gone so badly for Phil Bennett against Western Province, he was more than half-way to being chosen for the test team. Old had been on the substitutes' bench when England had played the Proteas and he had watched what had happened with dismay.

'I was praying that I wouldn't have to go on the field in that game,' he said, 'and the only match I didn't want to play in on this tour was this one against the Proteas.'

Alan Old must have been psychic, because he was injured so badly by a late tackle in the first half of the match against the Proteas that one of his knee ligaments was severed. It was stitched together in hospital. His leg was put in plaster and three weeks later, he was flown home.

Rugby players are used to taking hard knocks and they know that they are playing a game which always contains the risk of a serious injury, but the tackle which wrecked Old's knee was absolutely disgraceful, because it had no relation to the play at all.

Burton picked the ball up from a maul and passed out to Old who swivelled with his back to the opposition in passing to Evans in the centre. Evans had caught the ball and was in the act of passing it to Milliken when one of the Proteas' centres just put his shoulder down and charged into Old from behind. Old was hurled into the air by the impact and felt such a pain in his leg that he thought it was broken. He was helped to his feet but the Lions' players gathered round him could see that the ligaments of his knee were quivering in spasm because of the damage that had been done. Dave Goddess helped him off the field and within a few minutes, those inside the ground heard the alarm bell of the ambulance as it left to take Old to hospital.

Milliken moved to fly-half when Old went off and Bergiers came on as substitute. The surviving midfield combination then dropped more passes than they held, but it was hard to be sure whether this was caused by a natural instinct for self-preservation or whether it was due to square pegs being in round holes.

The Proteas had given notice of their intentions at the very first scrum. They made no real attempt to contest possession of the ball and as the Lions heeled it and held it, the whole of the Proteas' midfield ran offside. The referee gave a penalty kick and Old kicked the goal.

Much the same thing happened at almost every set piece and in every loose ball situation for the rest of the match. The Proteas made no attempt to play football. They just set out to break away and to spoil.

Old soon kicked another penalty goal but it made no difference. On one occasion, the whole Proteas scrum disengaged itself so the Lions' front row went clean through. There was then nothing to stop the Lions pack marching forward thirty yards to score, but they did not do so, and the chance of an historic try was lost. Perhaps Mervyn Davies thought that his pack might trip over its own feet. Anyway, he picked up the ball, even though the whole Proteas' scrum was standing alongside waiting to tackle.

The referee did not give a penalty kick on that occasion. Perhaps he thought that as there was no longer a hindmost foot, the scrum was over. Perhaps he was playing advantage, though it was hard to detect any advantage in being crouched over the ball with about eight players waiting to jump on you as soon as you went to pick it up. Perhaps the referee was just being kind to the Proteas.

There was no doubt that Mr. Katzenellenbogen was in a difficult position because if he had penalised the Proteas on their merits there would have been no game at all, and there might have been a riot. He simply could not see everything that was being done off the ball, but on the other hand, he had seen what happened to Old. He gave a penalty kick on that occasion and the Lions scored from it. Irvine kicked an up-and-under which Uttley lost in the sun, and when the ball came down, it bounced back off his head to the other forwards as they followed up. They did not allow themselves to be disconcerted by this unexpected and novel means of transferring the ball and they bunched in behind Slattery after Kennedy had given him a pass and drove him over the line for a try. Irvine could not convert the try but he did kick a penalty goal before half-time when the Lions led 13-6. Tobias had dropped a goal from a scrum for the Proteas and he had also kicked a penalty goal.

From the very beginning, some of the Lions forwards had known that they would not be able to stand on ceremony and they had gone about their business with a purpose that had drawn some protests from their own backs. However, when the team gathered to discuss the proceedings at half-time, the backs had seen enough to persuade them to withdraw those protests unconditionally. They were even offering the forwards encouragement.

The Proteas spoiling continued to be effective for another 20 minutes, in which they confined the Lions to a try scored by Brown from the front of a lineout, and another penalty goal kicked by Irvine. Then the Proteas tired from the sheer physical slog of holding their much heavier opponents and in the last 20 minutes, the Lions scored 17 points. Bergiers scored an easy try when for once the Proteas' defence lapsed on the blind side of a scrum and then Evans put in J. J. Williams from the open side of a scrum. Finally, Milliken scored after Ralston and Burton had set up a maul. Irvine kicked another penalty goal and converted the try scored by Bergiers.

The referee did his best to appear impartial. He penalised the Lions whenever he could. Even then, there was an enormous imbalance of penalty kicks in favour of the Lions and when the coloured spectators came over the fence near the end of the match and began to crowd the touch-line, the situation became rather tense. When Irvine went to convert the last try from near the touchline, a spectator tried to run on the field and push him despite a formidable cordon of coloured police. It was hardly surprising that Irvine missed.

It was also noticeable that at the end, the referee let the game go on until he was positioned on the touchline in the middle of the field right opposite the players' tunnel. He then blew his whistle and was off the field and into the tunnel so fast that not even the Lions could catch him, and some of them were doing their best. Max Baise had done exactly the same thing when he refereed England's game against the Africans at Port Elizabeth. I remember remarking that even Gerald Davies could not have caught him.

Teams from overseas want to help the advance of Rugby in the non-White communities in South Africa, and it is true that visitors are in the best position to do that, but the non-White authorities must fulfil their half of the bargain and stop using the games as a means of making a comparison between the ability of the coloured teams and some of the weaker White teams in South Africa.

Perhaps it was inevitable that the non-White teams would adopt this approach, at least in the beginning, but now that the principle of playing these games has been established, it is time that the the non-Whites stopped making political points and started playing Rugby. Neither England nor the Lions enjoyed their games against the Proteas, and that is the whole point of playing any sport. Fixtures are reviewed before every tour and no visiting team would want to go on playing matches against players who did what the Proteas did to Alan Old.

By the time the match ended, the ambulance taking Old to hospital had only just arrived. The journey took nearly an hour because to start with, the ambulance could not even get out of the ground. All the exits and all the approach roads and all the land round the stadium at Goodwood were jammed with parked cars. The ambulance bell which had been heard inside the stadium had been rung by the driver in a desperate attempt to clear the way.

Alan Old was accompanied to hospital by Phil Bennett, who also acted as a stretcher bearer. First he and the driver made Old as comfortable as they could, and then they set off. They had not gone 100 yards before they discovered that they could not move any further because of the parked cars in the way. They knew it would be hopeless to try to find the drivers so they did their best to open either the doors or the windows to move them out of the way. To make matters worse, the ambulance driver was not too sure of the best way to get to the Leeuwendal Nursing Home, which hopefully was their destination.

Someone suggested that if he turned round and went another way, he might do better, so he climbed into his cab and clunked the ambulance into gear and went into reverse. He had just got the vehicle on full lock when he backed into a parked car with such a clatter that Alan Old went almost as far into the air as he did when he was tackled. Phil Bennett first made sure that his team-mate was all right and then jumped out to see the extent of the damage. No one seemed too bothered about that and the driver drove forward again. He disentangled the ambulance from the other vehicle with a great scrunching and jerked forward on his way, with Alan Old hanging on grimly in the back. They did not get far along that route, either. They squeezed past the rows of parked cars, and sidled round tree roots and put their wheels on verges but in the end, they came to just as firm a halt as they had in the other direction. However, they did discover someone who knew a way round the impasse. Unfortunately, this meant reversing again. The driver was game to the last. Once more he climbed into his cab and once more he clunked the ambulance into reverse. Phil Bennett guided him backwards until it was time to turn, the driver looked into his mirror, and with a confident spin of his wheel, he backed straight into a concrete post. Once more Alan Old slithered across the back of the ambulance.

When they had sorted themselves out, they managed to work their way out of the car parks and on to the open road. They were only just in time. The match was nearly over.

Even then, their adventures were not finished because when they arrived at the Leeuwendal Nursing Home, Phil Bennett picked up one end of the stretcher and the driver picked up the other and they set off to find the right department. They were given to understand that it was on the eleventh floor of a certain building, and after much hopping about and pressing of lift buttons and manoeuvring of the stretcher through awkward doors, they arrived. They were then told that they had come to the wrong building and that the department for dealing with cases like this was somewhere else. So back they went to the lift, and after more hopping about and pressing of lift buttons and manoeuvring through awkward doors, they came to the ground floor again. Then they trudged across to another building and when eventually they arrived Phil Bennett was every bit as glad to get there as Alan Old, because when he put down the stretcher for the last time, he felt like joining him on it.

The specialist did not take long to make a diagnosis. He touched the side of the ligament and could tell at once that Alan Old had played his last match on the 1974 British Lions' tour of South Africa.

CHAPTER 12

Springbok Selection

JOHAN CLAASSEN and the other Springbok selectors met later that evening to choose the South African team to play the Lions in the first test at Newlands the following Saturday. They had been evaluating players in training camps, on internal tours and in trial matches for something like three months. It was not difficult to see that they were uncertain of those values, because there had been such a large turnover of players throughout the whole selection process. Men who had started out as potential Springboks in the training camp at Ellis Park in March had been falling out of contention at a disquieting rate.

The selectors were also divided about the style of play to adopt. With Johan Claassen reserving judgment, two of the selectors thought that they should pick Dawie Snyman at fly-half and run the ball and two more thought that they should pick Gerald Bosch and kick the leather off it. This was evident from the selection of the Springbok trial teams. Dirk de Vos and Paul Bayvel were the two scrum-halves and Dawie Snyman and Gerald Bosch were the two fly-halves. De Vos had played for years as a kicking scrum-half and had been so erratic on such a grand scale that one of his own selectors said of him, "At the end of one match, you want to build a monument to him. At the end of the next match, you want to shoot him."

Whatever else, Dirk de Vos' style of play could not possibly have helped Dawie Snyman to play a running game and while the Lions were beating the Proteas a few miles away at Goodwood, de Vos and Snyman were looking painfully innocuous in the Springbok trial at Newlands.

It was hard to understand this fragmentation of purpose by the Springbok selectors, because after all the arguments, Dawie Snyman had been chosen at fly-half in the "A" team. This seemed to indicate that Johan Claassen had come down on the side of the running game. Having done that, he might have given Snyman a scrum-half who was suited to his cause.

All this gave a strong impression of a divergence of opinion among the selectors and of a failure to grasp the essentials. Further evidence of this was provided by the strange story of Derek van den Berg, the Natal tight-head prop. Van den Berg had played against England in 1972, and had played well, but being a doctor in a hospital, he was extremely busy and perhaps not able to devote quite as much time to his Rugby as he would have liked.

Anyhow, he was invited to play in the Springbok trials, and so he went to the considerable trouble of arranging for other doctors to do his work while he took the time off to fly down from Durban to Cape Town to play in the trial.

Imagine his surprise and disappointment, therefore, when he emerged from the dressing room at Newlands changed and ready to play only to be confronted by a selector who said, 'What are you doing?'

Not unreasonably, van den Berg said with some mystification, 'I'm playing.'

'Oh no you're not,' said the selector. 'You're down here as a reserve.'

Van den Berg shrugged and went back into the dressing room to change back into his ordinary clothes. Having done that, he emerged from the dressing room with his kit-bag only to be confronted by another selector.

'What are you doing?' he said. 'Why aren't you changed?'

'I was changed,' said van den Berg patiently. 'But I've just changed back again because I've been told I'm not playing.'

'Who told you that?' he was asked. Van den Berg revealed all.

'Well, just you change back again and get ready to play,' he was told.

Van den Berg went back into the dressing room again, and took off his clothes again. By that time he must have felt like the lady called Ultra Violet who had been making such a name for herself as a strip artist and diverting so many of the readers of the Sunday newspapers in South Africa. While van den Berg was changing, the second selector went off for a discussion with the first selector. In the end, they reached a compromise. Van den Berg did play, but in only half the game. He could have been forgiven if he had felt that his time would have been better spent with his hospital patients.

This episode was fairly typical of the lack of clarity of purpose of the Springboks selectors. They were unsure of themselves, they were unsure of their players and they were unsure of their tactics, and they were in that situation because they were on new ground.

Johan Claassen had enjoyed his greatest triumph by going back into South Africa's Rugby past and picking some of the golden oldies to play against the All Blacks in 1970, and thanks partly to the unrealistic choice of tactics by New Zealand, the Springboks had won the series against an individually better team.

Claassen's instincts, therefore, must have been to go for age and experience. That was what he had done before, and it had worked. By 1974, however, South Africa had very few players with any appreciable experience of international football and therefore of proven international ability. All they had was age and innocence. Therefore, an entirely different selection exercise was involved. Instead of rearranging the products of the past, new players had to be found and they had to be moulded quickly into an effective combination.

To do this, it was essential to assess the strengths and weaknesses of the Lions in relation to South African Rugby, and it was essential to pick a Springbok team for the first test which could go forward with only minor modifications for the rest of the series. That meant that Johan Claassen and his colleagues had to make up their minds where South Africa could attack the Lions, where they had to defend, and above all, they had to make up their minds how South Africa were going to play. It soon became apparent that they had not perceived where they could attack the Lions or where they had to defend or how they were going to play. As an exercise in selection and tactical appreciation, the Springbok effort in 1974 was as sadly incompetent as much of the history of British selection and tactical appreciation before 1968.

Syd Millar had made no bones about the fact that the Lions were going to concentrate on the scrummage, and the Lions had already done well enough in the tight to show that this was an area where the Springboks would have to defend. The scrummage starts in the front row and South Africa needed a tight head prop who at best would make the Lions uncomfortable, and who at least would make them work. South Africa needed, in fact, a tight head who is what is known in the fight trade as a banger. By then, however, it was clear that the Springboks were already committed to Hannes Marais as captain, and whatever he had retained of his old technique, it looked as if he had lost the physical presence which in years gone by had made him such a formidable banger.

There was the added complication that Marais was only captain of Eastern Province on sufferance. It was obvious even to a visitor that Eastern Province preferred the captaincy of George Barnard, and as Ian Kirkpatrick was the coach of Eastern Province, as well as being one of the most influential national selectors, the Springbok selection panel must have known that their captain-designate did not enjoy the unqualified support of his province.

Whether David van der Merwe, of Boland, or Johnny Burger from Western Transvaal, or Johan Strauss, of Transvaal, or Hans Weber, of Northern Transvaal, or Martiens le Roux, of the Free State, were more effective tight heads than Marais was something the Springboks should have established back in the training camp and on their internal tour. Scrummaging is something which can be improved out of all recognition by practice, and although in the space of three months, South Africa could not have repaired substantial shortcomings in scrummaging technique, they should have been able to make the best of what they had.

Their failure to come to grips with this problem from the beginning was at the heart of the failure of the Springbok selectors throughout the series. For example, there was no indication that they even regarded Dawid van der Merwe as a serious contender, yet he had put Syd Millar himself out of the Lions' test team in 1968, and Fran Cotton regarded him as one of the best props he played against on tour. All except Strauss of the other props were similarly disregarded.

Again, once it became clear that scrummage was an area where the Springboks would have to defend, it became equally obvious that if they wanted to win any good ball at all, they would have to concentrate on the lineout. In this phase of the game, they had an outstanding jumper in J. G. Williams, but he needed to be supported with determination to make him effective. Similarly, the Springboks had at least one loose forward in Morné du Plessis who had shown himself capable of challenging for the ball at the back of the lineout and in the Western Province match against the Lions at Newlands the previous Saturday, Kobus Immelmann had demonstrated that it was possible to win a lot of ball from Bill McBride at the front of the lineout.

These signs were all encouraging for South Africa, and they were all as obvious as that towering hill or rock known as the Bishop's Nose on Table Mountain. At the very least, they should have done something to relieve the gloom and the pessimism in the country because they provided the Springbok selectors with a base from which they could work to build some sort of forward platform.

Johan Claassen and his colleagues ought to have seen, too, that if they could push their loose forwards through the middle of the field, as Western Province had done, Phil Bennett was physically not strong enough to help much with the defence, and that in turn would help the Springboks to commit J. P. R. Williams, which was another of their most urgent priorities. The Lions' full-back had shown himself to be so infernally good that the Springboks either had to bury him or to outflank him. If they could commit him to tackle or bury him in the ruck, they would have been in a position to move the ball quickly to the wings, where the Lions had shown that their defence could be penetrated.

After the game against Western Province, the Springbok selectors might have thought that the Lions themselves were in doubt about their choice at fly-half, and in that they were right, but the injury to Alan Old had settled that particular issue. Bennett was certain to be chosen in the Lions' test team.

All these considerations led to an easy appreciation of the Springboks' match requirements. They needed an aggressive tight head and a fully committed scrummage, but they needed to build their lineout and their platform for attack around J. G. Williams and Morné du Plessis. That meant that they had to provide those jumpers with support which was both determined and well organised. They also had to make use of the lineout peel to drive the ball through the middle of the field, and they needed a strong and a thrustful scrum-half to project their loose forwards into the midfield from the scrums.

The other essentials were to eliminate the avoidable mistakes which would lead to the Lions putting the ball into scrums and to eliminate any kicking which would set up J. P. R. Williams. The Springboks needed basically to play a midfield driving game off the lineout, and if they kicked the ball at all, they had to be absolutely certain of putting it into touch, or alternatively, of kicking it high enough and short enough to give a player like du Plessis the chance of challenging J. P. R. Williams for the catch.

In the Western Province game, the Springbok selectors had seen the shortcomings of du Plessis in defence and they had seen some of the rash things he did when kicking the ball, and so they ought to have known that they needed to play him on the flank as a lineout specialist and as a retriever of the ball from kicks. That in turn argued the necessity of choosing a grafter and a fetcher on the other flank, and above all, it argued the necessity of choosing an experienced number eight who was a top-class operator in defence.

To someone coming into the country from the outside, the selection looked straightforward. Tommy Bedford was the most experienced number eight in South Africa and a natural choice as captain, and Roy McCallum had just shown that he was exactly the sort of scrum-half that South Africa were looking for. What is more, Boland Coetzee had played well enough in the same Western Province team to demonstrate his capabilities as a grafter and fetcher, though it may have been that other forwards could have done Coetzee's job even better and provided more physical presence.

The key to this selection, of course, would have been the choice of Bedford as captain. This would not necessarily have meant dropping Marais, but it would have meant making a decision about whether Marais was worth his place in the team as a tight head and as a lineout peel support player. The other corollary of the selection would have been the dropping of Jan Ellis from the back row.

These two decisions were crucial to South Africa's forward play and to the tactical development of the series, but the Springbok selectors either did not see or would not accept that either of them might have been necessary. They had committed themselves to Marais as captain, and they had not even invited Bedford to the trials. What is more, it never seemed to occur to them to question the value of Ellis in the type of game that he would have to play, with the result that far from being dropped, Marais and Ellis were the only two Springbok forwards to play in every game in the series.

Later in the tour, it became apparent that there was an Afrikaaner hostility to Natal and to Rhodesia which was as unhealthy for the Afrikaaner and for South African Rugby as it was for the English speakers in Natal and Rhodesia.

Tommy Bedford's great crime had been that he had been outspoken about the urgent need for South African Rugby to reorganise after the Springboks' unsuccessful tour of Britain in 1969-70. He had recognised that British Rugby was going to stride far ahead of the game in the Republic. He had also stood aloof from the general euphoria after the Springboks had won all their matches in Australia in 1971. He thought that the lack of quality in the opposition ought to have been taken into account. It was not difficult to see that he did not share the general euphoria about Johan Claassen as a coach, either.

To make matters worse, Tommy Bedford had called Natal, 'the last outpost of the British Empire.' Apart from being very funny, this was a remarkably perceptive observation, and it should have been received with the tolerance accorded to a nice point, nicely made. After all, the Afrikaaner is in a position to afford tolerance now. He is in the majority, and he has the power, and he has had it for a generation. It is in his own interests to be magnanimous in victory over the minority English. It is pointless for him to get angry and stubborn and bloody-minded when Rhodesians and Natalians grumble that there is no point in them travelling to play in Springbok trials, because they never get picked even if they do play well. It would be much more constructive for the Afrikaaner to think about this and consider whether there might be a grain of truth in it. If there is, then it is up to him to do something about it. He has the majority. He has the power. He must know better than anyone that in the long run, there is positively no profit in further sub-dividing a divided country. Apartheid in sport in South Africa is slowly dissolving, and the rest of the sporting world is greatly encouraged to see the progress, but the aspect of sporting apartheid which is the pettiest and the most deeply entrenched is that between the Afrikaaner and the English. This was proved by what happened to Tommy Bedford on the British Lions tour of 1974.

In wider terms, it was also proved by the lowering of the playing standard of the English-speaking backs in South Africa. In the past, some of the greatest names in South African back play have come from the English-speaking community, but in 1974 they were painfully thin on the ground. Indeed, it soon became obvious that the Springboks were even worse off for international class backs than they were for forwards. The headlines were noticeably bereft of hot properties behind the scrum. There were not even any lukewarm properties behind the scrum. Positively no-one was saying, 'Wait until you play against so-and-so.' There had been some half-hearted support for some younger players like Gavin Cowley, of Eastern Province, but after the game at Port Elizabeth, no-one was very enthusiastic about them, either.

Graham Thorne, the New Zealand centre, had come to exactly the same conclusion. He had returned to South Africa after the All Black tour of 1970 and he had played three seasons of provincial Rugby for Northern Transvaal, so he was in a good position to make an assessment of the prospects. His verdict was that South Africa did not have a captain in sight. He thought that their forwards might turn out to be fair, but that their backs were only average, and that in any case, he could think of only three players who were reasonably certain of being chosen for the team. As he said, this was not a prospect exactly leaping with optimism.

The Springbok trial had not helped much, either. Dawie Snyman had played badly before he was injured and Gerald Bosch had had the better of the argument at fly-half, and matters were confused still further when Dawie Snyman's brother Jackie came into the 'B' team at half-time and played better than either of them.

The watching Lions, Ian McLauchlan and Ian McGeechan, thought that the Springbok scrummaging was high and loose, and even more important that the lineout play was messy and badly organised.

The fact that the Springbok selectors could arrive at a point four days before the first test and still be divided among themselves as to whether they should pick a team to run the ball or kick it only added to their difficulties, because instead of comparing like with like in the trial, they had put themselves into the position where they had to try to compare two completely different sorts of evidence. It was not surprising, therefore, that they took a very long time indeed to choose their team to play the British Lions in the first test. The meeting dragged on long into the night.

When the Springbok team was finally announced, it was seen that their selectors had decided to ignore most of the evidence of their trial and almost all the work they had done previously in their training camp and on the internal tour. Instead, they had accepted the match between the Lions and Western Province as the most reliable guide to both form and ability, and they had chosen seven Western Province players in the test team.

South Africa's decision meant that they had chosen Roy McCallum at scrum-half, even though he had not played in their trial at all, either as a first choice or a reserve. It was a brave decision and the correct one. The surprise was not so much that he had been chosen for South Africa, but that a player of his ability could have been ignored by the entire national selection process for three months. He had exactly the qualities that South Africa ought to have been looking for at scrum-half, and as he was 28 years old, he must have had them for years.

McCallum's brother Ian was also chosen at full-back. This gave South Africa their first pair of brothers in a team since Jaap and Dolf Bekker had played in 1953. It also gave rise to some sharp criticism from Natal. The fact that Ian McCallum had been invited to play full-back in the Springbok trials ahead of Malcolm Swanby had not been well received, because Swanby was preferred to McCallum by Natal. Again, it was an instance of Johan Claassen going back to the past to choose an experienced player. Ian McCallum was then 30, and like Derek van den Berg, he was a doctor and not as fully involved in the game and not playing as regularly as he might have liked, but his left-footed goalkicking had made an important contribution to the success of the Springboks against the All Blacks in 1970.

It was only sensible for the Springbok selectors to look upon goalkicking as potentially one of the deciding factors of the series. Goalkicking is always important, at any level and in any country, and every team touring South Africa in the past had noticed that almost invariably, they were given fewer kicks at goal than the home side. The only question was whether Ian McCallum's goalkicking was still as accurate as it had been in the past and whether his game at full-back still had the strength for international Rugby.

To some extent, the Springbok selectors were deluded by the trial. McCallum was considered to have had a successful match as a goalkicker because after missing his first three kicks narrowly, he had put the next four between the posts. No-one seemed to have thought of the psychological effect on both McCallum and his team if he had missed his first three kicks at goal in a test match and it did not seem to occur to anyone that if McCallum did miss three kicks in a row, he would be extremely unlikely to be asked to take the next four. Test match captains are not usually as patient as that. Against England in 1972, Piet Greyling had gone round the roulette board twice by the time South Africa came to take their seventh kick at goal.

One of the biggest problems facing the Springbok selectors throughout the series was that their choice of full-backs was so limited. Since the introduction of the restrictions on touch-kicking, the full-back had become the attacking pivot of the team and therefore it was surprising to see that so few full-backs in South Africa had followed the example of H. O. de Villiers. Most of them were semi-orthodox and all of them were very ordinary. This put South Africa at a crippling disadvantage, because J. P. R. Williams was easily the best player in the world in this position, and even though he was far ahead of any of his rivals at full-back in Britain, many of those were much better than anything South Africa could offer. Full-back always used to be one of South Africa's plus positions, but in 1974 it was one of their biggest minuses.

Another pair of South African brothers were also vitally involved in the selection, but they were rivals for the same position at fly-half. Dawie Snyman had been the front runner for the position in the event of South Africa deciding to play a running game, but he had not played well either for Western Province or in the trial and so it was surprising to see him selected, particularly as he retired from the trial injured. His brother Jackie Snyman had looked much the better of the two in developing a running game.

Perhaps Jackie Snyman's effort was obscured by the fact that the Springbok selectors had gone into the trial with their minds filled with the idea that they had to make a choice between Dawie Snyman and Gerald Bosch. This in itself was illogical, because Snyman and Bosch played two such totally different games. It would have made far more sense to have made a choice between Dawie and Jackie Snyman, or between Bosch and another kicker. In any case, the selectors must have been predisposed towards the running game, because they chose Dawie Snyman despite his shortcomings. All of this would have been just about forgiveable if they had chosen Jackie Snyman as the reserve at fly-half, but they did no such thing. They chose Bosch.

That made no sense at all, because if Dawie Snyman was further injured in the course of the match—always a possibility in view of his injury in the trial—Bosch would have had to go on the field as substitute and everyone playing on both sides of him would have had to change their games completely. Bosch's selection also made it impossible to maintain any continuity of approach in practice.

The selection in the back row was just as difficult to follow. It seemed to stem from the unjustified premise that Ellis, at the age of 31 and with no worth-while form behind him in the last two years, was an automatic choice. From that it followed that if South Africa wanted a jumper at the back of the lineout, they either had to play Morné du Plessis on the other flank or play him at number eight. As both Ellis and du Plessis preferred to play loose rather than tight, the selectors obviously felt that they had to get a grappler in somewhere and so they chose Boland Coetzee on the other flank and pushed du Plessis back to number eight. It looked an extremely doubtful combination for the type of game it would have to play.

The tight forwards were even less convincing. They were nearly all from the North, but they possessed none of the qualities of implacable determination and sheer physical hardness traditionally associated with the forward play of Transvaal and Northern Transvaal. This was the underbelly of the Springbok team and to have called it soft would have been an understatement.

For all his mildness, J. G. Williams was obviously required as a jumper. The selectors did not seem to regard Immelman as a serious contender, whatever he had achieved against the Lions, and in the absence of another genuine front jumper, it became all the more imperative to pick a real competitor alongside Williams. 'Moaner' van Heerden had displayed those qualities in the trial, but he was ignored. Instead, the selectors preferred Kevin de Klerk even though he was as slow to assert himself as Williams.

CHAPTER 13

Test Selection

MEANWHILE, the Lions had been busy choosing their own team. There is no doubt that their thinking had been shaken by the Western Province game, because whatever the selectors may have said to the contrary in public to bolster the morale of the other players, the team they chose to play in that game must have been the one they expected to play in the test match against South Africa the following week.

They had seen that team lose control of both the front and the back of the lineout and they had seen it lose control of the loose ball. Their back row had been almost totally eclipsed and Phil Bennett had been subjected to a most uncomfortable afternoon at fly-half in which he had been asked to do most of the things he finds most difficult without having the pleasure of playing to any of his considerable strengths.

The Lions' selectors were then on the point of dropping Bennett and choosing Alan Old instead. They had the memory of Old's record-breaking performance against S.W. Districts still fresh in their minds, and if he had come off the field unharmed after another convincing display against the Proteas, there was every reason to suppose that he would have been chosen for the test team. Remembering how Bennett had played for Llanelli and the Barbarians against the All Blacks, and for Wales against England, this seemed to be as much of a mistake as the demotion of Mervyn Davies and Fergus Slattery in favour of Andy Ripley and Tony Neary. On the one hand, you had proven ability at the highest level. On the other hand, you had only the promise of ability at that level.

With the exception of Ian McGeechan, the Lions had very few potential generals in midfield and Bennett was so exceptionally gifted in so many ways that it seemed far better policy to protect him in defence rather than sacrifice his talents as a counter-attacker and as a kicker and as a reader of the game. It was hard to imagine Bennett missing touch and losing the game as Old had done at the end of the match between Scotland and England, and it was equally hard to imagine Old kicking and playing as brilliantly as Bennett had done with a beggar's ration of the ball for Wales against England. The injury to Old was an appalling misfortune in every sense, but there is not much doubt that it spared the Lions' selectors from making a serious mistake. They had to settle for Bennett, and as the series unfolded, it became clear that he was the one midfield player who was capable of producing any inspiration in attack.

Even so, the Lions made six changes from the team that had played Western Province. They replaced the entire back row, they brought in Fran Cotton at tight head instead of Sandy Carmichael and they made two changes in the backs. Dick Milliken came into the centre in place of Roy Bergiers and J. J. Williams replaced Clive Rees on the left wing.

The changes in the backs were comparatively minor adjustments because in both cases, the two players involved were of similar physique and similar styles. Their strengths were roughly the same and so were their weaknesses. Milliken was not a good passer but he had shown the strength the Lions wanted in their midfield defence and he had shown the ability to take a tackle and keep on his feet to set up the ball for a maul. Rees was a cleverer runner than Williams and he was not much short of him in pace, either, but he lacked experience as a left wing. By then, the Lions had acknowledged their need for a mid-field general and they were hoping that Mike Gibson would be available to replace Alan Old. Gibson had said that he would not be available for another fortnight.

The changes in the forwards were a different matter. Ripley accepted that he had played badly against Western Province and regretted that his own personal lack of form had counted so heavily against Neary and McKinney. Ripley did not make his injured back an excuse, although it must have been a considerable handicap.

Neary was not so acquiescent. He was extremely disappointed to be dropped and said so. One of Syd Millar's great strengths was that he was so popular with all the players, but Neary told him in no uncertain terms that he thought the selection of Slattery was a question of the Irish looking after the Irish. Neary played in only five more games on the rest of the tour. McKinney suffered exactly the same fate, though he was such an eminently good-natured soul that it was hard to imagine him saying anything contentious even if he had felt indignant. Perhaps after that the management felt that it had to be seen that the Irish were not looking after the Irish, and McKinney suffered a little as a consequence.

Not that the management had any need to feel defensive about the selection of Slattery. He should have been first choice from the beginning. He was the fastest flanker, he was more aggressive

1. Gordon Brown scores the first try of the tour against Western Transvaal.

2. With the ball under his right arm and an opponent on his shoulder, Tom David makes a determined advance at Potchefstroom.

3. Mervyn Davies (No. 8) tries to pull van Eyck away from Stewart McKinney and Fergus Slattery (facing left) takes on Barnard as Gordon Brown (on the ground) kicks out in one of the fights in the match against Eastern Province.

4. Hannes Marais (No. 3) and the Eastern Province scrum in rare disarray against the Lions at Port Elizabeth.

5. Stewart McKinney (left) holds back the opposition as Mervyn Davies drives for the line against Eastern Province.

6. McKinney is the first to offer congratulations as Davies scores.

7. Mike Burton, Stewart McKinney, Fran Cotton and J. J. Williams watch Alan Old on the way to his record of 37 points against S.W. Districts at Mossel Bay.

8. J. J. Williams on the way to his record of six tries in the same match.

9. Clive Rees scores against Western Province.

10. Chris Pope scores for Western Province and there is nothing that Billy Steele can do about it.

11. Lions towing each other in training at Greenpoint in Cape Town.

12. Roy Bergiers, as one of the vanquished, carries one of the victors after the charity match against the girls of Cape Town University.

13. Roy Bergiers, in much more serious mood, cutting through to score against the Proteas.

14. Morné du Plessis has his kick charged down by Mervyn Davies in the first test. Both have their eyes tight shut as Jan Ellis (left) watches.

15. Phil Bennett kicks one of his three penalty goals against South Africa in the first test at Newlands.

16. Hannes Marais looks as if he intends Gareth Edwards no good at all as the Lions scrum-half makes one of his devastating kicks in the first test.

17. The first anti-apartheid demonstration at a Rugby ground in South Africa. University students protesting at the Lions' match against Southern Universities at Newlands.

18. The referee wags his finger at Gordon Brown and Tom David wags his finger at the opposition in the quagmire at Newlands for the game against Southern Universities.

19. The schoolboys in their boaters present a terribly English scene as Tom Grace scores against Rhodesia.

20. Andy Ripley, who helped to make the Lions' last try against Transvaal, looks for support as John Moloney and Tony Neary close up.

21. Phil Bennett cuts past the forwards on one of the runs that demoralised South Africa in the second test at Pretoria.

22. Bennett scores in the second test.

23. Dick Milliken and Ian McGeecha in the vintage car procession at Bloemfontein.

24. Gareth Edwards about to put a rolling kick past the scrum against Orange Free State.

·. Fergus Slattery snarls into score against the Griquas at Kimberley.

26. Tom Grace treads the same path to score in the same match.

27. Tony Neary bursts away to score against Northern Transvaal

28. Mervyn Davies caps a brilliant performance with a try against Northern Transvaal from the back of a lineout.

29. Fran Cotton tries a hal hearted lean and Mervyn Davies watches resignedl as Chris Luther kicks a penalty goal for Norther Transvaal.

30. Mervyn Davies is pulled away from a fight in the match against Northern Transvaal by Vic Booyens.

31. Davies points and says, "Just you watch it!" after having his head kicked.

32. Gareth Edwards and John Moloney running neck and neck from J. J. Williams and Andy Ripley at Mdantsane.

33. Twenty yards later, Moloney collapses with a hamstring injury

and he never stopped running. He was not such a good footballer as Neary and sometimes he made mistakes in his choice of play, but at least he was invariably in a position to do something, whether it was right or wrong. He also suited the restricted style of play adopted by the Lions because they did not make a great feature of their back row in attacking moves.

Some of the same arguments applied to Mervyn Davies. He seemed to be the only man in the touring party or anywhere near it who did not accept that Andy Ripley was necessarily going to play in the tests. He knew that he played tighter than Ripley and that his close tackling and close support play were better, and he was confident that eventually his merits would be seen and that they would be recognised. 'And even if they are not,' he said, 'at least I have the consolation of having played four tests in a great team in New Zealand.'

With that attitude, Davies was bound to succeed, because it meant that he was prepared to do the work which would put him back to the fitness levels he achieved in New Zealand and when he was playing for London Welsh. For whatever reason, he had lost that peak since changing jobs and returning to Wales and he had played a comparatively poor domestic season but having demonstrated his ability so many times at the highest level, he had only to accept the need for work and to rediscover the right attitude to be chosen for the tests. He did both.

Roger Uttley was chosen on the other flank, just as Carwyn James said he would be. That was a more challenging selection, but it was fully justified. Tom David was still not fit enough to be considered after his hamstring injury and McKinney knew better than anyone that he was lucky to be on the tour at all. In any case, McKinney was nothing like big enough to do the support job at number six in the lineout which Derek Quinnell had done so well in 1971 and which the Lions needed again in 1974. Uttley was not quite big enough to be a top class lock, and he was not quite quick enough to be a genuine loose forward, but in a pack which was in control of the scrummage, he was such a good utility forward that he was capable of forming a very profitable alliance with Gordon Brown in the lineout, even if it was a trifle unholy.

The Lions had learned in the Eastern Province game that there was positively no future in trying to play to the new laws in the lineout in South Africa, because the referees simply did not apply them. Fortunately, the hard core of the pack had been so thoroughly trained in the finer points of lineout illegalities in New Zealand that they were quickly able to adjust. They closed the gaps and they blocked and obstructed and indeed, they soon moved so far ahead of their rivals and the referees that it was rather like a contest between the Mafia and some small boys in a sweet shop. The referees allowed the ball to be thrown straight at the front jumper, instead of down the line of touch, and that suited Bill McBride fine. Some of the referees even allowed the ball to be thrown directly above the jumper when it was thrown to the back of the lineout. Their ratio of success in spotting lifting in the lineout was about one in eight and some of them never did fully comprehend the implications of jumping into an opponent while pretending to jump for the ball so that both jumpers missed it and the ball fell into the hands of the large gentleman behind. The Lions eventually came round to Carwyn James' view that it might be a good idea if the large gentleman in question was R. M. Uttley.

They knew that the lineout was the area where they were most vulnerable, and they also knew that if they were to choose Brown because of his scrummaging ability and his all-round utility as a forward, they would have to take steps to stop him being exposed by J. G. Williams in a straightforward jumping contest at number five. Brown had no illusions about his chances of success in a contest of that sort. He is basically a front jumper and although he had responded so well to the challenge of touring that he was playing as well as any forward in the team, he knew his limitations better than anyone. Hence the selection of Uttley.

Uttley himself knew equally well that he could be badly exposed in defence if the South African scrum-half and loose forwards ran at him on that side of the scrum. Derek Quinnell had been faced with the same problem in New Zealand, but he had been able to cover his lack of speed by playing always on the blind side. Uttley was not able to do that because Slattery did not like playing open side and blind side. Slattery preferred to play on the right which meant that for half the time Uttley would have to play as open side flanker. Still, Uttley is one of those cheerful and essentially practical people who is very high on the list of those you would be prepared to go into the jungle with, and he made up his mind to do the best he could for as long as the Lions wanted him to do so. At that stage, though, he would have been glad to know that it was going to take South Africa's tactical analysts three and a half test matches to work out that they might be on to a good thing if their scrum-half scuttled off to the right of the scrums.

The other change was in the front row. Fran Cotton had come on to the field in the first match against Western Transvaal as a substitute when Sandy Carmichael was injured and so had his first match practice of the tour as a tight head, even though he had been chosen originally as reserve to Ian McLauchlan at loose head. As Mike Burton, the other tight head, was also injured at Stilfontein, Cotton had a run in which he was able to play three of the first four games at tight head and so make a case for consideration in that position. He made a very persuasive case indeed. He had adjusted his game to suit Syd Millar's requirements so that he played much tighter than usual and put most of his effort into scrummaging and lineout support play. Very few props have the ability to be able to make a choice. They have to do either one thing or the other. They either have to play tight or loose. Cotton, however, could do either. He had developed considerably in physical strength since his tour of South Africa with England in 1972 and he had developed his knowledge of scrummaging technique. In his earlier days, he had been a prop who had earned most of his marks in the loose and who sometimes had some very uncomfortable afternoons in the tight. Even as late as 1972, he had lost his place to Mike Burton in the England test team to play South Africa because he had not been able to assert himself against Nick Bezuidenhout and Northern Transvaal in the week before the test match. Burton has always been uncompromising in his attitude, both physically and mentally.

Cotton learned from that. He had come from a family of distinguished Rugby League players, but it had always been his great ambition to become a British Lion. He must have felt that he was unlucky not to become one in 1971, because he was the official reserve prop for the tour, and the Lions in New Zealand lost two props with serious injuries. However, they replaced one with a lock and after consulting with the other tight forwards, they replaced the other with 'Stack' Stevens. The feeling then was that Cotton was not quite good enough in the tight to do the job the Lions wanted.

Cotton could have been forgiven for turning away to Rugby League in despair, but he swallowed his disappointment and kept plugging on. Indeed, when he got to South Africa with England a year later and lost his place to Burton, he was big enough to accept his limitations and determined enough to do something about them. This argued great strength of character and it had its reward when he played in the England team which beat New Zealand in Auckland in 1973. At the end of the match, he ran through half the All Black team selling dummies left and right. The England players thought that was the moment above all others which really proclaimed their triumph.

In the following season, Cotton demonstrated his versatility. He played for the North of England in an area trial and it was his destruction of the left side of the Midlands scrummage which led to the North's extraordinary win by 53 points to 12. Syd Millar had already been appointed as Lions' coach, and he watched that match. He said afterwards that he would have disregarded it completely as an evaluation of the ability of the Midlands players because it stemmed from a collapse in one position, but he was clearly very impressed with the player who had caused that collapse. By then, Cotton had shown that he had developed enough in physique and technique to be able to play either a running game or a scrummaging game and he was one of the few props in Britain who had shown himself capable of playing with equal facility at either tight head or loose head.

When he began his career, he had been given some memorable roastings at loose head in some very important games. For a time, he moved over to tight head and concentrated on that position. However, he did not allow himself to develop a fixation about playing on the other side of the scrum as so many defeated loose heads do and when he thought that he was equipped to do so, he moved back again. It was a remarkable story of persistence. South Africa had seen the same thing happen in their own country with a little chap called Gary Player. When he first tried to play professional golf in Britain, he was told he would never be any good at it, and the best thing he could do was give up the game and get a nice secure job in an office. Gary Player declined to accept that advice and went on to beat the world. Fran Cotton did the same and by the time he left South Africa in 1974, he looked certain to follow John Pullin as captain of England providing he did not accept one of the inevitable offers to turn professional. Looking even further ahead, it was not difficult to see Fran Cotton as captain of the next British Lions team in New Zealand.

At the same time as the team was announced, it was confirmed that the Lions had chosen Max Baise to referee the test match. That decision probably took them all of ten seconds. Baise had refereed two of the Lions' test matches in South Africa in 1968, when both Syd Millar and Bill McBride had been players, and he had shown the fair-mindedness which is the first thing that touring teams look for in countries like South Africa, New Zealand and Australia, where international matches are refereed by local officials. Referees in those countries often notice more of the offences committed by a touring side simply because they tend to watch the game as spectators as well as referees. Like everyone else, they are curious to know how the touring team plays and so naturally they spend more time watching the visitors than they do in watching the home team. That is the charitable interpretation of the refereeing bias so often encountered. There is a less charitable interpretation, of course, and sometimes that applies as well. Referees in the southern hemisphere have been known to blow for their country, and to blow as hard as they can. Max Baise had also shown that he was an extremely competent referee. That was a nice bonus.

Under the terms of the tour agreement, the South African Board submitted four referees to the Lions' management for each test match. It was then up to the touring team to choose one of them. If the Lions were unhappy about all four of the referees on any particular panel, they were at liberty to ask for another referee from outside the panel, but if the South African Board in turn did not approve of that referee, then they were entitled arbitrarily to appoint a different referee entirely. The Lions had done this in 1968, when they asked for Walter Lane, of Natal, to referee the second test at Port Elizabeth, but the South African Board did not accept him and they appointed a referee from outside who upset the Lions so much that there was not the slightest prospect of them ever making the same mistake again.

Strictly speaking, Baise should not have been on the panel for the first test at all. It was laid down in the tour agreement that a fortnight before the first test match, the Lions would have seen all the referees on the first international panel. That meant that the four referees on that panel had to be appointed to officiate in the first four games of the tour. The first panel, therefore, should have consisted of Piet Robbertse, Gert Bezuidenhout, Cas de Bruyn and Fonnie van der Vyver, but because of the misfortune befalling Mr. van der Vyver in the Eastern Province game, a point was stretched and Max Baise, who handled the fifth game, was brought on to the panel in his place. The Lions were pleased. It worked out well for them. It worked out well for Max Baise, too, because most of his rivals in South Africa agreed that he was the best referee in the country.

The Lions who had not been chosen for the test team swallowed their disappointment and made their way off to the University of Cape Town, where they played a Rugby match against the lady students for charity. The Lions had some difficulty in raising a team but it turned out to be such an enjoyable match against such attractive opposition that if it had been played again the following week, there is not much doubt that all 29 players, plus the manager and coach, would have been squabbling to get into the team. A selection meeting would certainly have been necessary, and it could have turned into quite an acrimonious affair.

As it was, the Lions managed to field a team of eight with the assistance of Nigel Starmer-Smith, who was covering the tour as a B.B.C. television commentator.

The ladies beat the Lions quite easily, thanks partly to the local rule which allowed them to run whereas the Lions could only walk, and thanks partly to some dastardly deeds which were committed by the referee. Sandy Carmichael was most palpably framed, if that is the word, when he emerged from one of the scrums and it was discovered that he had a brassiere in his pocket. He protested quite truthfully that it was a plant, but no one believed him and he was sent off the field in disgrace.

Andy Ripley played in spectacles, arguing that although they might have dazzled some of the pilots approaching the nearby airport, they were sufficiently high off the ground to constitute no danger at all to the opposition. Ripley provided one of the tour's richest moments in this match. Wearing a T-shirt proclaiming, 'I am so perfect it scares me', he foiled the ladies by standing quite still in the middle of the pitch and holding the ball high above his head in one hand. The ladies squealed and jumped round his knees, but no matter how hard they tried, they could not take the ball off him. This was not surprising, because the ball was about 10 feet off the ground. Ripley looked rather like Professor Dolittle surrounded by a pack of frisky young puppies.

Some of the Lions' efforts were not as altruistic. Giggling in the scrums indicated some activities not precisely envisaged in the laws of the game, or at any rate, in the Laws of Rugby Union football, and the tackling of one of the Lions' wingers was so protracted that it gave his opponent no chance to release the ball.

That evening, the touring party went to a cocktail party given by the South African Rugby Board at their headquarters at Newlands. It was a crowded gathering, made all the more significant by the presence of various members of the International Board who were spending a very pleasant week in Cape Town at the expense of the South African Rugby Board on their way back to Britain from the meeting of the International Rugby Football Board which had just been held in Australia. Most of the South Africans at the party were discussing the implications of the Lions' game against the Proteas the day before. They were saddened by the injury to Alan Old, and wondered if it would do more damage to the image of the coloured players representing the South African Federation. Many at the party gloomily recalled the niggling spirit of the game played by the Proteas against

England in 1972 and acknowledged that not many touring sides would play with the restraint of England and the Lions in the face of such provocation in the way of late tackling and persistent offside play.

Dr. Danie Craven had been disappointed when the coloured player Green Vigo had turned professional after the England game in 1972 and went to Britain to play Rugby League because he felt that Vigo was a good enough player to be selected for the Springbok Rugby trials on merit and this was what he wanted. Dr. Craven had pressed the South African government hard to allow his Board to introduce racially mixed trials and he was determined to go on with the struggle.

'This is central to the whole issue of South African sport,' he said. 'Mixed trials and mixed representation must come eventually, and I believe Rugby can lead the way. Our players are prepared to accept it and so are our administrators. Many of them have already done a lot to help the coloured and the African players. Most of them would welcome integration in our Rugby.'

No-one could question the importance that the South African Rugby Board attached to the issue, because those administrators who could not bring themselves to accept the idea of racially integrated Rugby had disappeared very rapidly from the scene. One of them was a man who had built a distinguished career in Rugby and who had worked successfully as a liaison officer with various touring teams. He was only a rung or two below Dr. Craven himself, and yet suddenly, his membership of the Board had come to an end. It was widely believed that this had occurred because he had not agreed with the Board's policy of pressing for racially integrated Rugby.

Dr. Craven said that he wanted to see South African teams touring abroad again. The Springboks had lost their tour of New Zealand in 1973 because of a political intervention by the New Zealand government and although that has only seemed to make the New Zealand Rugby Union all the more determined to fulfil their next tour of South Africa, Dr. Craven knows that some countries like Wales feel that they cannot tour South Africa again until they have had a reciprocal tour of Wales by the Springboks. He also knows that even if South Africa do fulfil all the requirements of choosing a racially integrated team from within a racially integrated domestic structure of Rugby football, there is still a strong possibility that the political opponents of South Africa will find some other excuse to raise objections to any projected tours and to try to disrupt them. That does not deter him. As he said, he sees this as the greatest issue facing sport in his own country.

CHAPTER 14

First Test

THE Lions' concern about their lineout was shown the next day when they trained at Stellenbosch on their way to have lunch at a wine farm. It was a miserable day, with rain blowing in the air, and the forwards went off to the top of the cluster of pitches at the foot of the mountains where Dr. Danie Craven has his home and where his beloved Stellenbosch University play their games.

With the timbered slopes of the mountain rising sharply behind them, the Lions practised four-man lineouts with the four men out of the lineout advancing on to the ball thrown over the top. It did not look very convincing, even as a last resort. The Lions practised other variations of the short lineout, too, though by then Table Mountain had been down to its ankles in cloud for days and it was obvious that the weather in the Cape had broken.

The day the Lions had spent in Stellenbosch on the 1968 tour had been very different. The sun had been warm and mellow, the roses had been miraculously still in bloom and the Lions had had nothing to do all day but eat and drink and take whatever other chances came their way as they lazed in the sun and laughed at Bob Hiller's jokes and reflected that the third test was over and they had just lost the series. Now the weather was grey and cool and the wine farm was being fitted in after training as one of those things that really ought to be done before it was too late and the series was just about to begin.

The atmosphere surrounding the Rugby was very different, too. Instead of contemplating one of those traditionally armour-plated Springbok teams which had too much strength both fore and aft for its opponents, the 1974 Lions were faced by a team which was so inexperienced that it looked wet behind the ears. Six of the players were new caps and all except two of the others were novices in international Rugby compared with the Lions. Even those two, Hannes Marais and Jan Ellis, struck no fear in the hearts of their opponents.

This was the crucial difference between South African Rugby in 1974 and South African Rugby prior to 1972. When opponents looked at those Springbok teams of former years, there were always players to fear, whether it was 'Mannetjies' Roux or Jannie Engelbrecht or John Gainsford or Dawie de Villiers or Piet Visagie or Mof Myburgh or Gys Pitzer or Hannes Marais or Frik du Preez or Piet Greyling or Tommy Bedford or H. O. de Villiers. In previous generations, the relative level was probably even higher. Quite apart from the pressure of playing against these Springbok teams, there was the anguish of this very personal contest which had to be faced. In 1974, this anguish did not exist for the Lions, except perhaps for Gordon Brown, and even he knew that the examination in front of him would be technical rather than physical. Otherwise it was the Springboks who were doing the worrying.

Naturally, there was still an apprehension about the collective unknown. It was one thing to look at the Springbok team and think that logically, it ought to present no problems, but it was another thing to experience the reality. Much had been made of the inspiration that South African teams drew from pulling on a Springbok jersey. Again, the development of team organisation has considerably reduced the impact which inspiration can have in international Rugby football, and indeed, one of the most noticeable developments in the last five years has been the way in which badly organised international teams can be exposed in relation to their own provinces. New Zealand had just provided a case in point. Taranaki, Wellington and Canterbury had all beaten England on their tour of New Zealand, but the All Blacks themselves had lost. Without this organisation, the sum can be equal to less than the parts. Naturally, it is difficult for a touring side to believe that in 1973, it might have been easier to beat New Zealand than it was to beat Wellington, or that in 1974, it might turn out to be easier to beat South Africa than it was to beat Western Province. At that moment, the Lions still had fresh in the minds the memory of the fact that Western Province had just rattled them, and rattled them badly. Therefore, South Africa ought to be even more difficult to beat.

Any team is always conscious of its own weaknesses, and the defence of one or two of the Lions' backs was sufficiently flimsy for those with experience of South African Rugby to know that if the Springboks could play with the vigour and the determination traditionally associated with them, those Lions backs could be bundled over and swept away and not even J. P. R. Williams would be able to plug all the holes.

Similarly, the handling of some of the Lions' backs was such that even in practice, without the pressure of opposition, they were making more mistakes in a morning than the 1971 Lions had made in a week. The one comfort was that J. P. R. Williams was playing with such a towering command of the game that even his team-mates who knew his qualities were shaking their heads with astonished admiration.

There was another comfort, too. The weather in the Cape was becoming progressively worse and the pitch at Newlands was beginning to look like Cardiff Arms Park on the day that South Africa drew with Wales in 1969. Some of the younger Lions who had only played international Rugby on the beautiful surfaces so recently introduced in Europe, thought that Newlands in 1974 was 'a disgrace.'

Admittedly, it was badly scarred if judged by its usual standards but after two days of cloud and rain and with the prospect of more to come, it was hard to see how it could fail to suit the Lions. It was obvious that the Lions wanted to confine the game to their tight forwards as much as possible and a wet pitch would do most of that work for them. Equally, a wet pitch was the last thing the Springboks wanted. They had picked a team to run the ball and if the conditions stopped them, they would have to turn round and try to do something for which they were not equipped.

Ironically, therefore, the battle positions for the first test were precisely the reverse of those traditional encounters between South Africa and the British Isles for the previous 80 years. The Lions had the tight forwards and intended to avoid mistakes by playing nine-man Rugby and playing for the pressure positions which, if occupied for long enough, would increase the chances of the Springboks making mistakes themselves. It was not the most dashing of gauntlets for British Rugby to throw down in view of the way the Barbarians had demolished the All Blacks in 1974, but it was exactly the way that South Africa used to play. The Springboks, for their part, had chosen a team to run the ball, which was exactly the way that the Lions used to play.

By the time Saturday came, the weather was so much on their side that when the Lions drove round the horse-shoe of motorway from their hotel at Sea Point to the ground on the other side of Table Mountain at Newlands, it was hard to resist the impression that God must be an Irishman. Really heavy rain overnight and in the morning had turned the pitch into a surface which was nearly as much liquid as solid.

To make matters infinitely worse, or better, according to your point of view, the authorities at the ground had gone ahead with the usual practice in South Africa of playing two preliminary matches before the big game. It is true that the second of these had made us sit bolt upright with surprise at seeing at least one good young player in South Africa, but even the sight of Peter Kirsten's marvellous handling ability at fly-half in the Western

Province Under-20 team did not alter the view that South Africa must have been mad to allow the games to proceed.

The practice of playing these preliminary matches used to agitate the Lions no end when they had to play against the steam-rolling Springbok packs of old but now that the Lions were driving the steamroller themselves, they adjusted easily to a much more conciliatory attitude. Privately, of course, they were saying that the South African authorities must be stark, staring, raving bonkers to allow the matches to be played, but if anyone wanted to ask, they let it be known that they fully understood the difficulty of disappointing all those people who had bought their tickets in the expectation of seeing continuous Rugby from one o'clock until ten past five! My word, yes.

With the pitch in the state it was, neither side had any option but to play nine-man Rugby, and when they saw the film of the match afterwards, the Lions must have grinned with delight as they saw themselves squelching out from the players' tunnel and saw the frowns of concentration on the worried faces of their opponents.

South Africa won the toss and decided to play with the wind behind them. Normally, a wind in South Africa (except in Port Elizabeth) is the lighest of zephyrs when judged by the standards of Europe but the wind in Cape Town on June 8, 1974, was a wind by anybody's standards. It fairly hurried down the pitch.

Bennett kicked off for the Lions and saw J. G. Williams catch the ball and set up the first maul for South Africa. In the first ten minutes the Springboks used their ball well, and Snyman kicked to the corners accurately enough to stretch J. P. R. Williams and the Lions' defence. De Klerk won some early ball at the front of the lineout, too, and later on, South Africa threw three balls to J. G. Williams in the middle which Gordon Brown thought were meant for du Plessis at the back. As Brown turned to follow the peel, he saw to his considerable surprise that each time this huge man Williams had caught the ball two-handed.

But if Brown was surprised by Williams' reach, the whole Lions' team was astonished to see du Plessis, the Springbok number eight, sprinting back to cover his full-back when the Lions threw the ball into the lineout. He did this even in the first half, when the Springboks had the wind behind them. There were occasions when he was lucky not to be penalised, because he left the lineout before the ball had left the line of touch.

Du Plessis did the same thing from the back of the scrums. This was even harder to understand, because from the very beginning, the Springbok tight forwards were in trouble. Sauermann, the

Springbok loose head, kept calling for more weight and his calls became more urgent as the match progressed. Marais, on the other side of the scrum, was not faring much better and with their number eight often departing with all haste, it was not surprising that the Springboks had very little weight coming through from behind to stop the Lions turning the scrum so that Edwards had the best angle for his kicks. Edwards had developed an effective kick in which he got over the ball and topped it as hard as he could so that it hit the ground a few yards away and skidded through the mud before rolling into touch on the blindside wing. There was nothing that du Plessis could do to stop these and even against the wind in the first half, Edwards won yards and yards of precious ground and kept the worst of the positional pressure off his defence.

The wind pushed the Lions into their own half, but with their scrummage gaining control and McBride beginning to assert himself against de Klerk in the lineout, Edwards was able to make sure that the Lions needed no great defensive heroics to keep the Springboks outside their 25.

The Lions did have one nasty moment when du Plessis and Ellis drove the ball through from the back of a lineout but they kicked on too far and Bennett was able to drop out safely from the 25.

Against that, the Lions nearly scored a try themselves. Windsor fed the ball back from Uttley in a lineout and Bennett set up a position on the right from which Steele nearly scored. Milliken was making ground as hard as he could on the inside, but even if Steele had been looking for support it was not quite close enough to be decisive and he was stopped just short of the line.

Midway through the first half, McCallum had another kick at goal from the left. The ball went across the face of the Lions' posts and was fielded by J. P. R. Williams behind his own line. He looked up and saw that there was only one defender between him and the Springbok line 120 yards away. Perhaps unconsciously, he thought of the Lions' game against Hawke's Bay in 1971, when in almost exactly the same place, he caught a kick at goal which brushed the outside of the far post and started a brilliant counter attack which ended with Gerald Davies scoring a try between the far posts at the other end.

The 1971 team, however, was geared to think in those terms. The 1974 team was not. As J. P. R. Williams passed to J. J. Williams behind his own line, the Lions' left wing was taken so much by surprise that instead of taking the ball upfield and to the left as fast as he could, he was startled into taking the ball across his own in-goal and back towards trouble. Muller caught him and tackled him and Williams had to concede a five yard scrum.

The Springboks won that well and took the ball first to the short side on the left, where they won a maul and then moved it back to the open side on the right. It was the best ball the Springboks won in the match, but Snyman did not appear to think of giving his backs the chance to score a try. Instead, he dropped a goal.

From that moment, the Lions never looked back. They took a tapped penalty kick in midfield, and after Brown had set up a maul, Edwards and J. J. Williams probed deep to the blind side. Roy McCallum took a penalty kick for South Africa from inside his own half, but kicked it too deep and the Lions found touch again. Thanks to McBride's efforts at the front of the lineout, the Lions were then winning as much of South Africa's lineout ball as the Springboks were themselves, and some clever kicking by Edwards and Bennett pushed them up the right touchline.

As Edwards went to put up a high kick from the lineout, Sauermann late-tackled him and was penalised. Sauermann, who was remembered for the way he nearly broke Jan Webster's hand with a kick in the England test of 1972, had kicked Edwards after the first lineout and one England forward among the Lions watching in the stand positively itched to do something about it.

Afterwards, he said, 'I told Fran Cotton about Sauermann. I told him to hit him straight off, but he didn't and sure enough, Gareth got kicked. And where would we be without Gareth? The man's just magic. I can't clap him or anything when I watch him play. I just sit there with my mouth open. Reverse passes, thirty-yard passes, brilliant kicks under pressure, strength, guts, tackle, speed—the lot. When he throws the ball out at Twickenham, it would finish up at London Airport if Phil Bennett didn't stop it.

'If I play next Saturday against the Transvaal, I shall have a go at Sauermann. He was so tired this Saturday that he couldn't even run at the finish, and I shall hit him so bloody hard next Saturday that he won't be able to run at the start.'

Max Baise did not see the kick at Edwards at the beginning of the match, but he did see the late tackle, and Bennett kicked for goal. It was a difficult kick, into the wind and from far out on the right, and Bennett pulled it across the face of the posts. He pulled it so far that it turned into a tactical kick which embarrassed South Africa severely. Du Plessis got across to it and went to kick for touch, but by then he was being challenged hard by Davies and, as the All Black Alan Sutherland had discovered in Dunedin, it is difficult for forwards who are physically anything but neat and compact to kick for touch quickly under pressure. Their legs are longer and heavier and they take longer to swing back. Du Plessis found the same thing and Davies charged down his kick.

Both players shut their eyes for the impact and when they opened them, they had lost sight of the ball. This was as well for South Africa, because it was sitting invitingly near the line and if Davies had known where it was, he could have picked it up and scored. By the time he had discovered its whereabouts, the Springboks were beginning to muster some defence, and although Davies picked up the ball, he was knocked down and could only crawl over the line with it. Davies said afterwards that he did not think that he had been tackled, and the film of the incident certainly suggested that he had a case, but the referee was not impressed with it and gave South Africa a penalty kick.

It did not take them far, and with half-time approaching rapidly, the Springboks mush have begun to suspect that they were going to lose. Even with the wind behind them, they were having to defend. Still, they were leading by three points, and if they could keep that lead until half-time and the wind then dropped it might enough.

Within a couple of minutes, even that hope was dashed and the suspicion that they were going to lose must have turned into an awful certainty. The Lions called a three-man lineout near the Springboks 25, and Snyman was caught offside in midfield. That kick was so close that Bennett had no hesitation about kicking for goal into the wind, and he succeeded. So at half-time, the score was 3-3.

The wind did not drop, either. If anything it grew firmer than ever. Bennett thought that it had changed direction and shouted across to McGeechan to tell him so, but after a few minutes, he was not so sure. He had an early opportunity to test it, because South Africa subsided quickly into defence and into a series of mistakes. First Snyman missed touch and then Ian McCallum had to make a mark from a kick by Edwards. McCallum did find touch with that kick but after the Lions had knocked on a peel from the lineout and had then been penalised in a scrum, McCallum missed touch on the left. Steele and Davies attacked up that touchline and Edwards came up in support on the blind side. As a ruck formed out on the Lions' right, Ellis and van Wyk went into it offside and the referee gave the Lions a penalty kick.

Even down the wind, it was not an easy kick, because the surface was so bad. In any case, it was from near the right touchline which was the more difficult side of the field for Bennett. He kicked it well but saw the wind take the ball away to the right of the posts and thought he had missed. Then late in its flight, it swung back again and went through the middle.

Bennett pranced back to the middle of the field on the tips of his toes. When he has kicked a good goal, he bounces back past the halfway line, flicking the ground away from beneath him. If he has kicked badly, he walks back initially, shaking his head in self-reproof, before breaking into a sad little jog. His satisfaction can be measured by the spring in his step, in much the same way that the judges of ice-skating and springboard diving assess the efforts of various competitors. Even out of the mud, his prance after that goal would have rated an average of at least 8.7 marks out of 10.

The second half was then only five minutes old, but it was already clear that the Lions were going to win the match very easily. Despite the wind and the mud, they had survived the first half with something approaching comfort. They had not been required to scale any heights in defence, or even any foothills. They had not been required to make any of those desperate, slithering, mud plastered tackles which ought to have been necessary to preserve their line. They had scarcely been required to make any tackles of any sort. It was very noticeable that as they gathered together at half-time, most of the Lions' backs had not even got their shorts dirty.

Once Bennett had put them into the lead, the feeling of comfort increased to the point where the Lions might just as well have been sitting in armchairs. Edwards changed his kicking tactics from driving the ball low under the wind to pumping it high downfield. All the Springboks could do was huddle miserably near their 25 as they covered back and found short touches. The match was an hour old before this running team was even able to pass the ball as far as its outside centre.

In the safety of their opponents' half, the Lions forwards could afford to take risks to increase their control of the lineout. Brown concentrated on jumping into J. G. Williams to leave the ball for Uttley behind him and McBride went on obliterating de Klerk. The snowball of Lions' possession grew bigger all the time.

However, perhaps the most decisive moment came in the scrums. Sauermann had been having an increasingly bad time against Cotton, and had been loud in his complaints, but in one scrum his difficulties became so acute that he literally squealed. 'That finished them,' said one of the Lions' forwards afterwards. 'They just collapsed after that.'

The Lions went on playing their game of possession and position, and all they had to do was wait patiently for the points. The Springboks became increasingly desperate and took some short penalty kicks which were such fiascos that they only proclaimed even louder their lack of leadership and their lack of organisation. From the first of these, Roy McCallum, Ellis and Marais got themselves jammed so conclusively up the right touch-line that Pope was flattened. I am almost certain that it was the first time Pope touched the ball in the field of play.

Against that, J. J. Williams was held only a yard short of the Springbok line after Uttley, Windsor, Edwards, Milliken and J. P. R. Williams had forced the ball on from a maul. The Springboks did manage to pass the ball down their threequarter line once, but Whipp and Ooosthuizen did not even reach the advantage line before the ball was submerged by the Lions' defence. Again the Springboks were awarded a penalty kick at a lineout in their own half, and again they tried to develop a move from a short kick but again they messed it up completely. Muller had to unload the ball to Coetzee who was engulfed by Davies.

It must have been humiliating for a Springbok captain like Marais, himself a prop forward, to choose to take lineouts instead of scrums in his own country and in front of his own people. It must have been even more humiliating for him to see even that tactic defeated so that he had to go back to taking scrums again even though he knew that the Springbok scrummage was under so much pressure that it put the whole team in peril.

That was what happened when the Lions scored their third penalty goal. South Africa tried to work the ball away from a wheeling scrum well inside their own half and du Plessis broke away offside as his scrum-half went to kick the ball through. Bennett kicked the goal and did such a hop and a skip that every judge present unanimously gave his prance 9.8.

It had been an afternoon of frustration for the whole Springbok team but for their loose forwards in particular, it had been the most emphatic of dead losses. For du Plessis and Coetzee especially it must have been a depressing contrast to the joyful romp of the week before. Ellis did not even have the memory of that to console him when he tried to carry the ball away one-handed from a maul after a lineout, Davies took it off him with the greatest of ease and turned it back to Edwards who took one glance at the posts and drove it between them with a piston thrust of a dropped goal. Edwards did not prance. He just turned away. He had buried the dead.

By that stage, J. P. R. Williams had so little to do that he advanced rather diffidently upfield and suggested to Bennett that perhaps they might do a scissors. Bennett told him to bugger off, and said that the next time he got the ball he was going to kick the bloody thing as far as he bloody well could. Bennett is not normally as abrasive and afterwards he was sorry he had been so abrupt. 'But the forwards had worked hard, and I wasn't going to take a chance of throwing it all away,' he said doggedly. Not that anyone was complaining. Not even J. P. R. Williams.

It was the first time that the Lions had beaten South Africa for 19 years, and afterwards, Dr. Danie Craven did not attempt to disguise his disappointment. At the reception after the match, he said that it was his duty to present caps and blazers to the six new Springboks who had played for their country for the first time that afternoon.

'I have to present a cap and a blazer to Chris Pope,' he said. 'He created a record by becoming the first Springbok ever to play for his country without touching the ball.'

That was not strictly true. Pope touched the ball twice, and he had at least one collection of bruises to prove it, but the point of the criticism was brutally valid.

When he came to Peter Whipp, Dr. Craven said, 'At least he did better than Chris Pope. He did touch the ball once.'

Dr. Craven turned to the burly Kevin de Klerk. 'He looks a big man here, but he wasn't a big man on the field.' And of 'Boland' Coetzee, Dr. Craven said, 'He is the old man of the team, and he played like one.'

The Springbok players looked thoroughly embarrassed. The Lions squirmed with them.

The Lions could not believe that beating South Africa could be so easy. Billy Steele said wonderingly afterwards, 'It was like playing in a practice match.' Mike Burton felt exactly the same after England had beaten South Africa at Ellis Park in 1972. 'I felt I hadn't done enough,' he said.

That evening, it was confirmed that the Lions were prepared to wait a fortnight for Mike Gibson to complete his business affairs before being flown out as a replacement for Alan Old. He was expected to join the touring party just before the second test in Pretoria, by which time it was hoped that Old himself would be out of hospital.

The Lions did not forget Alan Old that evening. They went to see him as soon as their coach left the ground after the match and they gathered outside his room in the hospital and sang, 'We have overcome.' Clive Rowlands, the Welsh national coach, had gone to see Alan Old. Both of them sat there in tears.

CHAPTER 15

Southern Universities

THE weather worsened over the weekend. Only the wooden slopes at the foot of Table Mountain were visible through the cloud and driving rain. The advance guard of Welsh supporters who had docked in the 'Windsor Castle' the previous Wednesday borrowed some waterproofs as they went out to play golf and wondered what on earth had happened to sunny South Africa.

The rain spared the Lions the discomfort of training on hard pitches but it started a minor epidemic of influenza which swept through the team in the next week. Ian McGeechan was chosen at fly-half for the match against Southern Universities. which was to be their last game in the Cape, and Andy Ripley was chosen at number eight but both had to withdraw from the team and stay in bed. Even Mervyn Davies went down with the same virus so that Roger Uttley had to drop back to number eight with Phil Bennett at fly-half.

Other players in the touring party were affected and some of the Lions who did play were far from well. Gordon Brown went into the second row in place of Uttley but he felt full of cold, and when he saw the pitch at Newlands, he thought that he would be lucky to get through the game without catching pneumonia.

After a week of almost ceaseless rain the surface at Newlands had to be seen to be believed. Surface, indeed, was the operative word, because so much rain had fallen on it that it was flooded. There was almost a deep end and a shallow end. Bobby Windsor took one look at it and thought that it was more suited to Mark Spitz. It was not difficult to imagine someone drowning in it because the pools of water stood deep enough to cover the nose and mouth of a player who might be buried face down at the bottom of a ruck. That nearly happened once to Dickie Jeeps, the former England and Lions' scrum-half, and he never forgot the experience.

The Lions felt that the pitch was not fit for play. No one could remember a Lions game in South Africa being cancelled because of a flooded pitch, and it was obvious that the officials at Newlands wanted the game to be played. A lot of tickets had been sold and nine of the players in the Southern Universities team had also played for Western Province the previous week. The locals remembered how close Western Province had run what purported to be the Lions' test team, and they wanted to see how they would get on against the midweek team. They naturally hoped that there might be some reaction after the Lions' test victory.

The man who had the uneviable task of deciding whether the game should be played was the referee, Dr. Justus Moolman. He had refereed England's game against the Griques and against South Africa in 1972 and two years before that, he had refereed in Wales for six months while he practised dentistry in Newport. He felt that the pitch was not dangerous and that he could see the marking lines so he decided that the match could be played. It turned out to be an historic decision, but for reasons which he could not have anticipated, because it was in this game that students of Cape Town University made the first anti-apartheid demonstration on a Rugby ground in South Africa.

There had been rumblings from the University for weeks. The students' union had proposed a move to take action against any students who agreed to play for Southern Universities against the Lions but this had incurred the wrath of the silent majority to such an extent that a special meeting had been called and this proposal had been overthrown by a crushing majority.

They settled instead for a more restrained form of protest and they smuggled into the ground a large banner proclaiming 'We are playing with apartheid.' It was stretched between two poles and even rolled up it could hardly have been the sort of thing you could have stuffed down your trousers leg unless you had been walking on stilts, but although the police had been warned that the students were likely to take some action. the banner was not detected. At an appropriate moment in the first half when the Lions were busy attacking at one end of the field and the attention of the police had been diverted, the students ran on to the field at the other end and unfurled their banner.

For a few moments, nothing happened because the nature of the pitch was such that once the ball had been manoeuvred to one end of the field it was likely to stay there for a very long time while it defied the attempts of most of the players to move it. That was what happened here. The Lions and the Southern Universities players gurgled and squelched over the ball in a determined little huddle in one corner while the students were strung out in the other half of the field. Neither interfered with the activities of the other in the slightest degree. There was plenty of room for both.

Some of the players looked over their shoulders in mild embarrassment while the muddy faced men in the middle of the maul apparently took no notice at all. The referee looked across and wondered just what he should do.

In the end, some outraged Rugby enthusiasts jumped over the fences and literally waded into the demonstrators with such ferocity that they were being dispersed long before the police had paddled on to the pitch to escort them away. On the whole, it was rather an interesting diversion, because it will be remembered long after the proceedings in the match have been forgotten.

It was a mistake for the Lions to play the match against Southern Universities at all. No one could have anticipated the Springboks' selection for the first test when the fixtures were made, but as it turned out, it meant that the Lions had to play half the Western Province team three times in ten days, and although most of them became close friends by the end of it, they were all sick of the sight of each other as players.

It would have been much better if instead of playing Southern Universities, the Lions had played a combined country districts team at Upington. One of the most disappointing features of the Lions tour of South Africa in 1974 was that they visited so few of the smaller centres up country like Upington. As a result, they missed half the fun of touring South Africa. Every British touring team enjoys the run of matches along the coast in South Africa, but they also enjoy the contrast of the Kalahari and the opportunity of meeting such splendid men as Jack Horn and 'Doc' Visser and Jack Young. A match at Upington at that time would have been a pleasant way of working uphill to Johannesburg for the match against Transvaal at the end of the week.

The Lions won the match against Southern Universities with the greatest of ease. Even though University teams in South Africa combine past and present students so that occasionally some really gnarled veterans somehow qualify for selection, Southern Universities were pushed all over the pitch by the Lions. The pressure on their line was inexorable and it squeezed out a series of scores.

Brown scored a try from the front of a lineout and Bergiers ran strongly to score after Moloney and Neary had worked an opening from a scrum. Irvine converted one of the tries and also kicked two penalty goals, which was far from easy in the appalling conditions. The Lions' only moment of hesitation came just after their concentration had been disturbed by the anti-apartheid demonstration. They dropped out of their 25 but lost control of the ball and McDonald drove through to score.

In the second half, the Lions consolidated their victory, if that was possible on such a pitch, by scoring two more tries. Both were push-overs, of a sort. One was an orthodox push-over when the Lions forwards pushed Southern Universities over their line for a try scored by Kennedy from a scrum at the end. The other was unorthodox because Irvine beat a man on the right and kicked ahead and when the forwards recovered the ball, they wedged in behind Uttley and drove him over the line. Irvine converted Kennedy's try.

At least the match gave Tom David the chance to see if he had recovered from his hamstring injury. Within five minutes, he and every other forward was as blackfaced as a coal-miner coming up after working a shift, but he surged through the match with such exuberance that no one was in any doubt of his fitness. The forwards as a whole played with far too much power and purpose for Southern Universities. In every position that the Universities had a player whom they thought had played well, the Lions had one who had played better. They concentrated their efforts and committed their opponents in such a way that Phil Bennett literally had time to go paddling behind them. He stood firmly behind them at one lineout splashing about in the water with such an apparent lack of concern that it looked for all the world as if he was paddling in the sea over at Camps Bay.

The day did not promise much comfort for South African Rugby. Apart from the emphatic defeat of Southern Universities by the Lions, it was also the day when Eastern Province announced that they had dropped Hannes Marais as captain and given the job back to George Barnard.

Amos du Plooy, the chairman of the Eastern Province selectors, said that it was unfortunate for Marais that he had been relieved of the captaincy at that stage. This seemed something of a statement of the obvious. Mr. du Plooy added that he still considered Marais the most suitable player to captain South Africa against the Lions.

This added to the embarrassment in which Hannes Marais found himself. He had been quoted as saying that he was prepared to withdraw from the Springbok team if the selectors wanted him to and everyone who knew Marais had no doubt that this was his attitude at the time, but he was prevailed upon to modify what had been quoted as his opinions. 'Parts of that report are inaccurate and misleading,' he said, 'and wrong interpretations have been put into what I said. I want to captain the Springboks and will continue to do so as long as I have the confidence of my team and the selectors.'

It all sounded very lame and very sad.

CHAPTER 16

Transvaal

CLIVE REES spent an uncomfortable night as the Lions said their farewells to Cape Town. His right hand hurt, so as soon as the touring party arrived in Johannesburg the next day, he went to hospital to have it X-rayed. As he stepped off the aircraft, he shivered with the rest of us. Johannesburg was freezing in a bitter wind blowing from the mountains.

When the results of the X-ray became known, Rees was entitled to shiver again. The plates revealed that he had broken a metacarpal bone in his right hand. The bone was not displaced and when his hand was put in plaster, Rees was told that it should not be too long before he was fit to play again. Exactly how long was another matter. A specialist went to the ground when the Lions trained at Ellis Park in the hope of seeing both Rees and the X-ray plates. He ended up by seeing neither. He did say, though, that if the bone was not displaced and it was a straightforward fracture, it might be possible for Rees to play again within three weeks.

The doctor passed this opinion from the warmth of the Glasshouse. This is the popular name for the comfortably appointed lounge of the Transvaal Rugby Union which looks over one corner of the pitch at Ellis Park. The lounge is enclosed with glass at the front, hence its name, but with seats all around and a bar at the back, and an eagle's eye view of the Rugby, it is some way removed from the image of a prison which might be conjured up by the name Glasshouse.

It was a good place to be on the afternoon in question. The Lions training below were wearing their red track suits and anoraks and even after warming up, they did not unzip the hoods of their windproof jackets. They looked more as if they were about to finish an assault on Everest rather than work through a training session. Syd Millar did not ask them to do much because it was late in the afternoon when they arrived. By then, the freezing cold of the night air was beginning to clamp round the stadium and the Lions had enough problems with influenza without turning them into something worse.

The well-being of the Lions was not uplifted by their hotel, either. It looked comfortable enough when they moved in, and as it was one of the five-star hotels in Johannesburg, there is no doubt that it could have been comfortable enough. However, the players and the management were spread over fifteen floors and for the whole of their stay, one of the lifts was out of action.

These delays were inconvenient enough, but Rugby players will put up with most things as long as their rooms are comfortable and the food is good. There was nothing wrong with the rooms. It was just that the food was inadequate. The Lions were not in the least amused to go into a snack bar for their first meal and find that they could have pea soup, chicken and ice cream. Nothing else. Just pea soup, chicken and ice cream.

The management of the hotel was apologetic. 'The Lions are staying here at a special rate,' said one of the under-managers, 'and that means the menu is restricted.'

Inevitably, protests were made, and the next day, the Lions were offered a choice of dishes. They could have either Irish stew or a fish called kingclip.

Unfortunately, if there is one dish that most Irish Rugby players cannot stand, it is Irish stew, and there were troubles with the kingclip, too. It was almost inedible. Again, the manager was called.

'What is wrong ' he asked. 'The fish is rubbery,' said the Lions, denting it slightly with a massive effort with their knives. The manager also had a go. The dent he made was not quite so big. He shook his head. 'Kingclip is a rubbery kind of fish,' he said. That came as news to some of us who had been enjoying kingclip for years.

It was a ridiculous situation. Here were the Lions being put into one of the best hotels in Johannesburg on the cheap, even though they had gone to a great deal of trouble to get to South Africa in the first place, and even though the team was earning millions of rand for the South African Rugby Board. The four tests alone made nearly a million pounds.

It was not the fault of the hotel. One look at the choice of restaurants in the building made it perfectly plain that it could have catered for the tastes of almost anyone. But the restaurants were barred to the Lions. The players were confined to a restricted menu in the snack bar. And what was the saving? The difference between the cost of bed and breakfast at the hotel and full board was R3 a day, which even at the appalling rate of exchange available to sterling at that time was less than £2. As one of the Lions said, 'This hotel must really have had to go to quite a lot of trouble to give us food as bad as that.'

What with one thing and another, the Lions were not much impressed by their first visit to Johannesburg and some of them were feeling sorry for themselves for other reasons, too. By then, the team to play Transvaal had been announced and some of the players who had been hoping to break away from the midweek circuit and be given the chance of playing in an important Saturday match had been left out yet again.

Mike Burton, Chris Ralston, Stewart McKinney and Tom David were particularly disappointed. Burton had been positively itching to play against Sauermann and he had been given to understand that he could look forward to that pleasure in the game against Transvaal. Burton's enjoyment of the prospect was heightened by the fact that the Lions had been told that Sauermaan did not want to play against them. The story went that after his unhappy experiences against the Lions in the first test, Sauermaan had lost face so much that he wanted to withdraw from the Transvaal team. Hannes Marais, the Springbok captain, had told him that he must not do that. 'You must take what is coming to you,' he said. Burton had intended to make sure that plenty would be coming to him, but when the Lions team was announced, Burton was not in it. He was in despair.

Chris Ralston was just as disappointed. 'At least you've been injured,' he said to Burton. 'I can't even get enough games to do that.'

Stewart McKinney must have felt even worse. He had gone four matches without a game and similarly Tom David was hoping to be selected after his vigorous display against Southern Universities.

At the time, it seemed as if the Lions could afford to encourage a few of their midweek players by choosing them because even with a depleted team, London Counties had drawn 12-12 with Transvaal the previous year. What is more, London had coped quite comfortably with the Transvaal pack. Against that was the fact that the match against Transvaal was a week before the second test and it would suit the pattern of selection to keep the bulk of the Lions' test players together and rest them in midweek.

No doubt Syd Millar and Bill McBride also remembered that Transvaal had been the only provincial team to beat the Lions in 1968. They decided to take no chances. They kept the bulk of the test pack together. The only changes they made were to bring Andy Ripley and Tony Neary into the back row. Ripley's selection might have been expected because he had starred for London Counties against Transvaal at Ellis Park the previous year. Neary may have been helped into the side by the influenza which had confined Fergus Slattery to bed.

The Lions thought that the match against Transvaal might turn out to be a punch-up, coming as it did in the week before the second test. Accordingly, they decided to rest Gareth Edwards. He was the key player and they knew that they could not afford to go into the second test without him.

For the match against Transvaal, though, it looked as if the Lions might have to settle for any fifteen players who happened to be somewhere near fit on the day because within 36 hours of arriving in Johannesburg, a combination of influenza, stomach upsets and injuries had reduced their ranks to 21 reasonably able-bodied men. Apart from Alan Old and Clive Rees, who were injured, Gordon Brown, Geoff Evans, Fergus Slattery and Ken Kennedy could not train and Roy Bergiers, Billy Steele and Mervyn Davies gave up at various stages. The next day, even J. P. R. Williams succumbed. He tried to train at Ellis Park but after warming up, he left the field. 'My legs just won't go,' he said. He went back to bed.

He did not get out of it until just before the match the following day, and although he felt far from well, he resolved that he was going to play. Tom Grace, Bobby Windsor and Gordon Brown did the same thing, so that when the players' bus left to go to the match at Ellis Park, it contained a mixture of infection and determination in roughly equal proportions.

The ground was full long before the Lions arrived, but that did not stop thousands more spectators piling into the ground. And why not? They had bought tickets for seats, and they were perfectly entitled to seek admission in the hope of finding the seats they had bought. For a large number of them, it was a vain hope. Anyone arriving at Ellis Park less than two hours before the kick-off stood about as much chance of reaching his seat, never mind finding it, as he had of buying a ticket for the second test.

Ellis Park in 1974 was like a spider's web for tubular steel scaffolding round an oblong of yellow grass, and to those who had to try to climb upwards and outwards to the edge of the web, it felt just about as strong. The further they went, the more hopeless their task became because the gangways were nearly all blocked with people who had given up the unequal struggle of trying to reach their seats or alternatively, of trying to persuade the people to move out of them who were sitting in them when they arrived. People could neither get into the seats nor get out of them. Anyone who wanted to answer a call of nature either had to contain it or release it underneath the seat. That was not unknown, either. Hygiene just did not exist.

Safety standards did not exist, either. In every match played by the Lions at Ellis Park in 1974, there could have been a major crowd disaster. Because the gangways were obstructed, there was no way people could have got out of the stands in the event of the need for a swift evacuation. Because of the hopeless overcrowding it only needed someone to lose their balance at the top of the stands and fall for an avalanche of people to slide down on the principle of a giant snowball. The single rail of scaffolding at the bottom certainly would not have stopped them.

The overcrowding was such that there was not even room for children to sit down. The accommodation consisted of planks of timber stepped up on the scaffolding. A row of people were expected to sit on each plank and on that same plank, there was also supposed to be room for the feet of the people sitting behind. Whoever calculated the width of the average seat and the length of the average thigh bone got his sums badly wrong, because there was nothing like enough room either to sit down or to get your legs in position. Even children could not sit with their legs at right angles to the seats they were supposed to be sitting on, because their knees would have been jammed into the backs of the necks of the people sitting in front. For adults, the situation was ridiculous. Yet for seats like that at the test match, the Transvaal Rugby Union charged eight rand, which is £5.

Toilet facilities at the ground were almost non-existent for women and everyone who walked underneath the stands went in peril of their lives from the coke tins and bottles cascading down the pin-table and metal scaffolding underneath the seats. Those who simply had their clothes ruined by squashed naartjies or urine which fell on them counted themselves lucky. Ellis Park in 1974 was a disgrace.

Fortunately, Transvaal's match with the Lions was not a disgrace. The fears that it would turn out to be as dirty as the Lions' match against Canterbury in Christchurch in 1971 proved to be unfounded. The match was hard but it was reasonably clean. No game of that nature is ever played without a few altercations, but at least they did not escalate into open war.

Transvaal had picked a heavy pack, with a man who had been recently a prop playing at hooker, and a lock on one of the flanks. In the first scrum, they even succeeded in pushing the Lions. This encouraged them to take the battle to their opponents, and they succeeded so well that they dominated the whole of the first half. Transvaal led 9-3 at half-time and they would have been even further in front if Gerald Bosch had kicked better at fly-half, or if van Wyngaardt had not missed a loose ball when he was diving to touch it down for a try near the posts.

The loss of the first test match and the bitter arguments between the North and South had turned Transvaal's match against the Lions into another Springbok trial, particularly as McCallum and Snyman, the Western Province half-backs, had been preferred in the test to Bosch and Bayvel of the Transvaal. The whole of the North had been up in arms when so many Western Province players had been chosen for the test, and when South Africa lost, the North made no attempt to restrain its sarcasm and its hostility. The fact that the test match had been lost by the front five of the Springbok pack, and that almost all of them had come from the North, was completely ignored. Transvaal would show them, and in particular, Gerald Bosch and his beautiful boot would show them.

Unfortunately for the North and for the Transvaal, Gerald Bosch and his beautiful boot did not show them at all, even though his forwards gave him every chance. In the first two minutes of the match, they forced the Lions to concede a penalty kick almost in front of their posts. Psychologically, it was the most important moment of the match. Nothing would have done more for the morale of the Transvaal team if Bosch could have kicked that goal, but he missed it. The beautiful boot failed.

At the level of football in which Bosch normally plays, he is given any number of opportunities to recover a mistake like that, but at international level, those opportunities rarely come again. The lost ground can never be recovered, and even though Bosch kicked three penalty goals before half-time, he knew and Transvaal knew and the Lions knew that he should have had more.

Bosch kicked his first penalty goal when McBride deflected the ball badly from a lineout and J. P. R. Williams was penalised for lying on the ball as he tried to retrieve the situation. He kicked his other two penalty goals when the Lions were penalised first for shirt-pulling and then for obstruction in a lineout. Against that, Bennett kicked a penalty goal for the Lions when Transvaal were caught offside.

The Lions had been pushed back so much in defence that they were glad to be still in contention. They owed most of that to Bosch, because above all else, a fly-half who is a kicker must be able to recognise those rare and precious moments when he has the ball and he has three men running against two or two men running against one. Those are the occasions when he must not kick.

Twice in that first half, Transvaal had an overlap. On both occasions, Bosch failed to see it. On both occasions, he kicked the ball away. He did much else that helped the Lions, too, kicking the ball into touch on the full or kicking away balls that could have been put to better use. His kicking was so obsessive that it was almost a reflex action.

Transvaal did have one moment of bad luck. Bosch dropped at goal from the left side of the field and missed to the right of the posts. The ball eluded the Lions' defence and ran loose in goal and if van Wyngaardt on the Transvaal right wing had not become over-anxious and mistimed his dive, he would have scored.

It was easy to sympathise with van Wyngaardt and to understand his anxiety. It was also easy to understand his lack of familarity with the behaviour of the ball. With Bosch at fly-half, the ball was something he only ever touched when he threw it into the lineout, and so it was small wonder that he poured all his artistic and athletic soul into that aspect of his game. Even Sir Laurence Olivier could not have thrown in with more drama or a greater sense of stage-craft. The deep stoop forward, the furrowing of the brow in concentration, the arch of the body backwards, the closing of the eyes, the dramatic pause at the top of the backswing, it was all there, it was all there.

Transvaal needed a much bigger lead than 9-3 at half-time because there were already signs that they would find it hard to defend. Sauermann had decided not to try to take on Cotton in the scrums so he moved away from his hooker. This is the easy way out of trouble for a loose head, but it creates grievous problems for the men behind because they are left with a void in front of them. Transvaal's problems in the tight were compounded, too, by the fact that Oberholzer, their number 8 and captain, often ran away from the scrums, just as Morné du Plessis had done in the test match at Newlands.

Within two minutes of the start of the second half, the Lions set up a scoring position, just as Transvaal had done in the first half. The difference was that the Lions took their chance, and it was worth six points, not three. Windsor set up a ruck to the right of the posts and the Transvaal defence was caught so fast asleep when the ball came back that Milliken was able to ignore an overlap to his left and step inside three men before scoring a try which Bennett converted. It was a bad lapse of concentration in defence, and it threw away all the work the Transvaal forwards had done in the first half. They looked sick and from that moment on there was not much doubt that the Lions would win.

Bosch dropped a goal from a strike against the head in a scrum but by then it was clear that the Lions were taking control. The referee did not see that Ripley had grounded the ball over the line from a five yard scrum, but it made no difference because from the ensuing five yard scrum, Bennett scissored with Milliken on the open side and the Lions' centre ran straight through the transfixed Transvaal forwards to put J. P. R. Williams over for a try on the blind side. Bennett could not convert but he did kick a penalty goal so that the Lions led 16-12. This meant that Transvaal would need at least two successful kicks at goal to overtake the Lions. There was never the slightest prospect of them scoring a try.

The extraordinary thing was that even with his team four points down, Bosch went on kicking the ball away. He did drop a goal from a lineout, but almost at once Bennett kicked a penalty goal when Transvaal were offside at a ruck. With the game almost over, the Lions led by four points and Transvaal had to score a try to win. That surely was the moment for Bosch to let us see whether Symons could run better than he could tackle or whether Cronje really was the best centre in South Africa. But no. He went on kicking.

The match had a fitting end. The Lions forwards tried to drive a loose ball through the middle of the field but overkicked it straight at Bosch. He preferred not to pick it up. He got out of the way. The Lions picked it up instead and Uttley sent Ripley on his way to make a try for Neary. Not one of Gerald Bosch's better days.

Fortunately for the Lions, the Springbok selectors were more easily satisfied. When they met that night, they reacted with such enthusiasm to Transvaal's performance that they made no fewer than six changes in South Africa's team to play the Lions in the Second test in Pretoria the following week. They chose Bosch and Bayvel at half-back, which committed the Springboks to an entirely different tactical approach, they brought in Frederickson at hooker and Bezuidenhout at loose head and they moved du Plessis to the flank to make room for McDonald at number eight. They had to make a change in the centre because Oosthuizen was injured so they selected Jackie Snyman, normally a fly half. It looked strange to see two runners like Snyman and Whipp outside a kicking fly-half like Bosch, but no one seemed to bother about things like that. Off with the old and on with the new.

CHAPTER 17

Rhodesia

THE LIONS flew up to Rhodesia the next day. They went reluctantly, not because they had any qualms about giving aid and succour to an illegal regime, but simply because all touring parties have a rooted objection to leaving any hotel to go anywhere at 8.30 on a Sunday morning, even to go to Victoria Falls.

Herman Visser had dark forebodings about the whole operation. He wanted to send some heavy luggage straight on to Pretoria and to keep only the essentials for the trip to Salisbury. 'Something is sure to go wrong,' he said. His fears were amply justified. It turned out to be the usual 8.30 for 9.45 business. Groaning bodies heaved themselves out of bed from seven o'clock onwards and the depleted lift service tried unavailingly to keep up with the movement of baggage and personnel from their rooms to the foyer and then to the restaurant and back to their rooms.

To make matters worse, the buses did not turn up. They had been sent the day before, but had been told they were not needed. Apparently no one had said that they should come back the following day. By the time this had been discovered and rectified, the foyer of the hotel was barricaded with bags and bodies in various stages of disrepair.

The blare from Andy Ripley's cassette tape recorder stunned the senses even more but even that was not enough to drown the yelps of anguish which came regularly from the direction of the cashier's desk as various sufferers saw the size of the bills for the various odds and ends they had consumed.

The Lions flew up to Victoria Falls in two Viscounts. Approaching from the air, the first thing you see of the Falls is a cloud of spray hanging over the trees in the distance like the billows of smoke from a woodland fire. The intensity of the spray and the consequent visibility of the Falls depends on the strength and the direction of the wind. That day was not a good one for looking at the Falls from the air.

The Lions landed at lunch-time on the air-strip cut out of wooded country near Victoria Falls and stepped out of the aircraft into the most gorgeous warm sunshine. They were told that they could leave their valuables on board and they went through customs so painlessly that most of them did not realise that they had arrived in another country. They were happy just to go outside the tiny waiting room of an airport and sit in the sun to await the arrival of their team-mates on the other aircraft.

This took rather longer than expected. Aircraft number two had just taxied into position ready to take off from Johannesburg when someone realised that they had left all the touring party's passports behind.

When the Lions were reunited, they were driven ten miles to a landing stage on the Zambesi river, pausing on the way to admire an elephant which had obligingly wandered near to the road as if to convince the Lions that they were now in the middle of the real Africa.

The riverboat was like something off the Mississippi, except that it did not have paddles. It was a lovely colonial craft, with two open decks and a staff of white uniformed Africans to steer the boat and serve the food. At that point, just above the Falls, the Zambesi is about a quarter of a mile wide and the waters of the river made a beautifully serene background as the Lions climbed down some steps to the landing stage and stepped aboard.

The Lions quickly climbed out of their number two dress of shirts, ties and day blazers and stretched themselves out in shorts and slacks in the sun. Our hosts told us that the perfect weather was a marked contrast to that endured by the Lancashire team when they had visited the Falls on their tour of Rhodesia and South Africa a few weeks earlier.

The riverboat glided smoothly away from the landing stage and nosed quietly upstream leaving some envious air hostesses looking down from the hotel on the bank. As it did, the smell of grilling steak drifted back from the bows and the Lions realised that they were hungry.

The T-bone steaks served by the chefs were about the size of the sails of a child's yacht, and you needed a plate the size of a dinner tray to carry all the meat and the rice and the salads that went with it. Some of the Lions sat in the sun on the top deck. Others sat in the shade below. It was a nice point as to which situation was the more attractive. On the top, there was an unbroken view of the river and the sun was so warm that it quickly dried up the colds and the sniffles acquired in Cape Town and Johannesburg. Down below, the view was not quite as commanding and the vitamin D content was markedly lower but at one end was the bar and at the other end was the food, always considerable compensations to Rugby players.

The Lions sat back happily and thought that if this was giving aid and succour to an illegal regime, they why on earth had not someone suggested it earlier? Alun Thomas looked at the river bank sliding past. 'It's beautiful,' he said. Indeed it was.

The river bank on the port side was very close indeed. Prudently, the coxw'n was keeping as much water as possible between us and Zambia on the other side of the river. We had heard all about the two Canadian girls who had been shot while visiting the Falls. Some of us had half expected to be greeted by a couple of ground to air missiles from Harold and Marcia as we banked to look at the Falls before landing. Fortunately, we were spared any form of artillery and we slid through the water as peacefully as Ratty and Mole in 'The Wind in the Willows.'

Well, it was as blissful and as peaceful for a time, while the Lions cooed quietly over their steaks, but as they sat back and reached for a beer, their natural high spirits began to assert themselves.

At that point, we could see some rapids ahead of us upstream, and we steered across to an island in the middle of the river. The Coxw'n asked the Lions on the top deck to sit down, so that he could judge his approach to the landing stage. He made it perfectly. We barely brushed the wood as the force of the current slowed us to a halt.

The crew made fast and before they could hitch the first of their cloves, some grey monkeys tumbled out of the woods and climbed along the guard rails. They were extraordinary creatures, because the testicles of the males were bright blue. The animals were also quite tame. Dick Milliken was considerably startled as he went ashore with a partly eaten apple in his hand when a monkey jumped up and took a bite. Milliken looked sadly at the apple and realised it was now unclean. Philosophically, he tossed the apple to the monkey, which caught it beautifully before racing up a nearby tree to devour the fruit. 'Better catch that monkey and put it in the centre on Tuesday,' said someone.

The return downriver was somewhat noisier, with the occasional beer bottle bobbing along in the wake. One man who was in no condition to enjoy himself, however, was Mike Burton. He had suffered an eye injury in a club game against Newport at the end of the previous season and it had become reinfected. Burton is an uncomplaining man, but it was so painful that he just lay down across three seats on the lower deck. 'I thought I was going to die,' he said later.

The coxw'n took the boat past the jetty and across the river in a graceful arc before turning upstream to come alongside the bank again. Once more he accomplished the manoeuvre perfectly. The

Lions had to be photographed with the crew of the boat before they left.

Another of the attractions of the Victoria Falls is a crocodile farm where these creatures are reared artificially to ensure their survival. They are kept in pens containing shallow pools of water and they vary in age and size from one year when they are about 18 inches long, to monstrous gnarled veterans of something like 20 feet. It felt like midsummer in Britain, but to any self-respecting Rhodesian crocodile, of course, it was the middle of winter and therefore perishing cold. When crocodiles are cold, they are comparatively inactive, though Mervyn Davies soon learned how fast they can turn and bite when he picked up one of the babies. It flicked round in a flash and nipped him across the knuckles.

Gareth Edwards examined the blood and the teeth marks sympathetically. 'You should suck it to draw out the poison,' he said, and suited his words with action. Instead of sucking the wound, though, he bit it again.

'Aaaaaagh,' yelled Davies, wringing his finger. 'I've been bitten by Edwards. Gangrenous!'

The Lions were then driven down the river bank to within a short distance of the Victoria Falls. As they stepped out of the coaches, they could hear the thunder of the water half a mile away and as they walked along the leafy paths towards the gathering tumult, the spray from the crashing water drifted through the trees and turned them into rain forests.

The Falls are even more beautiful from the ground than they are from the air. Different aspects of the Falls are presented as the path winds through the trees on the top of the cliff on the other side of the gorge across from the crashing water. In places the path goes so close to the edge that people with no head for heights feel dizzy. 'We've nothing like this in Troon,' confessed Gordon Broon.

On the way back, we found the statue of Livingstone, and Gordon climbed up and stood on the base alongside the giant figure. 'I know you'll not believe it,' said he, 'but we're related.' When the hoots of derision died down, he said, 'It's true.'

As we walked back to the coaches, Roger Uttley said, 'Imagine walking half way across Africa, and hearing nothing for months on end except the birds and then hearing the noise of that water. Just faintly at first. He must have wondered what it was. Then it grew louder and louder as he got nearer and nearer. And then he came to the edge of the cliff and saw that.'

Some of the Lions slept as they were driven through the late afternoon to the airstrip ten miles away. John Moloney slept, too

When he got out of the bus, his head was circled with shaving cream. Edwards had struck again. Moloney would have probably got into the aircraft still wearing his halo of shaving cream if the bus driver had not told him about it. He wiped it off as Fergus Slattery came tearing back from the village bearing yet another statue of your man Andy Capp in greenstone. Slattery discovered how cheap the greenstone was when he toured Rhodesia with the Penguins in 1973, and seemed to be cornering the market.

The Viscount took off for Salisbury with five or ten minutes to spare before the last of the light faded. Night flying out of Victoria Falls was not then possible because the landing strip did not have runway lights.

Gareth Edwards then settled himself back to sleep, and several beady eyes waited to exact revenge. He seemed aware of the threat, because he opened his eyes and wagged a finger at Tom David. 'I'll 'ave yew,' he said.

Flankers have said this to opposing half-backs down the ages in an attempt to discourage them, and apparently, T. P. David is apt to say the same thing to G. O. Edwards whenever Llanelli play Cardiff.

'But you 'aven't 'ad me yet, 'ave yew?' taunted G. O. Edwards.

'No,' said T. P. David. 'You never get the ball when you're playing for Cardiff against Llanelli, do yew?'

Edwards survived the trip unharmed, but the same could not be said of the manager. He had lost his blazer, with all sorts of valuables in it. Or rather, his blazer had been removed. 'It must have happened when we were at the Falls,' he said. 'But they said it would be safe to leave our stuff on board.'

With the officials of the Rhodesian Rugby Union and the usual loyal party of Welsh people waiting to meet him, he had to put on his raincoat to step out into the night.

The welcome for the 1974 Lions was not as tumultuous and as ecstatic as that which greeted the Lions in 1968. The airport was not crowded with thousands of cheering Rhodesians as it was then. Rhodesia has now become used to its independence and to living with sanctions. After all, ten years is a long time. The affection for Britain is just as strong among the older generation of Rhodesians, so much so that they are far more loyal to the Queen than many of the British, but naturally, to more or less of the younger Rhodesians, kinship with Britain is just a childhood memory.

This is all rather sad, and it was even sadder to arrive in the centre of Salisbury and find that Stewart Meikle's magnificent colonial hotel had been pulled down, with its balustraded verandahs round a central lawn. In its place had been constructed a perfectly adequate but absolutely nonedescript modern hotel. There was only one of the old Meikles, just as there was only one Raffles and only one Shepheard's, but there are countless thousands of the new Meikles, functionally efficient and totally unmemorable, all over the world.

However, we had to smile when we walked into the lobby. Outside, it was a warm summer's night, with the temperature simmering in the high sixties, and yet the staff were shivering in woollen cardigans with electric fires to warm their legs. To them, of course, it was winter, and it was cold.

It certainly was not cold the next day, when the Lions went up to the Police ground to train. The weather was as perfect as it had been at Victoria Falls, and the manager went out in his track suit for a run. He had found his blazer, too. Or rather, it had been returned. He nodded towards the players. 'It was that lot,' he said resignedly. 'Apparently, it was an anti-disciplinary measure.'

Alun Thomas was strict about appearances and had sent Geoff Evans back to his room to change when he had climbed on to the players' bus wearing a pink shirt instead of the white shirt required in the number two rig. The next day, the manager himself had appeared in a striped shirt on a number two rig occasion. Hence the tit-for-tat of the missing blazer. It was the first overt sign of a deteriorating relationship.

That day, Syd Millar decided to have a fitness session. As the sprints lengthened the signs of anguish began to grow. In the end, Fergus Slattery dropped on his hands and knees and was quietly sick.

Apart from Alan Old, who was due out of hospital in Cape Town that day, the only players who missed training were Bill McBride and Mike Burton. McBride had a strained calf muscle, and Burton arrived soon after it started, with his head swathed in bandages and wearing dark glasses like someone suffering from first degree burns.

He had been chosen to play against Rhodesia the following day, but the eye specialist had discovered an ulcer on the line of the original scratch on his eyeball, and although it was responding to treatment, it seemed extremely unlikely that he would be fit for the morrow. In his absence, J. P. R. Williams played at tighthead in the practice scrums and, as always, he set about the task as if he really meant it. There are no self-effacing chuckles when John Williams lines up against the forwards for a physical contest on the practice field. He has a go.

He had done the same thing in New Zealand in 1971, but on this occasion, he found considerable difficulty in staying where he wanted to stay. His feet developed a nasty habit of leaving the ground. He shook his head. 'Seems to have been a development in technique somewhere,' he said.

Rhodesia discovered the same thing the following day. When they ran on the pitch, they looked as if they were the left-overs from the schoolboy match which had just finished. Physically, they were dwarfed. They jerked back in the first scrum and went backwards at an ever-increasing pace throughout the match. In one scrum in the second half, the Lions advanced so rapidly that they were on the point of breaking into a trot.

It was clear from the beginning that Rhodesia had anticipated that this would happen and so their coach, Ian McIntosh, had decided to try to break up the play as much as possible. Rhodesia kept the ball moving as quickly as they could by throwing one-handed torpedo passes across half the width of the field. The theory of this was praiseworthy, but unfortunately for Rhodesia, the execution was rather less effective. The torpedo passes certainly went a long way, but they rarely went where they were intended. The result was that the ball was often knocked on, or the player due to receive the ball either had to wait for it or reach for it or go back for it. By the time these adjustments had been made, the point of the exercise had been lost because the Lions' defence was in the position it would have been if the passing had been quick and orthodox and accurate. When Rhodesia made outright mistakes, of course, like knocking the ball on, they merely transferred the scrum from one part of the field to another.

Neither Mike Burton nor Bill McBride was able to play. Burton had been subjected to a fitness test in the morning in which he had been required to look at the sun with his injured eye. 'They said, 'It's watering, you're not fit,' said Burton indignantly. 'I told them their eyes would blessed well water if they had to look at the sun out here.' He sighed heavily and counted all the games he had missed. 'What will they say at the Coach and Horses in Gloucester?' he said. 'They will say, "You went on a Lions' tour, and how many games did you play? Six? Seven? What were you doing?" But it's not my fault, is it? I had a broken leg in Stilfontein, a broken heart in the Transvaal and now I've got a broken eye in Rhodesia.'

Burton's place at prop was taken by Sandy Carmichael, while Roger Uttley added yet another game to what eventually became the highest total of the tour by substituting for Bill McBride.

The Police Ground at Salisbury is open and sunny and rather

like the sort of arena where you would watch show-jumping or a gymkhana in Britain. Whole sections of the low stands were filled with blocks of the reds and the blues and the greys of school uniforms. The difference was that half the Rhodesia Air Force seemed to be keeping a watchful eye on proceedings. The Prime Minister of Rhodesia, Mr. Ian Smith, watched the game, just as he watched the Lions in 1968, and his air force burned many thousand gallons of precious petrol and paraffin to assure the visitors that all was well.

The Lions won the match very easily by 42 points to six, but they did not play particularly well. They made far too many mistakes and they kicked badly. This illustrated better than anything the falling standard of Rugby in South Africa, because in the previous season, Rhodesia had reached the semi-finals of the Currie Cup and were only beaten by Northern Transvaal, the eventual winners.

The only Lion who did draw considerable satisfaction from the match was full-back Andy Irvine. He scored 22 points himself and played so well that he went a long way towards rehabilitating himself after the uncertainties of the early part of the tour.

He started with a penalty goal kicked after Rhodesia had been drawn offside and he followed that with a fine dropped goal from 45 yards. Rhodesia were under fierce pressure in front of their posts, and Paul Semple got himself into such a scrape that far from kicking the ball anywhere near touch, he only succeeded in depositing it straight upfield, somewhere near the halfway line, Irvine fielded it and dropped a goal.

Ian Robertson, the Rhodesian full-back, then kicked two penalty goals to bring his side level. He must have been hoping for rather more in the way of opportunities to prove to the South African selectors that he was worth his place in the Springbok team. He would have needed a fairly emphatic performance, because Robertson had made no secret of the fact that he shared the general view that it was absolutely pointless for Rhodesians to take the trouble to attend Springbok trials, because they never got picked anyway, even if they did play well.

Unhappily, for Robertson, his forwards were under too much pressure in the tight to give the backs in front of him any room for errors, and they made so many of those in their rather frantic attempts to break up the formal pattern of play that his own efforts had to be concentrated on clearing up the mess. Rhodesia tried to introduce some lineout variations but these usually led to mistakes, as so often they do, because they had not been practised enough to make them infallible. Similarly, Rhodesia hoped to disrupt the Lions scrummage by wheeling it. With their physique, this was always a vain hope. They might just as well have tried to budge Table Mountain.

Still, Rhodesia must be given credit at least for thinking positively about the game, for accepting the areas in which they were bound to be beaten and for trying to push the game into those areas where they had some hope of success. They failed, but they earned full marks for a brave try.

Rhodesia's position of parity did not last long. Fran Cotton brought the ball away from a lineout maul on the right touch-line, and Ken Kennedy switched Cotton's pass quickly inside to Sandy Carmichael. By then, Gareth Edwards was sprinting hard on the outside and Carmichael gave the ball to him so quickly that the Lions' scrum-half was able to break clear and sell an outrageous dummy in goal before scoring between the posts. Irvine converted.

While this was going on, Mervyn Davies was involved in a little contretemps and those who suspected that the look of indignation and outrage on his face were reminiscent of the crocodile farm at Victoria Falls were not far wide of the mark. In the maul which led to Edward's try, Davies had collected another bright set of teeth marks. This led him to reflect that in the space of three days, he had been bitten by a crocodile, by Gareth Edwards and by a Rhodesian. The aggravation which attended the third bite distracted some of the attention from what proved to be the most entertaining try of the match.

Tom Grace scored two tries on the Lions' right wing. Roy Bergiers and Andy Irvine made the opening for one by creating an overlap from a lineout won by Chris Ralston and Gareth Edwards made a chance for a kick ahead with a determined break from the blind side of a scrum.

A long break by Ian McGeechan in the first half was supported by Geoff Evans who set up Billy Steele for a try, and Fergus Slattery took advantage of some confusion between the Rhodesian full-back and fly-half as they changed positions to charge down a kick by Lendrum and follow up and score.

Slattery played as if he was not in the least inconvenienced by his moment of intestinal upset on the practice field the day before. His involvement in his Rugby was rarely less than complete and when he is playing behind dominant tight forwards, his quite exceptional speed makes him a thorough nuisance to all his opponents. The grimace of effort which he makes when he is sprinting also makes him an alarming prospect, particularly as the gumshield he has worn since his teeth took such a clattering against Canterbury in 1971 adds a sharks-tooth dimension to his snarl.

The last try was scored by Irvine. He caught a missed touch and dodged past the defence with a nice mixture of real pace and clever running. He scored the try close enough to the posts to make the conversion a formality, and as he had already kicked two more penalty goals, he sent his total of points for the tour soaring from 29 to 51.

It was in the game against Rhodesia that Irvine graduated from being a doubtful quantity under the high ball to being a possible selection on the right wing for a test match. At that time, senior Scottish players in the team remembered his lack of success on the wing in his earlier days and advised firmly against considering him as a winger. However, his strength and his pace and the cleverness of his running, as well as his tenacity in defence, meant that he was at least as well equipped in the skills as any of his rivals and the extra 15 yards which he could add to the range of the Lions' goalkicking gave him an added advantage. Irvine did have a passing weakness on one side of his body but that was not the greatest of handicaps for a wing, because at least he was always alert to the possibility of making the ball available for his support, which was a thing that Billy Steele sometimes forgot to do in moments of stress.

After the match, the Lions went into the clubhouse at the ground to meet Mr. Ian Smith and to have a drink with him. He was as affable and as cordial as he had been in 1968. He said he had thoroughly enjoyed the afternoon. He did not look as if he was in a ferment, but then, neither did his country. The peace and the quiet and the privacy made a welcome change from the bustle of South Africa, and it strengthened the feeling that when the Lions go back to South Africa in 1980, the Four Home Unions should follow their policy to its logical conclusion and ignore the political hou-ha about Rhodesia, if any still exists. Salisbury is much the most sensible place for the Lions to have their pre-tour training camp. It is on the way to South Africa, and so represents two hours less flying, and it has the ideal combination of altitude, climate and congeniality of atmosphere for a touring team to prepare.

It is also a good place for buying copper. John Moloney seemed to be intent on cornering the whole of the Futures section of that particular commodity market. Peter Larter had demonstrated himself to be the keenest shopper in 1968, but on this tour, John Moloney and Fergus Slattery challenged him hard for his title.

CHAPTER 18

The Second Test

THE climatic contrast with the previous Sunday could not have been more complete when the Lions stepped out of their jumbo jet at Johannesburg on the way to Pretoria and the second test. Instead of the bitter cold and searching wind that had made them step briskly up the steps into the aircraft three days earlier, they were caressed with the warmth and gentle zephyrs of summer and these were made even more agreeable by the drive to Pretoria. This is only 40 miles from Johannesburg but it is downhill all the way and the drop of more than a thousand feet softened the padded edges of South Africa's winter even further. The only people who were not enchanted were Hermann Visser and his baggage men. The Lions had left them behind at the airport.

By the time the Lions arrived in Pretoria, most of the Springbok players were already there. The International Rugby Football Board decrees that teams playing a home international must not meet more than 48 hours before the game, but the Springboks had got around that neatly by holding their trial game in Cape Town on the Tuesday before the first test. In Pretoria, they did not even bother to use an excuse. They just turned up on the Wednesday.

The Springboks had already been forced to make another change in their team. Gert Muller had withdrawn because of injury and his place on the left wing had been taken by Gerrie Germishuys, of the Free State. That brought the number of changes in the South African team up to seven.

The Lions, by contrast, made no changes at all. They resisted any temptation which might have existed to play Andy Irvine on the right wing and they continued with their experiment of playing Roger Uttley on the flank. They had the reassurance of knowing that the Springboks had chosen Gerald Bosch at fly-half, so there was not much danger of South Africa moving the ball quickly to the wings and exposing Uttley's defensive limitations. They also had the reassurance of knowing that the Springboks had chosen a very loose back row, which again meant that Uttley's determined driving in the tight-loose would be seen to its best advantage.

The events of the games against Transvaal and Rhodesia had settled the minds of the Lions' selectors about the centres, too. Dick Milliken had done the job required of him against Transvaal and both Roy Bergiers and Geoff Evans had been injured against Rhodesia anyway.

Those of us who hoped to watch the Springboks train were disappointed. They went off to work out their master plan behind the walls and locked gates of a prison. They had done this sort of thing before. Even their training camp before the tour started had been held in private. It all seemed slightly ridiculous. It must have been embarrassing for the Springbok players, too, particularly when they were told that they must not have any contact with the outside world and that they must concentrate so exclusively on their preparations for the match that they must not even read the newspapers. The thought of the Springboks creeping furtively out of their room and looking anxiously up and down the corridors reminded me of a spy comedy in which Bing Crosby, as one espionage agent, sidled up to Bob Hope, as another espionage agent, and asked out of the side of his mouth, 'Have you got the papers?'

Bob Hope looked cautiously up and down the street.

'Morning or evening?' he said.

Not that the Lions could afford to laugh too much. They were almost as cut off from the outside world themselves. They were in a hotel which had only four telephone lines manned by one operator, and with upwards of thirty journalists and photographers trying to get calls out of the place, and with ten times as many girls trying to get calls into the place, the day to day business of the management and the other guests came to a grinding halt.

Alan Old rejoined the touring party in Pretoria. His leg was in plaster but the ligament injury was a straightforward severance without any complications and it had been stitched together. The doctors were confident that he would make a good recovery.

At almost the same time, Mike Gibson also arrived and immediately went out to train. He thought he would be fit enough to play in the following game against the Quaggas. He looked fit enough to play in the test itself.

The weather continued warm and pleasant on the day of the match. The conditions therefore were absolutely perfect for the team and the running style of play the Springboks had left behind in Cape Town. This time, however, they had been committed to trying an entirely different combination of players at loose-forward and in midfield and they had been committed to playing in an entirely different style.

The mystification engendered by all this was soon heightened by the sight of Ellis scuttling up to the front of the lineout. It seemed as if Johan Claassen had some compulsion to stop his loose forwards doing their proper job. In Cape Town, with his scrum in great difficulty, he had assigned du Plessis, his number eight, with the task of retiring from it at great speed to cover the kicks of Edwards to the blind side wing. This only increased the difficulties of the sore-pressed Springbok scrummage and it enabled the Lions' forwards to give Edwards even better controlled ball with which to pick his spot to embarrass the Springbok defence with his kicks. In Pretoria, the tactics seemed to be to move Ellis to the front of the lineout so that he could put pressure on Edwards, but to be fair to Ellis, he looked thoroughly unconvinced about the wisdom of the whole exercise. He often seemed to be in doubt as to whether he should be at the front of the lineout or at the back, and Cotton soon stuck out his bulky backside to stop Ellis getting at Edwards in any case. This meant that Ellis was able to contribute very little of value to the South African cause, and even worse, it deprived the apology of a Springbok midfield defence with one of the most vital elements of its cover.

As if all that was not bad enough, the Springboks then kicked the ball away with such gusto that they gave Bennett, the Lions' fly-half, an unbroken supply of the possession he loves best to start the counter-attacks of which he is such a master. Those counter-attacks, of course, went straight through the middle of the field, where Ellis would have been if he had not been moved elsewhere . . . Six years earlier at Loftus Versfeld, Ellis had broken Barry John's collarbone. In 1974, he did not touch Bennett all afternoon.

All these considerations were revealed much more quickly than they usually are in international matches, though the first mistake was made by the Lions. They had won four of the first five balls of the match when McCallum, the Springbok full-back, went to find touch on the left and missed. Steele tried to gather the ball near the right touch-line but did not pick it up at once and instead of rolling it into touch he tried to advance. He ran straight into the arms of Germishuys and du Plessis and saw the ball swept away from him. The Springboks moved the ball quickly across field to the right but knocked it on as they moved it back inside.

The Lions could only find touch from the scrum and J. G. Williams won a good lineout ball for the Springboks which Bosch kicked diagonally. This kick did not extend J. P. R. Williams in the least. Brown jumped into J. G. Williams at the next lineout and the Lions won the ball but again they had to find touch and at the next lineout Williams again won the ball cleanly.

Instead of kicking, Bosch slipped past Slattery and Bennett. It was a good break, made all the more damaging by the surprise of it, but instead of working back towards his support, the Springbok fly-half ruined all his good work by kicking the ball straight at J. P. R. Williams. Old habits certainly die hard, and in Bosch's case, they proved very expensive.

On the first occasion that Brown jumped into J. G. Williams, the Lions' lock did not provoke any retaliation from that gentle man, but when he did it again, Williams was moved to do something about it. He hit Brown, and although he did not do it with any real conviction, it did at least indicate that the Springboks realised that they were being taken out of the lineout and had planned to do something about it. The strange thing was that they did not do more, because their attempts to discourage Brown were only sporadic.

Almost at once, the Lions had a chance to take the lead. They were given a penalty kick about 35 yards from the Springbok posts and nicely to the left. This ought to have suited Bennett perfectly, because he draws the ball to the left as he hits it with his instep. In practice on the Thursday, though, Bennett had been hooking his place kicks a bit too much, so he decided to aim off more to the right. He hit the ball exactly where he intended but pushed it straight to the right of the posts. The ball did not hook in its flight at all.

The Springboks dropped out from their 25 and the Lions kicked the ball into touch on the full on the open side. The Springboks knocked the ball on in the lineout and this gave the Lions a scrum ideally situated on the left side of field for one of Edwards' attacking kicks for the blind side wing.

Edwards executed the chip kick perfectly and made McCallum look horribly badly positioned. The ball bounced before McCallum could reach it and it bounced badly enough to beat him. J. J. Williams reached the ball first and with Pope on the Springbok right wing failing to get back to cover his full-back, Williams was able to kick ahead and score. It was such a simple try that it must have made the whole Springbok defence feel thoroughly sick. Again, Bennett pushed his kick at goal past the right post. Again, the ball did not curve in its flight. He shook his head and frowned. There was positively no prance as he went back for the kick-off.

It did not take Bennett more than a couple of minutes to get back on his toes, because in that time, he could have scored a try himself. Milliken ran a long way before setting up a ruck and Bennett shot away to the left in perfect balance and in perfect position to set up another try. Bennett looked as if he could have scored himself, but he gave the ball to J. J. Williams on the left wing. Williams should have side-stepped the cover and come inside where there was plenty of room to score but instead he went for the corner and did not manage to ground the ball properly.

At that stage of the game, the Springboks could have been overwhelmed because almost at once, J. G. Williams was penalised in a ruck down in the right corner where South Africa had already suffered so much grief. Again, it was an easy kick by Bennett's standards, and again, it was perfectly placed for him, but again, he pushed it to the right of the posts.

The Springbok goalkicking was no better. J. G. Williams even lost his scrum-cap in one moment of indignity in the lineout and the referee gave South Africa a penalty kick about 45 yards from goal on the left. It was in a good position for Bosch to kick with his right-footed draw, but Marais, presumably trying to keep the pressure off his young fly-half, gave the kick to McCallum. In the event, Marais only put more pressure on McCallum, who despite his seniority, looked even less capable of withstanding that pressure than Bosch. McCallum had already made some important mistakes without the compensation of a really good piece of play to encourage him and set his mind at ease. McCallum looked distinctly fraught as he made his preparations to kick at goal and then looked even worse as he sliced the ball wide of the left post with his left foot.

For a time, the Lions' tactical and touch-kicking was not much better than South Africa's. J. P. R. Williams fielded a missed touch kick by Pope and started a counter-attack with Slattery, but at the other end, McGeechan had to scurry to retrieve a badly sliced kick by Edwards and then Germishuys perpetrated an even bigger mis-kick than the one which had given him the ball in the first place.

South Africa were determined to have the last word, though, and when they missed touch again on the left, J. P. R. Williams caught it and passed the ball inside to Bennett in yet another broken field situation. Bennett jinked away to the left and then side-stepped back towards the centre with J. J. Williams sprinting diagonally behind him to take a scissors pass. There was then nothing between Williams and a try between the posts, but Bennett's pass was not one of his best and Williams knocked it on.

At that point, it began to look as if the Lions might be letting South Africa off the hook. They had missed 16 or 18 points and the game was not 25 minutes old, but the ease with which Bennett made his run and the total lack of interference from the South African loose forward and midfield defence must have made the Springboks realise that unless Bosch could kick some goals, and kick them pretty quickly, the Lions could probably afford to be prodigal and still win with something to spare.

Within two minutes, even that hope was dashed. The referee gave the Lions a scrum because the Springboks delayed too long in throwing the ball into the lineout but he penalised the Lions in the scrum. This penalty kick was to the right of the posts and therefore more suited to the left-footed McCallum, but Marais gave it to Bosch instead. Rather predictably, Bosch pulled the kick across the face of the posts, and as the Springboks re-formed to face the drop-out from the Lions 25, it was not too difficult to see that neither McCallum nor Marais nor Bosch felt that things were exactly going their way.

As if to rub it in, the Lions promptly scored a try and converted it. First Bosch missed touch and then J. P. R. Williams missed touch and finally McCallum raced up the Springbok right wing and hoisted a high kick which was fatally too far ahead for him to re-gather. All it did was pull him right out of position as he followed up, and Bennett saw this at once as he dropped back into his 25 to collect the ball.

In an instant, the Lions' fly-half had assessed the field in front of him and begun a curving run away to his right and back into the centre of the field. He nearly cleared the screen of forwards following up but was just caught by Marais with a desperate lunge from behind. By then, Bennett was close to the tight forwards and McBride was able to turn the ball to Davies. The Lions' number 8 was tackled quickly but McBride doubled behind him and moved the ball on to Brown who passed the ball out to Edwards.

The movement was still working towards the right, and Edwards kicked towards the right touchline where Uttley followed up and tried to gather. It looked as if he knocked the ball on and this impression was strengthened when he swung a disappointed kick at the ball. The referee was unsighted, though, and he missed the knock-on. By then, McCallum was back in position in defence and he hesitated, looking towards the referee. Some of the Lions hesitated, too, but J. J. Williams who had come right across from the left wing, sensibly played the whistle and booted the ball even further on. Still the referee did nothing, so Williams raced after the ball and scored a few yards in from the right corner flag. It was a much more difficult kick at goal than some of those Bennett had missed but from the way he went about it, he was confident of success and his kick amply justified that confidence.

So after 30 minutes, the Lions led 10-0 and although they had not played particularly well, their opponents had made so many mistakes and had left their midfield so full of holes that the score could just as easily have been in the high twenties. The Springboks were winning some ball from J. G. Williams in the lineout but they were either kicking it away or making mistakes, so that on the one hand they were playing to Bennett's strength as a counter-attacker and on the other hand they were enabling the Lions to have threequarters of the put-in at the scrums, which was the point of their greatest forward strength.

The Lions used their scrummage possession to give McCallum and his wings a desperately uncomfortable afternoon. There was one priceless moment when the Lions held the ball in the back row of their scrum and Edwards stood up and had a long, hard look down the right touch-line. He looked first at Germishuys and then at the space behind him as if to say. 'Whatever are you doing up there, my man? If I kick the ball behind you, you are up the creek without a paddle.'

Edwards bent down as if to pick up the ball, and Germishuys scurried off backwards to cover the space behind him. But Edwards did not pick up the ball. Instead, he peered over the top of the scrum again, like a walrus emerging from the waves and stared at Germishuys as if to say, 'Whatever are you doing back there, my man? If I run the ball to the blind side and pass to the wing, there is no defence to stop me and you are down the creek without a paddle.'

Again Edwards bent down as if to pick up the ball, and Germishuys scurried back upfield as if his life depended on it. Edwards had poor Germishuys going up and down like a yo-yo before eventually he called for the ball and put the poor man out of his misery by kicking it down behind him.

McCallum looked just as uncomfortable at full-back for South Africa. To make things even worse for him, he sustained a shoulder injury in going down to stop a forward drive by the Lions.

Bosch dropped a goal off the near post from his favourite position on the left side of the field when he was given a ball from a lineout, but within a minute, the Lions might have scored again. They worked a good ball from a scrum to the blind side wing where J. J. Williams had J. P. R. Williams running in support inside. It looked as if an exchange of passes would have produced a fairly straightforward try, but the Lions' winger kicked ahead and the chance was lost.

The Springboks were so busy in defence that they failed to recognise chances even when they presented themselves. Just before half-time, Ellis came away from a maul in his own 25 and if he had assessed the situation properly, he would have realised that he could have created an overlap for his left winger by running straight at the first of the Lions' backs who were moving up in defence.

Ellis had no such thoughts. He was indulging in his favourite ploy of carrying the ball in one hand. This may look very cavalier but it ought to have been coached out of him years before, because it minimises the chances of the ball-carrier making an accurate pass, it predisposes him to kick and it maximises the chances of the opposition taking the ball off him in a maul.

Sure enough, Ellis kicked, and everyone said, 'Hooray.' No-one said it louder than the Lions' backs, because although Ellis found touch near the halfway line, they had been spared an embarrassing moment in defence.

He nearly had to pay an even higher price for his folly. A scrum followed the lineout, and the Springbok scrum-half so delayed his put-in that his hooker lost his timing completely and Windsor took the ball against the head. Milliken drove hard for the Springbok line and first Slattery and then Edwards were held up only a few feet away.

Worse followed, the Springboks were given a five yard scrum, but Bayvel missed his fly-half with something to spare when he went to pass to him and hurled the ball straight over the dead-ball line. The expressions on the faces of the Springboks revealed their thoughts more clearly than any words. The Lions then put the ball into a five yard scrum, and the Springboks were only saved by the fact that the referee gave them a penalty kick. Even then, the Lions might have scored again because just as the half ended, Milliken missed a pass when the Lions had a 3-2 overlap.

Hannes Marais did his best to whip up his men at half-time, when the Lions led 10-3, and there is not much doubt that if the Springboks had been good enough to exert any territorial pressure for any length of time, they might have overhauled the Lions on penalty goals alone. In the first half, the Springboks had three penalty kicks and the Lions had two. In the second half, the Springboks had ten penalty kicks and the Lions had three. Five of the Springboks' penalty kicks in the second half were kicks at goal, despite the amount of time they spent in defence.

Within two minutes of the start of the second half, referee Cas de Bruyn had penalised the Lions for stepping offside at a wheeling scrum and Bosch had kicked his first penalty goal. Even with the score at 10-6, however, the Springboks were not able to exert any pressure. A teasing, tantalising kick by Bennett squirmed away from McCallum and South Africa were pushed back on to defence again by a switched drop-out from the Lions '25'. The Lions made a lot of ground up the right wing with this and set up the position from which they scored their third try and settled the match.

Snyman tried to work the ball out of defence, and passed inside to McDonald, but the Springbok number 8 lost the ball in a maul and Slattery broke away on the right. He went towards the touchline and swivelled to give Bennett an inside pass. Bennett threw a dummy and with Steele unmarked outside him on the right, he had a two against one situation and a certain try for the taking. Strictly speaking, Bennett should have made the try for Steele, but perhaps mindful of his experience with J. J. Williams in the first half, he saw that McCallum had come across too far in an attempt to make an interception so he beat him on the inside with a side-step and scored.

As Bennett went past, McCallum stuck out a leg and caught the Lions' fly-half on the instep. The injury was so painful that Bennett could not take the conversion kick, and while Edwards was making his preparations to do so, Bennett had a look at the damage inside his sock. He saw a lot of blood and a nasty deep cut which eventually required five stitches. However, he had a pad put on it and decided not to go off because he felt that his foot would not stiffen up while he stayed really warm and kept it moving. Edwards missed the conversion kick, so that after eight minutes of the second half, the Lions led 14-6.

In the next three minutes, the Springboks made two more mistakes which should have cost them tries. First they kicked the ball straight to J. P. R. Williams, who surged through the middle of the field and left Slattery with a double overlap on his right. Slattery was tempted to go for the line himself, though, and was tackled and South Africa got away with it.

Their luck did not last long. Du Plessis threw a pass back to Bosch who was under such pressure from Bennett that he could not kick and had to unload the ball to McCallum. The Springbok full-back was in difficulties himself and got so little power into a left-footed kick towards the left touchline that the ball went straight to Edwards near the 25.

Edwards squared his shoulders and snorted off down the right touch-line and came very close to scoring himself, but when he was checked, he passed to Gordon Brown who was roaring up in support and the Lions' lock went over for a try. By then, Bennett felt sufficiently recovered to take the kick at goal, but he missed.

The looseness of the Springbok play was hard to believe, because within three minutes, the Lions could have scored again from a strike against the head. Bosch did kick another penalty goal after a scrummage infringement, but everyone knew that it was no more than a temporary respite.

Whatever encouragement the Springboks might have felt was quickly dissipated when McCallum's distinguished international career came to an end in a miserably ignominious episode. First he ran off the field, and then he ran back on again, and then with frantic signals coming from the Springbok selectors in the stand, his captain waved him off again. It looked as if Hannes Marais was giving him out, just as a cricket umpire might, rather than sending him to the doctor. McCallum was in no obvious pain when he made his spritely retirement, and he looked in no greater discomfort from his shoulder injury than he had for the previous twenty minutes. Sadly, McCallum's departure from that test match, and probably from international Rugby, earned him the biggest cheer of the day. How different it all had been four years earlier when he had helped to defeat the All Blacks.

When McCallum went off, McDonald went to full-back in one of the more bizarre positional adjustments of an incredible afternoon, and Brown won a lineout for the Lions on the right. The Lions' backs had called a move, presumably with the idea of testing McDonald's capabilities as a full-back, but when the ball came back, McGeechan changed his mind and dropped a goal instead, as if to show that whatever Bosch could do with a right-footed drop kick from the left of the field, McGeechan could do equally well with a left-footed drop kick from the other side of the field.

That put the Lions ahead 21-9 and it put them in such command of the game that even the crowd at Loftus Versfeld gave it up as a contest. When the Springboks took the kick-off after the dropped goal, a wag on the terraces brought a roar of laughter when he shouted, 'Hooray. You're in their half!'

Dawie Snyman came on as a replacement for McCallum and was just in time to see Brown galloping out of his 25 with far more confidence of penetrating the opposition than had been demonstrated by any of the Springbok threequarters. However, Brown rather spoiled things by kicking ahead. This kick was not well-directed and Germishuys was able to start a counter-attack which built up a position from which the Lions were penalised for being offside in midfield. Bosch took a kick at goal and hit a post. Uttley caught the rebound but missed touch and Ellis tried to develop a counter-attack with his backs.

As they did so, Dawie Snyman went down and stayed down with an ankle injury. He had only been on the field for six minutes to follow the McCallums and make the second pair of brothers to play in successive tests for South Africa. He could not continue and had to be helped off the field.

He had no sooner gone than J. J. Williams and Edwards attacked down the left and although Edwards over-ran the ball, such was the exuberance of the occasion, and such was his self-confidence that he indulged in one of the favourite party tricks he used to produce when partnering Barry John and flicked the ball back over his shoulder with his heel. It was such a cheeky thing to do that somehow it seemed to sum up the game.

Leon Vogel came on as replacement for the injured Dawie Snyman. No sooner had he arrived than he flattened Bennett with the most extraordinary late tackle. This knocked Bennett out. He had been feeling pretty ill-used before that, because apart from his sore foot, he had been thumped hard into the ground by McDonald and had bitten a lump out of the side of his tongue. 'I hate the taste of blood,' said Bennett ruefully. 'Particularly my own.'

When Bennett had recovered consciousness, he worked up enough of a sense of outrage to feel cross about what Vogel had done and he did not need too much encouragement from Dr. J. P. R. Williams to take the kick at goal himself. It was from the right side of the field, but he put it over with some determination.

By then, Whipp had gone to full-back and the crowd were streaming home in thousands. They scarcely even looked at the final indignity which their team heaped upon itself.

J. G. Williams won a lineout in his own half, and the Springboks half-heartedly tried to move the ball in midfield. The Lions were up very fast in defence and forced a maul which the Springboks lost. As the ball came away, Bennett moved it to the left and Milliken set off apparently to get as far as he could before he was stopped by the screen of defenders in front of him. At that stage, there was nothing untoward about the situation at all. It was only transformed by what the Springboks did to themselves, because as Milliken advanced, three of them, among whom Ellis was prominent, seized him by the jersey and positively hauled him over the line. Milliken may have been surprised by such hospitality, but he was not overwhelmed by it to the extent that he forgot to put the ball down for a try. Bennett could not convert.

There was just time for South Africa to take the kick-off and just time for them to make one more mistake. The ball did not go ten yards, so it was a scrum back, Lions' ball, Lions' heel and the Lions' match.

The Springboks' defeat by 28 points to 9 was the worst they had suffered in their history, but even then, it did not reflect the extent of their disorganisation. The Lions scored five tries but they missed six kicks at goal and they missed seven chances of scoring tries. The Springboks could have been beaten by fifty or sixty points, and against that, they did not once even threaten to score a try themselves. It was the worst performance and the most extraordinary capitulation in modern international Rugby, and it only confirmed the suspicions formed on the England tour two years earlier that for the time being at least, South Africa had dropped out of the rankings as a major Rugby playing country. The Lions led 2-0 in the series and rejoiced.

After it was all over, it was hard to resist the thought that having been in purdah for three days, the Springboks would be doing themselves a favour if they stayed that way for the next three weeks. Johan Claassen had not allowed them to read any newspapers. It would have been an act of humanity not to allow them to read the newspapers in the morning, either, or on the Monday, or for a very long time to come. He could have been forgiven if he had not wanted to read them himself.

CHAPTER 19

Game Park

SOME of the Lions were rather the worse for wear in the morning, but most of them managed to muster in the pleasantly warm sunshine in front of their hotel in time to catch the buses taking them to an airport near Pretoria where two DC3's of a commercial airline were waiting to fly them down for a three day rest at the Kruger National Park.

Now Dakotas are something of an acquired taste. Their impressive safety record is always advanced to sooth the fears of those who are doubtful of the advisability of flying in aircraft which were going strong in the war thirty years ago, but they are very far removed from the huge modern jet aircraft which take off and land so smoothly that the champagne in the glasses of privileged passengers in the first-class department is scarcely disturbed. It is not quite true to say that in a Dakota, you feel the need for a brown leather helmet, a pair of goggles and a parachute, but you do get the elementary feeling of flying by the seat of your pants which was so familiar to gentlemen like Bleriot and the Wright brothers. As I say, this now has a limited appeal and people like Bill McBride and Bobby Windsor, to name but a few, decided that they would rather make the journey by road, even at the 50 miles an hour speed limit on the South African motorways.

The others gathered round the aircraft at the side of the grass runway and played football while they watched their baggage being separately weighed on what looked like a pair of bathroom scales, and stowed in canvas webbing pens in two holds fore and aft of the small passenger cabin. This is never the most encouraging of starts for a flight, but the Lions took some small consolation in the various crates of beer which had been so thoughtfully provided by a representative of South African Breweries who was well versed in attending to the needs of touring Rugby teams.

The flight to the game park from Pretoria took the better part of two hours and it was well into lunch hour before the aircraft bumped and yawed through the air pockets to land at the airstrip near the Skukuza rest camp. Skukuza was only two or three miles away, and the party soon split up into various groups who were fitted into combies and driven into camp in time for a late lunch in the restaurant.

The accommodation at the rest camps in the game park consists of rondavels, which are small round buildings, plastered and painted white both outside and in, and with conical thatched roofs. They contain the primitive essentials of a bed and a basin with somewhere to hang your clothes, and a series of wash-houses, with showers and baths and other essential facilities, are built at regular intervals to serve different groups of rondavels.

South Africans pride themselves on the simplicity of these camps. The game park itself is a huge area, the size of Wales, and the only concession to civilisation is that a few of the dirt roads have been tarred. Otherwise, the country is as God made it and as the elephants have left it, dotted with small trees as far as the eye can see like an orchard in winter. Many of the trees in the dried yellow grass are broken where the elephants have casually pulled off branches to eat the surviving leaves.

Winter in the Kruger National Park, though, is very different from winter in Cromarty. The area is sub-tropical and although it was warm enough in Pretoria, the drop in altitude made it warmer still in Skukuza. The mosquito netting on the doors of the rondavels looked a wise precaution, and Dave Goddess, the team-masseur, even took anti-malaria pills.

The warmth immediately made the Lions think in terms of swimming pools, and Tony Neary was surprised to find that they are not fixtures at all the rest camps in the game parks.

Most of the players spent the afternoon sleeping or settling in, but some who were lucky enough to be near the car park climbed into a bus which went out by chance on a game drive and saw one of the prizes of the visit, a leopard padding along the side of the road for a long way while it allowed itself to be photographed. Leopards are shy creatures, but this was within a mile of the gates of the camp.

The camps are all fenced off to keep out the very real lions and the other big game in the park and the gates of the camp are locked very firmly each night at dusk. Woe betide any car-load of game viewers who are late for the evening curfew. The gates are not opened again until dawn, when a patient queue of combies waits to drive out for a glimpse of the animals before they move away from the water in the river-beds to go into the bush to sleep in the middle of the day.

Not that many of the Lions were very anxious to do that. At least, not on the Monday morning. A group of them had diverted themselves with a game of Thumper the night before, and at the same time, had provided a great deal of amusement for the visitors to the camp. The principle of the game is that a group of players sits round a big table and each one works out an individual signal. It may be a twitch of the nose, or the wink of an eye, or a flick of an ear, but whatever it is, it is the personal signal of the player involved. The idea is to make them as subtle as possible so that they are difficult to detect.

One player is assigned to start the game, and he calls out, 'What's the name of the game?' Back comes the reply 'Thumper.' 'How do you spell it?' T-H-U-M-P-E-R, THUMPER, and everyone then bangs the table like mad as if they were playing bongo drums and watches like hawks for the signals to be passed from one player to the next. The player who starts the game will select another player to pick up his signal simply by looking at him while he is thumping away at the table, he will give that signal. It is then up to the next player to pick up that signal accurately and to reproduce it before passing on his own signal to someone else. The penalty for failure is to drink a glass of beer straight off, which means that the bad players become progressively worse to the vast delight of everyone until they either fall under the table or are noisily sick.

The extraordinary thing is that people who don't much care for drinking beer can often be inveigled into the game, even though they have to suffer dreadfully as a consequence. Some of the players were shrewd operators and were caught very few times. Even Mervyn Davies, who 24 hours earlier had set out to break Sean Lynch's 1971 British and Irish Rugby Union Celebrating Record, had had a sleep and was in surprisingly crafty form. There he sat, with two days' growth of beard and a soft floppy hat, looking like something out of Gauguin, but he had far too many marbles for most people when it came to a game of Thumper.

The game revealed some unsuspected adepts. Fergus Slattery played the game like the expert tourist he is, and after a sticky start, Geoff Evans sat quietly in the background, decoding and transmitting signals like the codebreaking department in the Royal Navy. That's what comes of going to the Manchester Institute of Science and Technology.

The crowd gathered round the game under the patio lights became so big and was so vastly entertained that Ian McLauchlan suggested that the Lions should have a silver collection. He suggested it twice.

Inevitably, the innocents are the ones who suffer most at the end of a game of Thumper, and Billy Steele retired from circulation for 24 hours. Roy Bergiers in the end decided that he just could not pour any more beer down inside him so he poured it over his head. Later, much later, J. P. R. Williams could not work out what had happened to his bed. He wandered about for hours, with an infinite patience, while he tried to trace a rondavel with a bed in it. 'I know there's one somewhere,' he kept muttering.

So there was. It was stapled into the thatch over his head. But who would think of looking for a bed on the roof of a rondavel? I think he ended up sleeping on the floor, and was probably quite oblivious to the real lion that roared outside the camp all night.

Bobby Windsor was only too well aware of the lion outside and the other animals wandering about. In the pitch black of the night, he could not find his room either. He knocked on Tom David's door, and was told to go away, but he wouldn't, and in the end he made such a heart-rending plea about the spookiness of the night and the mysterious rustlings of the animals that they let him in.

For a touring team, one of the advantages of staying at Skukuza is that there is a training pitch in the village near the camp, and after an early morning game-drive for the hardier souls, the Lions played football and had a short training session. This was something of a surprise. There were one of two absentees. That was not a surprise.

The training pitch is outside the camp and it is not fenced, so the proceedings are likely to be interrupted every now and then by a warthog or a group of grazing impala. Warthogs can be belligerent, but fortunately the one that wandered along the dead-ball line as the Lions were training stopped only to look and then trotted off busily somewhere else. It paid no attention to those of us sitting in something resembling a bus shelter by the side of the pitch.

Phil Bennett was among those present. He was unable to train because of the injury he had sustained when scoring his try in the second test. He confessed that his foot was sore but at least he had the comfort of knowing that it was the remarkable game that he had played that had revealed the true dimensions of the gulf between British Rugby and the game then being played in South Africa.

'I've fancied my chances of running like that for some time,' he said 'The Springboks kick so much ball away. They're like New Zealanders, their loose forwards are not very good at tackling backs. They don't hold off and wait for you, and push you where they want you to go, like they do back home. They come straight at you, running flat out. They are suckers for the side-step. Being big men, they can't change direction.'

Bennett was convinced that he could have scored himself when J. J. Williams hit the corner flag and he made no apology for scoring instead of setting up Billy Steele. 'McCallum had got too far across to try to cut me off from Billy and I knew I could beat him on the inside. The only trouble was McCallum stuck out his foot as I went past and his studs caught me on the instep, just where I kick the ball.'

Bennett's estimate of the ability of the Springbok team was echoed even more forcibly by Brian Vaughan, who was the manager of the 1962 Lions team in South Africa. He had come down to the game park as part of a holiday trip, and although he was very careful not to intrude upon the preserves of Alun Thomas, he said that he thought that the best team the Lions would meet on tour would turn out to be the one they played each day in practice. It turned out to be a perceptive judgment.

'This Springbok team does not compare with the ones they turned out up until 1970. I think the Springboks are missing international competition. You really sort out what you've got when you are on tour. But I don't think that is the explanation of their decline. They just don't have the players now. South Africa has gone soft. They are not doing their physical work on the farms as they did. The farms have all become mechanised. I suppose it was bound to happen.'

It was harder than usual to find big game in the Kruger Park. Normally, the animals move close to the rivers in the dry season and the roads running close to the banks are ideally placed to catch the herds moving to and from the water. At that time, though, the bush was not as dry as it normally is. There had been a lot of unseasonal rain and the waterholes away from the river had not dried out.

That evening, the camp authorities at Skukuza gave the touring party a braai-vleis, and very good it was, too. The grilled meats and salads and jacket potatoes and lots of those sweet long kebabs disappeared so rapidly that the cooks had to rush off and prepare some more. That splendid representative of South African Breweries was with us still and on that night he surpassed himself by producing a few cases of best red wine. The Lions had caused something of a commotion by asking whether they could have strawberries for extras in the restaurant. The management had to have a conference about it, even though the South African Board were making more than £300,000 on one test match. A bit different from Carwyn James's style in New Zealand. He reckoned to drink a bottle of best French red wine every night with his dinner, and if he had players as guests, as he invariably did, he ordered two or three bottles. No conferences were necessary at the braai, though. Everyone just tucked in.

In the morning, the Lions trained again at Skukuza and Mike Burton and Stewart McKinney, who had become comrades in arms through having so much medical treatment together and through playing so often in the same team, decided that they were putting on a bit too much weight and that they would run up to the training pitch from the camp. They were out of sight of the camp and going down the hill into the country when they noticed that the place had suddenly become very deserted and that there were no Africans about. All they could hear was the clip-clop of their training shoes on the road. Suddenly, they heard a rustle in the bushes, and McKinney shot past Burton as if he was finishing the Olympic 100 metres final. 'What's the matter?' puffed Burton. 'It's only a wart-hog.'

'Ai've never seen a warrrt-hog with a mane like that,' said McKinney, in his rich Ulster accent. They arrived at the training pitch several pounds lighter.

The training was moved up a couple of gears from the gentle jog of the day before and the team chosen to play the next match against the Quaggas practised together. Mike Gibson was put straight into the team alongside Roy Bergiers in the centre with Tom Grace and Clive Rees on the wings. Bergiers was having some trouble with a back injury and it seemed foolish to risk Rees so soon after breaking his hand.

Mike Burton had been promised a game, too. The Quaggas had announced that they had chosen two tight-heads in their front row and the one who had been named to play at loose head was none other than Johan Strauss. Burton was looking forward to the encounter with much relish. Fran Cotton was at loose head in the Lions' team, with Gordon Brown and Chris Ralston at lock and Tony Neary, Tom David and Andy Ripley in the back row.

Cotton had been chosen as captain. He turned out to be the only new Lion who was given that honour on tour but in a team which was orientated almost entirely towards the forwards, he had impressed all the most influential people with the strength and purpose of his play. The only regret was that Cotton's advance had been made at the expense of Sandy Carmichael. The latest selection meant that Carmichael would have played only 4½ games out of thirteen.

After lunch, the touring party drove to Pretoriuskop, another rest camp 40 miles away. Tony Neary had heard that there was a swimming pool at the new camp. So there was. Unheated. Despite the warmth of the day, the water was cold and not too many were tempted to extend their bathing beyond lying in the sun.

The afternoon was enlivened considerably by Thys Mostert, the chief game warden at Pretoriuskop. He suggested that the touring party might like to drive out to the rhinoceros farm where these animals were being bred to preserve the species in the park. He and two of his colleagues took a group out in three trucks. It turned out to be a very wild ride indeed. As soon as the trucks had turned off the dirt road into the farm and the gate had been shut behind them, Thys led a drive across rough country which would have been familiar to the long range desert group in the last war. The high-chassis trucks, built incidentally in Japan, and not in Coventry, charged through the bush as if it did not exist. We raced alongside the herd of stampeding rhinoceros like cowboys rounding up cattle and no matter how the animals twisted and turned or into what thickets they ran, Thys Mostert laughed and spun the wheel of the leading truck and kept us alongside. There were times when we ran over saplings that looked as if they would carve us through the middle like a cheese wire but Fergus Slattery, who never missed anything worth doing on tour, hung on to the rail over the cab of the truck and revelled in the ride. So did Alan Old, even with the discomfort of having his leg in plaster. It must have reminded him of his ambulance ride to hospital after the Proteas' game. Mervyn Davies also sat stolidly in the back, with four days' growth of beard on his chin and his planter's hat jammed so firmly in position that even at forty miles an hour over rough country it defied all Thys Mostert's attempts to dislodge it.

Thys was a character from another age. He had a pilot's licence and flew light aircraft from a nearby airstrip and he lived and loved his life to the full. When we had finished photographing the rhinoceros, he drove across country to where his staff were preparing for a game drive. He wanted to net the rarer species among the small animals so that he could mark them and release those surplus to requirements. This involved staking and netting a long line across the side of a hill and driving the animals down the valley the other side and up into the nets. To do this, he stationed a line of workers with sticks and set them off beating the ground and shouting to drive the animals in front of them. The Lions joined them, even though some of them were far too lightly shod and clad to walk through the bush. The line of beaters went down the hill and up the other side but most of the animals detected a gap in the netting at the bottom of the valley and ran through it. When the drive ended with no animals in the net, Ian McGeechan shook his head sadly. 'The forwards let us down again,' he said.

CHAPTER 20

Quaggas

THE Lions flew up to Johannesburg early the next morning, after one last drive looking for game. A bus containing some of the players went past us and a few miles further on, we saw that it had stopped. They were all leaning out of the window and pointing excitedly. Brian Vaughan thought that there was something suspicious about it all, but we stopped too, and looked. As Brian suspected, there was nothing to be seen. It was all a plot hatched by your man Tom Grace. He grinned mischievously as the bus pulled away again.

After much anxious reconnaissance by Alun Thomas and Syd Millar, the Lions had decided to change their hotel in Johannesburg and move to the Landdrost. It was a happy choice. The Landdrost was a hotel in the new Southern Suns group which in 1974, at any rate, set clearly the most reliable standard in South Africa. As it had first been suggested by Dewi Griffiths and Alun Williams, from B.B.C. Wales, it was hard not to think of it as the Llanddrost, and every time thereafter, I had the greatest difficulty in leaving out the second 'l' whenever I had to write the name.

Graham Evans, who was running a series of package tours from Wales to support the Lions, had no doubts that all the hotel accommodation for the touring party should have been based on the Southern Suns group throughout South Africa.

The Landdrost certainly bore out what he said. The manager put the players into two floors just above the dining room where the players ate *a la carte*. This evoked purrs of satisfaction all round. 'The only danger about this place is that we shall eat too much,' said Ian McGeechan.

The only aspect of the accommodation at the Landdrost that surprised the Lions was the fact that they were sharing the hotel with the Quaggas. Mike Burton was quite taken aback to stroll round a corner and find himself face to face with Johan Strauss. From then on, they wandered around the foyer peering from behind pillars and trying to fix each other with the evil eye. Those who remember Robert Newton's splendid performance as Long John Silver in the film of 'Treasure Island' many years ago will have some idea of the rolling eyes and the flashingly fierce squints as they glared at each other. Robert Newton was much taken to saying, 'Ah, Jim laaad,' whenever he saw the young Jim Hawkins, who was suitably petrified by the performance, and it would not have been in the least surprising if Mike Burton, with his West Country accent, had not popped out from behind some marble column and breathed, with infinite menace, 'Ah, Johan laaad,' as poor Strauss went about his business.

'You wait till oi've finished with him,' said Burton with satisfaction. 'E'll be off on a waltz of his own.'

The Quaggas had managed to pick a useful team, despite the fact that some of the leading provinces would not release their players. Indeed, the selection could have been historic if the Quaggas' committee had been allowed to choose two of the coloured players from the Proteas' team, as they hoped.

They had watched the Proteas' game against the Lions with this view and the Quaggas were under the impression that if the matter was handled tactfully, the South African government would allow them to choose a multi-racial team to play against the Lions. This would have been a tremendous step forward and a great coup for the Quaggas club.

The word quagga means zebra and the Quaggas Rugby club operates on the same principle as the Barbarians. To a visitor from overseas, this had always been very confusing because there was also a South African Barbarians club which was quite separate from the Quaggas. To make things even more confusing, one of the leading lights of the Quaggas is 'Chick' Henderson. He is a South African who studied at Oxford University and who played for Scotland and who is a loyal and enthusiastic member of the parent Barbarians' club.

Fortunately, this gigantic tangle was unravelled at the time the Lions were in Johannesburg. The Quaggas had just built a private stand at Ellis Park and they celebrated its opening by announcing that they had amalgamated with the S.A. Barbarians.

When the Quaggas' fixture was put into the Lions' itinerary in place of the game against the very weak union from N.E. Cape, there were mutterings from the Lions about it being a fifth test match, though why on earth they should have been worried with South African Rugby as low as England had showed it to be was hard too see. However, when the Quaggas team was announced, it turned out to be such a nice balance of young players and promising players that no one could have taken exception to it. Indeed, with the exception of the front row, it looked the most intelligent exercise in selection that the Lions had encountered at representative level.

The pity was that it did not contain the Proteas players whom the Quaggas had hoped to include. Most people connected with the tour knew that something of this sort was in the wind, but they said nothing about it in the hope that it would go through. Unfortunately, one of the Johannesburg papers printed the story the week before the match and the South Africa government withheld permission for the Quaggas to choose the Proteas' players. This was a matter of as much regret to the Lions as it was to the Quaggas' committee. Logically, it had seemed the next step forward after England's games against the Africans and the Proteas in 1972.

Still, the Rugby public in Johannesburg rightly sensed that the Quaggas had picked a good team, and they bought tickets in such numbers that the authorities had to rush away and print some more. The first print was 40,000, but by the time the match started, there were 55,000 people in Ellis Park. That was a world record for a midweek match.

Fortunately, Bergiers recovered from his back injury and so the Lions were able to play as selected. They could not have had a more encouraging start either. They kicked off and the Quagga with the ball was driven into touch on the right. The Lions threw the ball long, and were immediately awarded a penalty kick. It was from about 35 yards range, and Irvine kicked the goal.

The Quaggas were not deterred. They threw the ball long at another lineout, and although the Lions won it initially, they kicked the ball away in the ruck and the Quaggas were able to turn the ball back to the blind side wing where Thoressen broke away and was only stopped by a fine tackle by Irvine.

From the following lineout, the Quaggas did almost the same thing except that they won the ball themselves and set up a maul near the touch-line instead of breaking through. Bayvel threw a bad pass from the maul but Kirsten picked it up beautifully. The Lions backs were so anxious to kill the threat that they ran a long way offside in front of their posts and Kirsten kicked his first goal.

One of the most important considerations for a team playing against a pack of superior scrummagers is to concentrate on avoiding the mistakes which lead to scrums. This might seem a statement of the obvious, but in so many of the Lions games, it did not seem to have occurred to the teams they were playing. In the Quaggas match, though, play went on for nearly ten minutes before the home team made a mistake which led to a scrum. Kirsten accelerated beautifully away from a maul but the man outside him over-ran and when Kirsten went to throw a long pass, it was forward.

That gave the Lions the chance to settle into a scrum, which they did at their leisure. It was most noticeable that they never tried to hurry these things. If the scrum was a little crooked, so much the better. It took time to straighten up. If the front rows got in a tangle and fell on the floor, then better still. That meant that even more time was spent with the front rows in contact, and all the time they *were* in contact, the Lions props were busy working away at their opponents.

Burton was obviously enjoying himself. Strauss was packing in an unfamiliar position and even in the first scrum, he looked uncomfortable. Another scrum followed almost at once, and Strauss looked more uncomfortable still. Significantly, the Quaggas had to yield a yard in that scrum.

They still heeled the ball and David was left some way adrift as Cronje and Cowley dummied through. Grace had to cover across.

Kirsten then tried to drop at goal from about 40 yards, but his kick was so short of power that it dropped straight to Bergiers, who linked with Gibson and launched a counter-attack. Gibson kicked ahead from the right touchline, where he was obstructed. The referee did not see this and eventually the Quaggas were awarded a penalty kick on their line.

They worked their way back upfield and forced Irvine to make a mark from which he kicked a beautiful touch. This set up the position from which the Lions scored their first try. The ball went loose from the lineout and Ripley kicked it on past the defence. He whirled himself into his full stride and beat the Quaggas to the ball as it rolled into goal. Whether he touched it down properly is another matter. The ball was popping and bobbling and Ripley went down on it in a clatter of arms and legs. The referee ran back, looking very thoughtful. Ripley's body had obscured his vision and the referee had a very long think before he blew his whistle and signalled a try. Irvine converted.

The Quaggas loose forwards were playing most effectively. They drove and controlled the mauled ball well enough to embarrass the Lions and were disappointed not to be given a try when Strydom, their hooker, drove over in the right corner. However, this did look like the correct decision. Strydom was turned on his back and the ball was still on his chest.

Against that, the Lions should have scored after Irvine had made a long break to the left. Rees missed the pass when he had an overlap and Stephenson, the Quaggas right wing scrambled the ball away. Stephenson also ran round Rees and began a spell of pressure by the Quaggas which led to their try. McGeechan missed touch on the Lions right and Kirsten flicked the ball down the line. The Lions were missing a man in defence but might have covered the gap if Rees had not come inside. As soon as he did, Stephenson galloped round on the outside and ran round.

He grounded the ball a few yards to the right of the posts and it was then that Bayvel made a mistake in his captaincy which he must have regretted since. No doubt the Quaggas had decided in training that the left-footed Cowley should take all the kicks to the right of the posts but the right-footed Kirsten had already kicked one goal and was playing with such assurance that it was clear that we were watching the birth of a new star. He looked such a class player, except in defence, that he reminded me of Bev Risman when I first saw him playing as a youngster for Lancashire. Perhaps it was easier for us to see this from the side than it was for Bayvel in the middle. The tide in the affairs of Peter Kirsten were coming to the flood but Bayvel did not take it. He gave the kick to Cowley and Cowley missed. It was a very important mistake. Cowley also missed a penalty kick at goal from much the same position.

Still, the Quaggas had scored try for try and were losing only 9-7. They were sufficiently encouraged to keep attacking, and Irvine had to produce a fine tackle to stop Coetser after the full-back had swept past Grace on the left. The crowd were well pleased.

They were not so well pleased in the five minutes before half-time, however. The Lions attacked on the left, where Ralston dropped a pass without being stopped for a knock-on and then Brown was stopped on the line. Whether Brown grounded the ball properly is open to speculation but there is not much doubt that Ralston knocked on and the crowd bombarded the referee with peel from the fruit known locally as naartjies when he awarded a try. Naartjies are a large form of tangerine and it was as well that the flesh of most of them had already been consumed before the peel was thrown because the Lions themselves stopped a few.

Irvine could not convert the try and just before half-time, Kirsten had another drop at goal for the Quaggas. Again his kick lacked power.

By then, the crowd knew that they were watching a game, and not a procession, and as there were 55,000 people at Ellis Park, they were able to offer raucous and delighted support. The Lions were fortunate to be leading 13-7. Scores of schoolboys went on the field at half time and cleared up the naartjies. They were suitably applauded.

The Quaggas began the second half well. Kritzinger was playing a useful driving game at number 8, and he was so well supported by his locks and by Fourie and Pypers on the flanks that they were able to set up some of the controlled ball from the maul which so often in South Africa had been almost the exclusive preserve of the Lions. This tied in the Lions loose forwards and it put pressure on their midfield. McGeechan had a kick charged down and Bayvel and Kirsten started an excellent passing move which led to a lineout on the Quaggas right.

By that time, the lineout was even more of a shambles than usual. As he had demonstrated in the Western Province game, Mr. Gourlay's definition of the line of touch was so flexible as to cover a corridor about three yards wide, and as long as the ball was thrown somewhere into the corridor, he deemed it a straight throw. That being the case, of course, the throwers naturally threw the ball straight to their own forwards and equally naturally, the opposition had to jump a very long way across to get anywhere near it. Most of the time, they were allowed to do this with impunity, just as they were allowed to perform almost comical feats of lifting, but occasionally he would award a penalty. He did so when Ralston jumped across on this occasion. The kick was to the right of the posts, but Bayvel gave it to Kirsten and Kirsten obliged with a goal straight through the middle.

The Lions' tactical kicking was beginning to look rather frayed and even their kick-off after the penalty goal was poor. However, they had begun to push forward in the scrums which reduced the opportunities available to the Quaggas' loose forwards. Kritzinger was penalised for picking the ball out of a retreating scrum and Irvine had a long kick at goal which he only just pushed to the right of the posts.

The Lions also confused the Quaggas' defence when Grace moved out very wide on the open side wing and ran on to a kick by McGeechan. The ball bounced badly, otherwise it would have exercised the Quaggas considerably to cover the danger. Still, the Lions were more than grateful when a Quagga forward aimed a chop of a blow with his forearm as a maul developed from a dropout from the Quaggas' 25. The referee gave a penalty and Irvine kicked the goal to push the Lions' lead up to 16-10.

After only 12 minutes of the half, Bayvel went down with what looked like a hamstring injury and although he had it strapped, he soon decided that he could not continue and was replaced by Schutte. Bergiers also suffered an arm injury and Gibson received a peremptory knee in his face from Pypers as the Lions' forwards drove him through. Pypers had shown in the Transvaal game that he was an uncompromising soul.

Midway through the half, the Quaggas all but scored again. Coetser again broke through from full-back and Irvine stopped him with another fine tackle but the ball went loose and there was enough Quagga support in the vicinity to make things so awkward for the Lions that they were more than relieved when David managed to stick out a leg and kick the ball into touch near the corner flag.

Rees had already knocked his injured hand and the gamble of playing him so soon after breaking a bone finally came to grief when he tried to make a tackle. His hand was kicked and although he did not know it at the time, the damaged bone was refractured. He had his hand strapped but within a matter of minutes, he knew he could not continue and was replaced by J. P. R. Williams. Within a matter of hours, Rees had had an X-ray and he knew that his tour as a player had come to an end.

Rees had no sooner departed than the Quaggas were awarded a penalty kick at another lineout. This was near the halfway line and it was on the right side of the field, but Kirsten indicated that he proposed to try to drop kick for goal. This inevitably caused a certain amount of surprise and delay while the touch judges scurried round and while Kirsten ascertained the exact point from which he should kick. His earlier efforts at drop kicks had not suggested that he had the necessary power, but this young man clearly knew what he was doing. He was not disturbed by the wait, either, and he found the right timing and the right trajectory to loft the ball so that it fell just over the bar. It was a beautifully judged kick.

With ten minutes to go, therefore, the Lions led only 16-13 and there was everything to play for. Kirsten must have been cross with himself for missing touch at that point because he knew the Quaggas had to exert as much pressure as possible and first J. P. R. Williams and then Grace pushed the Lions into an attacking position. By then Irvine was on the left wing in place of Rees but strangely Cotton did not call him up to take a kick at goal when the Lions were given one about 30 yards from the posts. The Lions chose to take a tapped penalty instead and were repulsed by a good touch kick by Kirsten.

The match had kicked off at the dangerously late hour of four o'clock and five minutes from the end, the light had almost gone. Even so, the crowd could still see well enough to become highly indignant when the Lions were awarded their third try.

Gibson began the movement with a break through the middle. When the ball went loose, Irvine swept it to the right with one hand. The ball did not go forward on that occasion, even though the crowd thought that there had been a knock-on, but when the ball came back to Gibson again and he passed out to the right, it looked very much as if David knocked on when he was in a position to score in the corner. The referee still allowed play to go on, and Brown came up in support again and scrambled over the line. The referee had another long think but again he gave the Lions a try and the crowd stormed in fury. They threw everything at Mr. Gourlay that they could lay their hands on and he covered his ears with his hands as the missiles hurtled past. Cotton told Irvine to wait until the commotion had died down before attempting the kick at goal. Irvine did so but still missed the kick.

The last few minutes of the match were played in a hubbub of outrage which was only partially mollified when the referee penalised Neary for being offside and Kirsten kicked his fourth penalty goal of the match.

Whatever else one might have said of Mr. Gourlay, he certainly proved himself to be a brave man because his positional play at that stage of the game indicated that he was quite unconcerned with the possible behaviour of the crowd. After watching Mr. Katzenellenbogen in Cape Town in 1974 and Max Baise in Port Elizabeth in 1972, I confess I was paying as much attention to this as to anything else, and when Mr. Gourlay blew his whistle at the end of the game, he was away in the corner of the field on the far touch line and as far from the safety of the players' tunnel as he could have been. In no time, the crowd had jumped over the fences and had streamed on to the field to besiege him. One of the spectators attacked him and bowled him over. Mr. Gourlay lay on his back covering his head with his arms while various people went to his assistance.

The most prominent of these was Gordon Brown, who grabbed the referee's assailant as he made off and held him for the police. However, the police let the man go when Mr. Gourlay said that he did not wish to press any charges.

At the reception afterwards, Mr. Gourlay was most philosophical about it all. His left eye was blackening from one of the blows he had received, but he had a drink with Gordon Brown and thanked him for his efforts, and said that he could understand the disappointment of the crowd. As his refereeing showed, Mr. Gourlay was clearly a very tolerant man, and a talk with him afterwards showed that he was thoroughly nice with it. The only exception he took was to a criticism offered by the chairman of the South African Referees' Society, Mr. Wouter du Toit, who took Mr. Gourlay to task for not awarding Strydom a try, even though his own view of the incident was from a range of at least 100 yards.

'How could he possibly have seen what happened better than I did?' asked Mr. Gourlay. 'I was right on the spot and I could see quite clearly that Strydom was on his back with the ball trapped on his chest. Strydom could not move the ball at all. Even when the other player climbed off him he was still on his back and the ball was still on his chest.'

That was not the end of the incident by any means. Mr. du Toit was first quoted as saying that the assault of the referee and the behaviour of some of the crowd was one of the most disgraceful incidents he had seen on the Rugby field, but when he returned from a business trip, he indignantly denied that he had said any such thing and added for good measure that the crowd was 'justifiably incensed' because Mr. Gourlay had 'looked for trouble with his bad decisions.'

'Two tries by the Quaggas were disallowed by Mr. Gourlay,' he continued, 'and he allowed the Lions a try he should never have allowed. It was obvious to me and to every knowledgable Rugby fan that these were wrong decisions and it must have been especially obvious to those people in that corner.'

'Naturally, I do not approve of referees being assaulted but this was an isolated case and the crowd were justifiably incensed.'

This was an astonishing attack by any standards and every referee in South Africa jumped to Ian Gourlay's defence. 'You soon find out who your friends are at a time like this,' he said.

Trevor Warman, the chairman of the Natal Referees' Society, said, 'There will be anarchy and mob rule at Rugby matches if this sort of top-level opinion is allowed to be accepted.'

Basil Medway, the president of the Natal Rugby Union, made another fundamental point. 'I think it is absolutely wrong for a referee, particularly one in such a senior position, to criticise another referee. Whether or not bad decisions were made, there can be no justification for the assault.'

Mr. Warman said that he intended to raise the matter at the next executive meeting of the South African Referees' Society. It sounded as if it was going to be a lively affair.

Even then, Ian Gourlay was still turning the other cheek. He admitted that he was surprised by Mr. du Toit's remarks, but said, 'Whatever I say now will make no difference. People will see a match the way they want to see it. The quicker the whole affair blows over the better.'

He was probably right.

CHAPTER 21

Orange Free State

AS soon as he knew that Clive Rees would not be able to play again on tour, Alun Thomas was given permission by the South African Board to telephone Albert Agar in London and ask for a player to be flown to South Africa as a replacement. 'I am sure I have no need to tell you who we have asked for,' he said.

The Lions had asked for Gerald Davies. As Davies was the best winger in the world, it might have been thought natural that the Lions should approach him about his availability. However, there is no point in asking even the best winger in the world to play for you if you do not intend to make use of his talents, and the 1974 Lions had already given clear indication that the use of the winger in attack and counter-attack was not a fundamental of their tactical plan.

In the games where the Lions had felt themselves to be threatened, J. P. R. Williams had stayed back and had played as an orthodox full-back. He had not been encouraged to set up overlap plays for his wingers, except in training, even though he towered so far above all the players then masquerading as full-backs in South Africa that the comparison was positively brutal. The Lions never used combined full-back and wing-threequarter plays to launch counter-attacks from inside their own half, either.

What is more, having won the first two test matches from within the framework of such a restricted style of Rugby, it was extremely unlikely that the Lions would change their approach. That week, I had a letter from one of the best known coaches in Britain saying that Mike Gibson 'would be worth ten more points' to the Lions. I replied that the Lions did not need those ten points. It was clear even then that the Lions did not need the passing skills and the footballing brain of Gibson to release the options open to an attacking full-back, because they had no intention of using an attacking full-back anyway. And if they did not need Mike Gibson, they certainly did not need Gerald Davies.

At that time, the Lions had more need of a third scrum-half to provide cover for Gareth Edwards and to make absolutely sure that he could be kept fit and fresh for the big games. Edwards had already played far more matches than was good for him and as it had already been established that he was the key player in the style of Rugby adopted by the Lions, he had become the most important member of the touring party. Therefore, he was the key player most in need of protection and most in need of cover, particularly as John Moloney had looked rather prone to injury.

The Lions could have given themselves extra cover on the wing by moving Geoff Evans into that position. It was apparent that he had no part to play in the team as a centre because he was a runner and the Lions wanted crash-ball merchants and tacklers in the middle.

The other consideration was that Phil Bennett was suffering from an injured foot and also from a bruised knee cartilage. It was not difficult to see that for the next two or three weeks, and possibly longer, the Lions could find themselves in trouble if they did not bring in some cover for their goalkicking. The only way they could do that was by choosing Andy Irvine on the right wing, which was another argument in favour of bringing out a third scrum-half as replacement rather than another winger, even a winger as good as Gerald Davies. With the Lions playing the sort of Rugby they were, the extra 20 yards range of Andy Irvine's goalkicking was likely to be of far more use to them than the running of Gerald Davies.

In any case, the discussions about Davies turned out to be academic because the hopes of persuading him to join the touring party proved fruitless. When he was first asked, Davies thought that he would be able to accept the invitation but within half an hour, he had changed his mind. As David Duckham had already committed himself to Coventry's proposed tour of Bermuda, the Four Home Unions asked Alan Morley if he was available to fly to South Africa immediately. Morley said that he was. He had played on the wing for England on their tour of South Africa in 1972 before losing his place to Peter Squires and he jumped at the chance of becoming a British Lion in South Africa in 1974.

If the arguments about Gerald Davies were academic, the arguments about the need for goalkicking cover certainly appeared valid when the Lions trained at Ellis Park before leaving for Bloemfontein. Phil Bennett had been named to play in the match against Orange Free State the next day but he was limping so badly that it looked one of the most optimistic selections of the tour.

Bennett did resume training for a while but eventually stopped and his place in the team practising for the match was taken by Ian McGeechan. The questions about the goalkicking posed by this move were not answered satisfactorily, even though a whole barrage of aspiring goalkickers opened fire at the end of the practice. Stewart McKinney, J. P. R. Williams, Ian McGeechan and Gareth Edwards all had a go and McKinney was the most successful but none of it looked very convincing.

A notable absentee that morning was Gordon Brown. His right foot had come into such violent collision with the spectator who had assaulted Ian Gourlay that he could hardly walk. 'I think I must have staved in every toe in my foot,' he said.

When they had finished training, the Lions left for Bloemfontein. This is the centre of the Afrikaaner heartland and it is also the centre of South African railways. For those reasons Bloemfontein is a place which most English speaking visitors find very much an acquired taste.

In 1974, though, the Lions' visit was relieved by a new hotel built sufficiently far from the network of railway sidings to provide some insulation against the mournful whistles of the locomotives and the clatter of the shunting which is forever going bump in the night. Some of the finest examples of railway antiquary are to be found either in Bloemfontein or going through it, and for train spotters it must seem like paradise, but as I say, for the rest of us, it has a distinctly limited appeal.

The Lions were taken into the city by a procession of vintage cars. There were so many of these that they made the collection at Beaulieu look quite inadequate. The cars were all in such superb condition that it seemed as if their owners had been stimulated to prove that whatever the railways could do in the way of antiquary in Bloemfontein, the vintage car enthusiasts could do even better.

The game against Orange Free State was really close all through and the Lions only saved themselves from defeat by scoring a try in injury time. They might not have done even that if the Free State had been capable of thinking as intelligently at the end of the match as they did while they were planning for it.

Free State concentrated most of their efforts on containing or diverting the Lions' forward drives and on either killing or stealing their rucked ball. Sakkie van Zyl had told his players not to build a platform for the Lions to ruck against but to go with the direction of the ball. It probably worked no better than anything else, but it was valuable as another peg on which the Free State forwards could hang their belief in themselves.

They also took advantage of Gert Bezuidenhout's lax refereeing to go down in offside positions to kill the ball in the rucks. This was something widely done in Britain ten years previously but it can only ever be done at a stiff physical price, as Glyn Davidge found when he was kicked black and blue by the All Blacks in Newport in 1963. Not that Davidge complained. Newport won.

Free State took heavy punishment, too, but like Davidge, they probably counted it worth while because they finished up in profit in terms of possession. They blocked much of the Lions' rucked ball and stole a fair bit themselves.

The Lions also had a bad time with their kicking. McGeechan found the touch-line as elusive as it had been in the game against the Quaggas, and Edwards even missed touch with a penalty kick. In addition, the Lions made mistakes when they tried to peel the ball and drive it from lineouts, and J. P. R. Williams was kept busy by the Free State full-back and fly-half in chasing long diagonal kicks to the corners. Even in the scrummage, le Roux made life awkward for McLauchlan and although they were often pushed, Free State usually managed to scrape their ball back somehow. The Lions' scrummage was not as controlled as it had been, possibly because of the lack of recent hard practice. Ray McLoughlin said in New Zealand in 1971 that scrummaging was something that needed constant hard work, otherwise it could disappear almost overnight, and Carmichael admitted after the game that he had felt the lack of practice.

Free State scored first, after 25 minutes. Slattery was penalised for being offside and Snyman lined up the ball carefully to kick a penalty goal. Slattery soon had his revenge. He caught Sonnekus in possession from a lineout and drove him over the line. The Lions were given a five yard scrum, which they drove and controlled really well, and at just the right moment, Davies picked up the ball and scored unopposed on the blind side.

The fact that Davies was unopposed provoked a bout of fisticuffs because Swart, the Free State captain, felt that he had been held in the scrum by Slattery. The kick at goal after the try was nicely placed for McGeechan's left-footed draw but he hit the ball badly. He missed the kick and promptly retired as a goalkicker.

Free State began the second half well. By then, Snyman knew that he had the feel of the game and apart from his kicking, which had a lower percentage of error than the Lions, he had a keen nose for a gap. He had already made one break from his line in the first half and he made another after a subtle little dummy which was so damaging that Grobler should have scored after taking Stander's pass. The Free State number eight seemed to hesitate, as if not sure whether to go for the line or look for more support and Edwards cut him down with a scything tackle. Free State should also have made more of a five yard scrum position. They called a move in the centre which went wrong and were lucky to retain possession from another scrum.

Even so, they made another chance with a number 8 move

from that scrum. On that occasion, Grobler did his part well enough but Germishuys lacked either pace or determination or both. Free State's only score was a dropped goal. It was scant reward for the pressure they exerted in the quarter of an hour after half-time.

The dropped goal came went the Lions lost control of a lineout won by Ralston in defence. Sonnekus popped it out to Snyman, who started to move to the left. He looked up and saw that the way was blocked by the Lions' cover defence, so he turned back towards the touch-line and hooked over a dropped goal with his right foot.

The Lions were soon given an opportunity to regain the lead. Verster was penalised for being offside in a lineout, and J. P. R. Williams kicked for goal from about 38 yards, out on the left. His kick was short and pushed to the right. As it bounced in goal, the ball stood on its end and bounced back away from the defender waiting to touch it down. He crawled forward on his knees, clawing for the ball. He was not able to reach it before J. J. Williams followed up and touched it down.

The Lions were indignant when they discovered that the referee had already penalised Free State for charging the kick and had awarded another kick, ten yards closer to the posts. Williams took the kick again, and again took great care in lining it up, but that time he pulled it to the left of the posts.

Apart from that, the Lions were jarred out of their usual control. When they tried a lineout peel, Free State won the maul and Snyman ran it beautifully. Fortunately for the Lions, the ball was knocked on in the Free State centre.

It was another long penalty kick to touch by Edwards which set up the position from which the Lions regained the lead. Free State were penalised again in the lineout and McBride asked McKinney to take the kick at goal. McKinney had kicked at goal as well as anyone in practice and as it was from the left side of the field, it suited his six steps backwards and one step sideways style of instep kicking. The ball curled round between the posts and the Lions led 7-6.

Free State drove the ball on well from a two-man lineout to push the Lions back in their half and although Edwards made some advance with a kick from a lineout, J. P. R. Williams sliced a kick and Davies was penalised for being offside in a ruck as he tried to retrieve the mistake. Snyman kicked the penalty goal and Free State led again, this time by 9-7.

At that stage, less than ten minutes of the match remained, and the 65,000 crowd could see their team achieving the first victory over the Lions. Their roars of encouragement rolled back and forth in the bowl of the stadium like claps of thunder.

For the first time, too, the Free State scrum looked reasonably comfortable. Le Roux had taken everything that McLauchlan could throw at him and although he was badly battered, Bestbier looked almost relaxed. Like Windsor in the Lions' own scrums, Bestbier was one of those hookers who used a hand flap signal to indicate when he wanted the ball put in the scrum, but his scrum-half Sonnekus was inexperienced and did not always respond immediately to the command of his master. There were times early in the match when Bestbier was flapping away at Stander's back like a particularly agitated chairman trying to establish order at a particularly unruly annual meeting. Some referees penalise hookers who use that type of hand signal for slipping their binding. Bezuidenhout did not seem to mind.

Free State's scrummage control was then so much improved that Snyman was able to pick his spot as he aimed a long rolling kick to touch. This pushed the Lions back deep into their half.

By then, the Lions were desperate. Evans made a half-break and led a frantic charge out of defence and Carmichael, McBride and Davies made a lot of ground with a lineout peel. Just before that, J. J. Williams had kicked ahead and the Lions thought that a Free State defender had run the ball into his own goal before touching it down.

The Lions knocked the ball on from their lineout peel. It seemed as if they had lost their last chance. However, in going back to save, the Free State lock Stoffel Botha was so badly concussed that he staggered around bow-legged when he tried to stand. He had looked a terrible mess even before that. He was so badly cut near the right eye that his head was swathed with a double layer of bandages to try to staunch the bleeding. He could only see out of one eye, and that eye was so hazy that he did not know where he was.

Poor Botha knew only one thing. Somehow, he had to get back into the scrum. He climbed to his feet and aimed himself in roughly the right direction. He lurched to his right in a semi-circle and collapsed to the ground again. The Lions' scrum waited and watched. They had intended to strike for the ball when Free State put it in to the scrum, but as soon as they saw that Botha was not going to recover, they decided to go for an eight man shove instead. Botha was led protesting to the touch-line and as the referee turned to restart the game, a burly Free State substitute forward ran hopefully across the field towards the scrum. The referee waved him off. A doctor had to certify that Botha was unfit to continue before the substitute could be allowed on the field.

Free State were fatally short of footballing brains on this occasion. The delay while Botha was treated was very considerable, and it was quite obvious from a range of 80 yards that Botha was badly concussed. Had Free State rushed a doctor across to examine Botha, he could have decided there and then that Botha was unfit to continue. You had only to take one look into that one visible eye to see that the player was badly injured.

Alternatively, Free State could have pulled one of their powerful backs into the scrum, or even two. It was their ball, and they had only to hold the scrum in control and heel the ball and kick it safely to touch to win the game. Swart, their captain, did not think of this. He had been fairly heavily battered himself, and either through exhaustion or sheer lack of mental application, he did not see the opportunity which was there to be taken. He folded himself wearily on to the side of the scrum and let events take their course.

Botha sat on the touchline in despair. The scrum went down, and as soon as Free State put in the ball, the Lions rocketted them backwards. It was one of the three best scrums they had in the whole game, and Free State were jerked off the ball so fast that Edwards almost had to run after his forwards. Davies picked up the ball at number eight and slipped it to Edwards who threw a dummy as he hurtled to the blind side. Even so, Edwards realised that he would not reach the line himself, and he threw the ball back over his shoulder hoping that support was there. It was. J. J. Williams had anticipated Edwards' problem and had come inside from his wing. Behind him, Davies was closing up as an added insurance. Williams took the ball though, and planted it gleefully over the line for the winning try. As Williams lifted his arms in triumph, Botha held his head in his hands.

McKinney could not convert the try, but it did not matter. J. J. Williams had scored in the third minute of injury time and the match was over.

The Lions were lucky to get away with it. Their lack of a goalkicker had nearly cost them the match. Syd Millar looked highly relieved when he praised Free State for being so fit and determined and giving the Lions their hardest game. Jake Swart, the Free State captain, looked at his bandaged and battered players and smiled, 'The Lions won the Rugby match and I think that at this moment, they would win a beauty contest between the two teams, too.'

It was an apt comment.

CHAPTER 22

Kimberley

THE Lions drove to Kimberley for their match against Griqualand West. This made a pleasant change from the monotony of flying, and although a bus trip from Bloemfontein to Kimberley in winter is never going to put the scenic drives through the Swiss Alps out of business, it was interesting to see that the uplands of South Africa looked just as vast and just as yellow and just as empty from the ground as they did from the air.

When the Lions arrived in Kimberley, they were entertained to an excellent braai-vleis by De Beers at their country club and later, some of the England players in the team went out to sample again the ineffable delights of the flood-lit putt-putt course which they had first tasted two years earlier.

Kimberley at night does not exactly swing, particularly on a Sunday, but again the construction of a new hotel had brought diversions and a change of scene to a town which, more than any other in South Africa, still embodies the Klondyke spirit of the mining history of the country. The Lions were not staying in the new hotel but the more intrepid of the explorers in the party soon found it and two of them even struck gold.

This takes some doing in Kimberley. It is much easier to find diamonds, especially if you have the good fortune to be introduced to a man like Fred Rossouw, who is one of the chief diamond appraisers in the town. Fred entertained a party of Lions for a whole morning in his office and found them such willing pupils in the study of the finer points of the various colours of stones, of their flaws and of their different cuts that the likes of Andy Irvine were soon sufficiently well informed to have a good haggle in Hatton Garden.

The meeting had been arranged by Mattie Human, another old friend from previous tours and another of those men who do so much to make tours of South Africa such a pleasant experience for Rugby teams.

The focal point of Kimberley, of course, is the Big Hole. This is the hole more than a quarter of a mile wide and hundreds of feet deep which thousands of claim-holders dug through the rock with pickaxes at the turn of the century to find those precious chips of pure carbon known as diamonds which were embedded in the blue ground of the most extraordinary geological funnel in the world. They dug out literally tons of diamonds from that giant funnel of rock until just before the first world war when they hit an underground spring and the diggings flooded.

It is a fascinating place. A diamond diggers drinking shanty has been reconstructed and fitted out just as it was eighty years ago. They have some of the original ladders that were used to climb down into the Big Hole and they have some of the leather buckets that were used to haul up the rock to the surface for sifting.

At the other end of the scale is the luxurious railway coach which used to take Cecil Rhodes on his opulent journeys round South Africa. This coach was built and equipped at enormous expense in America and it is complete with dining room and smoking room and what must have been one of the very first railway sleeping compartments. The cut glass and the silver is laid out on the table just as it was and the Illustrated London News of the time lies on one of the upholstered seats. The appointments and the fittings are in marked contrast with the stark simplicity of the first house ever built in Kimberley, a two-roomed prefabricated timber walled structure imported in sections from England. It looks like a garden shed.

Visitors from Europe who have become accustomed to wholesale vandalism and petty theft find it extraordinary to see so many priceless mementoes of the past hanging on walls from which they could be so easily removed. The cheque for five million pounds made out by Cecil Rhodes and De Beers for the mining company owned by Barney Barnato working the Big Hole in 1887 is enclosed in nothing more pretentious than a picture frame screwed to a wall.

Some of the Lions preferred to go shooting. They were taken out to a nearby farm and equipped with rifles with telescopic sights and sent out in open trucks to do their worst. They nearly had a nasty accident before they started. One of the Lions found out the hard way that the position of the marksman's sighting eye is very critical in the use of a telescopic sight. If you are too far away you can see nothing. He had the rifle cradled into position to fire and was scanning round for something to fire at when something blurred swam into vision. When he brought the target into focus he discovered that it was Ian McLauchlan's head.

The most thrilling chase of the afternoon came when one of the trucks saw a giraffe running along behind a line of trees and set off in pursuit. As they bumped and swayed along, Bobby Windsor had the rifle and was being homed in on to the target by Mike Burton, two of the fastest guns in the West of Griqualand.

'Go on, shoot,' yelled Burton.

'Are you allowed to shoot these things?' asked Windsor, looking up from the rifle.

'Of course you are,' bellowed Burton.

Windsor loosed off a volley of fire and looked up. The giraffe had dropped behind some trees.

'It's down,' shouted Windsor.

But then the giraffe appeared beyond the trees, still going at much the same speed. Windsor took aim and let go with another broadside from the truck careering along behind. The head of the giraffe bobbed down.

'Look, it's ducking as well,' said Windsor, and fired again.

Still the giraffe kept going.

'What are you doing?' shouted Burton through the wind. 'Go on. Shoot it.'

'I've 'ad 'im six times,' protested Windsor, 'and look at 'im. 'E's still bloody running.'

Windsor was still blazing away when the 'giraffe' emerged from behind the trees and came to a stop. It was a long stack of new, whippy timber tied to the back of a lorry and inclined in the air off the roof of the driver's cab at just about the angle of the neck of a giraffe. As the lorry went along, the flex in the wood made the top of the planks bob up and down, just like the head of a running animal. The African driver climbed out of his lorry and looked up at his timber in amazement. It had been shot to pieces.

Much the same thing happened to Griqualand West on the Rugby field, but that surprised nobody. England had scored 60 points against the Griquas in 1972 and Piet Visagie, the former Springbok fly-half who was then coaching the province, said gloomily that his team was better then than it was in 1974. Most of the locals thought that the match should be moved to the cricket ground because the new scoreboard which had been built there was more capable of moving quickly into three figures.

Whether the Lions were playing well enough to reach a score like that was another matter. They had met much stiffer resistance in the previous two games and had had some of their weaknesses exposed. They were also worried about the fitness of Phil Bennett, who had felt so badly about his withdrawal from the match against the Free State that he had spent a most miserable night afterwards. Bennett's cartilage injury was causing so much concern that Alun Thomas admitted that he might not even be fit to play against Northern Transvaal on the Saturday. 'We daren't take any chances with the third test the following week,' said the manager. Bennett had consulted a specialist and had been told that he could go on training but he looked unhappy when he tried and he moved only with considerable difficulty.

The rest of the Lions had not looked much better when they trained in Kimberley on the day before their match against the Griquas. This reassured the townsfolk who watched the practice. They had been worried that the Lions might beat the record of 97 points which they had set against S.W. Districts at Mossel Bay. That would have been the last straw in what had been a headlong decline in Griqua Rugby since they beat Northern Transvaal to win the Currie Cup in 1970.

By that stage of its career, De Beers stadium was beginning to look as forlorn as the team playing on it. The pitch was encircled by a cycle and running track with a shallow saucer of scaffolded seats round the outside. The one concrete grandstand was behind that saucer of tubular steel and planks, and was a very long way from the pitch. The stadium was set in the suburbs, not far from the edge of the yellow, empty plains all around.

The atmosphere of rejection was not confined to the ground. The crowd on the day of the match was thin. There were plenty of seats to spare. It was not hard to see why. Kimberley had tasted considerable success in South African Rugby in the recent past and had seen enough of the good days to be spoiled for the bad.

Their disenchantment was soon confirmed. The Lions played facing the flat sun that is invariably such a nuisance with late afternoon kick-offs in South Africa and quickly established an attacking position in the Griquas right hand corner. From there, Moloney went sniping off across field on a diagonal run to the right which continued uninterrupted until he scored. Irvine converted, so that after three minutes, the Lions led 6-0.

Grace just had time to have a kick charged down and Moloney just had time to make another break before the Lions scored again. They made their second try, or rather, had it made for them, from the same position on the field from which they had scored their first. Milliken, Irvine and Gibson moved the ball to the right of a ruck and Evans struggled over the line to score while towing various half-hearted attempts at tackles behind him. Again, Irvine converted. The crowd said, 'Ho, ho.' They were not in the least surprised.

Griquas' play in the first 20 minutes bore an air of hopeless resignation which was amply supported when they dropped out from their 25 following an unsuccessful kick at goal by Irvine.

They tried a switched drop-out and planted the ball straight in the arms of Milliken. This committed them to another anxious period of defence from which the Lions scored again. David took the ball from the open side of a scrum and although he was checked short of the line, he re-gathered his strength and forced his way over near the posts. Irvine converted.

The Lions were in that comfortable position where none of their mistakes were being penalised, so that even when Evans directed a pointless kick from a lineout straight at the opposing full-back, Smith made such equally poor use of the ball that the Lions were able to come straight back and score. Irvine came into the line to make an overlap and Grace stretched away to score a try. Irvine missed the conversion. Almost at once, the Griquas were awarded a penalty kick for barging in the lineout and van Eck hit the ball well to kick a goal.

Perhaps tempted by their early successes, the Lions struck for their opponents' ball in the scrums more often than usual, with the result that the Griquas' forwards were not demoralised by being pushed back. The Lions did not use the ball decisively in midfield, either. On one occasion, Irvine went streaking through outside Milliken, but instead of giving his full-back the ball, the Lions' centre dummied to him and was tackled standing still.

The Lions pulled themselves together with a rush launched by Ripley. He kicked the ball on and chased after it so hard that he caught the ageing Smith in possession. The Lions won the maul and Burton burst forward to set up another. As the Griquas scrambled back to try to hold the new threat, they went offside into the maul and were penalised. Irvine kicked the goal from close to the posts.

The Griquas were visibly encouraged by the resistance they had offered in the ten minutes before half-time, so that although the Lions led 25-3 and would obviously win the match very easily, their opponents began the second half feeling that they might have the temerity to play the occasional bit of football themselves. This feeling was strengthened when the Lions began to over-elaborate and Irvine was heavily tackled. The Lions had to chase back and were penalised for going offside into a ruck. Van Eck took the kick at goal again, but he pulled the ball wide of the posts.

The Lions switched the direction of the 25 drop-out and Grace gained a lot of ground on the right. From that position, the Lions first made an overlap for Grace to score a try which Irvine converted with a fine kick from far out, and then almost at once, Slattery broke away from the loose and snarled all the way to the corner. Two cover defenders ricochetted off him as he subsided in goal. As they went hurtling past he kept the ball cradled to his chest as he slid into a sitting position. He took some care not to ground the ball. As soon as he saw that the coast was clear, he jumped to his feet and was about to run round to score between the posts when he saw that the referee had already given him a try. Slattery looked mildly surprised and then mildly annoyed because the angle of the kick was wide enough for Irvine to miss.

As far as the Griquas were concerned, a score of 35-3 was no more inhibiting than a score of 25-3 and they proceeded to score a very fine try indeed. Their midfield backs executed the slickest of loops and Wiese on the right wing half outflanked the defence before kicking ahead. He still needed a good bounce of the ball to score but it stood up most obligingly and he ran close to the posts before scoring a try which he converted himself.

The Lions reacted with such indignation that they scored 16 points in four minutes. David burst from a maul and sent Grace on his way for his third try and almost at once a long lobbed pass by Gibson put Grace clear again. Grace's tour had never really recovered from the handicaps imposed by his early injury but by then he was thoroughly enjoying himself. He ran hard enough to reach the corner where he shook off a cover defender in goal before running round to score his fourth try between the posts. Irvine converted that try and within a minute, had run so hard himself to make an opening for Ripley to score that he allowed Gibson to make the conversion.

Losing by 51 points to 9, the Griquas soldiered on. What is more, they produced another excellent try. They missed out a man in the centre and the full-back came in to make an overlap and Wiese scored again. He could not convert the try but he did scrape a penalty kick over the bar when the Lions were offside in a ruck. This gave Wiese the satisfaction of scoring 13 points against the Lions, which in itself was a record.

The Lions scored three more tries. Steele took advantage of a kick which bounced awkwardly for the defence to score the first and right at the end, he side-stepped in off his left foot and then went the other way after Gibson had taken a ball from Ripley and swept it along the line. Steele was sometimes known to the Lions as 'Dancer.'

The other try was scored by Kennedy after David had made a long weaving break from midfield and had been supported by Moloney. It looked as if the ball was knocked on at the end but the referee was not well placed to see and he let it pass. Irvine kicked all three conversions and the Lions won 69-16.

CHAPTER 23

Northern Transvaal

LATER that night, Mike Burton learned that he had been nominated as duty boy for the next day. This came as a nasty surprise because he had been celebrating the win over the Griquas with some emphasis, and he knew that the two days on which the touring party moved each week were always the most difficult for the duty boy. It would be his job to round up all the players and make sure that they were on the bus to the airport and then he would have to count them again and make sure that they were all in the airport building and that they had their tickets and he would also have to make sure that they were all on the aircraft.

Apart from that, the duty boy was responsible for circulating the rooming list at the next hotel and he had to make sure that all the players were on the bus for the training session in the afternoon. That meant he had to find out who were going for medical treatment and who were not and if after all that, there was an official reception in the evening, he had to make sure that everyone was present and correct for that, as well. The job is done in rotation by all the players and naturally, some are very much more efficient at it than others, but on travelling days especially, it is all go.

Burton emerged bleary-eyed in the morning, not at all sure that he would be capable of meeting the challenge. His suspicions were soon confirmed.

He managed to assemble all his flock at the airport but noted with some alarm that W. C. C. Steele was fluttering in the background. Steele had lost his wallet and there was some talk of him going back to the hotel to see if he could find it. Burton hopped from one leg to the other, trying to keep abreast of the latest developments.

When the flight was called, the touring party went on board the aircraft, with the players and management sitting towards the front. Burton went up and down in some agitation, counting heads. Feeling as he did, his mathematics were none too good but try as he might, he kept finishing up one short, even though he did remember to count Alan Morley, who had just joined the team. The cabin crew shut the doors of the aircraft and it started to taxi off the apron towards the runway. Burton began to look desperate. He knew that the other players often tried to create situations which would make him give them a laugh, because by then he had become the chief entertainer in the party, but no matter how hard he looked, he just could not find Billy Steele.

He decided that there was nothing for it. Bracing his shoulders, he turned towards the captain's cabin and entered. He leaned deferentially over the captain's shoulder as the aircraft was being cleared for take-off and he revealed that the Lions were a player short. The captain said, 'I'll send a message.'

'That's no good,' said Burton.

The captain shrugged. 'We'd better go back, then,' he said.

The huge jet stopped and turned back towards the airport building. Those Griqualand West officials waiting to wave the Lions on their way wondered what crisis had stopped the take-off as the Boeing came whining back to the apron. The doors were opened and the steps were wheeled back in position. The captain disembarked and everyone went to look for Billy Steele. No sign of him. Then someone had a bright idea. They switched on the cabin microphone and said, 'Will passenger Steele please raise his hand?'

A puzzled hand surfaced from behind a newspaper at the back. Passenger Steele had been there all the time. He had recovered his wallet and had been one of the last passengers to board the aircraft. Burton sat down sheepishly. The captain re-embarked and raised his eyebrows. Burton nodded. The Boeing went on its way.

By then, the Lions had already accepted that Phil Bennett would not be fit to play against Northern Transvaal and so they chose Ian McGeechan at fly-half with Andy Irvine to cover their goalkicking on the right wing. It was the first major positional experiment the Lions had made since they moved Roger Uttley to the flank in Cape Town.

The Lions chose all but two of their eventual test team for the match against Northern Transvaal. Mike Gibson took McGeechan's place in the centre and Tony Neary was given a game on the flank in place of Fergus Slattery, who had played in three of the previous four matches. The Lions were also glad to see that Gordon Brown had stopped hobbling and that his injured foot had recovered sufficiently for him to resume his place in the second row.

The Lions trained twice at Loftus Versfeld when they returned to Pretoria. The weather was as agreeable as that which had prevailed for the second test, but the training sessions turned out to be rather less sunny and placid.

The most dramatic moment came at a scrummaging practice on the first afternoon. Sandy Carmichael was scrummaging at loose head against both Fran Cotton and the pack chosen for the match and Cotton took objection to what he thought was unnecessary pressure on his neck after the ball had been heeled. The upshot of this was that he hit Carmichael. These things sometimes happen in intensive scrummaging practices, particularly when that practice is sustained for a matter of weeks between players who are rivals, but it caused no end of a furore and filled the newspaper posters for a day.

The other side of the coin in scrummaging practice occurred the next morning when a scrum collapsed and Chris Ralston wrenched a shoulder. He was obviously in distress and had to retire but when he drawled, 'The pain is excruciating," like a butler announcing that dinner was served, the precise choice of his language in the context of his very apparent physical anguish made all the other forwards fall about laughing. Ralston looked wounded, both about the unseemly merriment and about the pain in his shoulder. He was unable to train for three days.

In the same training session, Geoff Evans pulled a hamstring. The Lions' backs were finishing off the morning's work with a pyramid of sprints when he felt a twang and pulled up. When he walked off the pitch, only two weeks and four days of the tour remained for the midweek team. It seemed unlikely that he would be fit to play again.

The atmosphere in Pretoria at that time was slightly unreal. It was as gentle and as balmy as the weather. There was none of the stridency and the hardness that British teams have come to associate with the place. There was none of the usual gloating clamour to buy tickets to see the Lions crushed. Pretoria seemed to know that even though Northern Transvaal were the Currie Cup champions, and even though the Springbok selection for the third test could hinge on their performance, Northern Transvaal ought to be beaten fairly decisively. I had never known the city as quiet before a big match. I had never seen rows of empty seats before in those huge stands which stretch away to the blue of the sky like steel staircases. Pretoria simply had no faith in the Northern Transvaal backs.

Northern Transvaal were as reluctant to use their backs as the Lions, though with more justification. They waited for kicks at goal and when McGeechan moved offside as Northerns won an early scrum, they were rewarded. Full-back Luther took the kick and was successful.

McGeechan kicked a good open-side diagonal deep into Northern's right hand corner which the defending side could only help into touch. The Lions threw the ball long and Davies won it easily. As he did so, he was pushed in the back and the Lions were given a penalty kick 10 yards from the Northerns line. Irvine took it back to the 25 and kicked the goal.

Northerns knocked on in the maul from the kick-off but Windsor was penalised as the Lions put the ball in the scrum, so Luther immediately had a chance to restore Northerns' three point lead. Davies and McLauchlan stood ten yards in front of Luther while he lined up his kick at goal; then, as he went back to take the kick, they took a careful pace to the right to try to change his orientation and put him off. Whether it was successful or not no one knows, but Luther pulled the ball in the direction in which McLauchlan and Davies had moved.

By then, the referee had already warned Gordon Brown for jumping into J. G. Williams and so the Lions had to be very discreet in their own half. This meant conceding most of the lineouts to Williams, but even so, much of the ball that Northerns won from the lineouts in the first half was badly controlled and the Lions often succeeded in forcing a ruck from which they were able either to exert pressure on the Northern half-backs or to simply advance before killing the ball and so being given a scrum.

When Williams caught the ball two-handed, the Lions did not have these options and their instinctive move into a defensive position in midfield carried the risk of penalty kicks. That was what happened when the Lions ran a ball into touch. Luther took the penalty kick and aimed off a bit to allow for the sidesteps by McLauchlan and Davies and duly kicked his second goal.

Both teams kicked badly and made a lot of mistakes and showed not the slightest inclination to use their backs while they manoeuvred for attacking positions. The next one took some time to develop and when it did the Lions were able to hold it because Luther twice made mistakes in his 25. First he fumbled the ball into touch and then he dropped a pass from a scrum in front of his posts. Booyens had to scurry back to kick from behind his own line and find a hurried touch near his right corner flag.

The Lions almost invariably tried a peel or attacked direct from the back of the lineout in this type of situation and as it was already apparent that Davies was the only source of lineout possession upon whom the Lions could rely that day, McLauchlan called a throw to the back. The outcome could not have been more straightforward. Davies simply caught the ball and fell over the line to score a try which Irvine converted. With a little more than ten minutes to go before half-time, the Lions led 9-6.

From a lineout, Davies tapped the ball back and for the first time, made a mistake with the angle of his deflection. Oosthuizen, the Northerns' number 8, burst on to it and was well supported by van Heerden in a passing rush. Milliken did well to bring off an interception in defence and was glad to concede a scrum from the maul. The Lions were even more pleased when Northerns kicked the ball through to them in that scrum and McGeechan was able to find touch.

The lineout that followed was an explosive affair. A fight started near van Heerden and both packs waded in with boots and fists flying. Davies was pushed to the ground and while he was there, Booyens, the little Northern Transvaal fly-half, kicked him in the face. This enraged even Irvine and he and Booyens stood snarling at each other while the referee tried to regain control. At the end of it, Eloff, the Northerns flanker, suffered a torn ear and after a further delay for repairs and lectures, the Lions were given a penalty kick.

Soon after half-time, Luther missed touch and kicked the ball straight down Gibson's throat. J. P. R. Williams came up in support and it seemed as if at last the Lions might be able to create something worth remembering. They won a maul, with the line gathering for an attack to the right. Edwards rather disappointingly kicked the ball into touch on the short side, and the backs dropped their hands in despair.

Northerns were given another penalty kick in the lineout and Luther found a long touch. Neary won the ball at that lineout without being able to clear the ball from a maul. The Lions were given a scrum and Northerns were given a penalty kick. For some reason, McLauchlan and Davies stood still, and Luther kicked his third goal to level the scores at 9-9.

Another sharp volley of anonymity followed. Northerns kicked into touch on the full from a lineout, the Lions threw the ball in crooked, Northerns opted for another lineout and also threw crooked. They seemed to be put off in their attempts to use the short ball by Cotton's practice of standing at the front of the lineout with his arms raised like a Messiah calling the faithful to prayer. The Lions were given a penalty kick at the scrum which followed and promptly missed touch. Luther caught the ball and put it away.

The Lions tried a throw to the front of the lineout and once again threw it crooked. Northern Transvaal again preferred to take another lineout, and again won a good ball which once again they kicked straight to J. P. R. Williams who rolled it back into touch.

By then, the game was rather like a parody of that Rugby song, which has, as one of its verses, 'You'll find touch, I'll find touch, we'll both find touch together. We'll be all right in the middle of the night, finding touch together.' The only difference was that it was the middle of the afternoon, and hardly anybody could find touch to save their lives.

That particular miss proved expensive for Northerns. The Lions kicked it through their lineout to advance a few yards, and although they knocked it on in the next lineout, Northerns lost the ball at the scrum and it popped out of the far side as the front rows collapsed. Edwards picked it up and twisted back to the blind side wing, where J. J. Williams took it on before giving a scoring pass inside to Neary. Irvine could not convert.

Within two minutes, Northerns were snapping at the Lions' heels again. They kicked off deep and Edwards was penalised for not putting the ball straight into the scrum on his 25. Luther took the kick at goal and although McLauchlan and Davies shuffled sideways rather desperately, Luther was much too close to be put off. The Lions' lead therefore was cut to one point, at 13-12.

Both sides went on wasting the ball. Northerns knocked on in a lineout and although Davies picked up from the scrum and launched Edwards, he kicked to the short side instead of trying to keep the ball alive. Northerns won the lineout, even though they had taken the ball into touch and Booyens could think of nothing better than to kick the ball dead for a 25 drop-out to the Lions. J. G. Williams caught that and established a maul which progressed into a scrum from which Booyens again kicked the ball deep, no doubt simply to keep the Lions on defence in the hope that they would make a mistake.

The Lions dropped out from their 25 and Brown staggered away from the maul with a look of sheer disbelief and considerable pain on his face as van Heerden stuck a knee hard into Brown's backside. Brown was sore for days. The referee saw what had happened and McGeechan put a penalty kick into touch. The Lions could not escape from their half, though, and Milliken was put under such pressure as he tried to deal with a bad ball that his kick was charged down and Northerns rushed it into touch. They drove round the back of that lineout and Luther was held in the centre. Still, Northerns were given a scrum in an excellent position for a drop at goal.

Again it took several attempts to get the ball in and out and when eventually Northerns heeled, Booyens could have dropped a goal if he had had the footwork to make himself a bit of time and room. He stood heavy-footed though, and allowed himself to be rushed into a hopelessly unbalanced kick which missed with something to spare.

Northerns concentrated on holding their attacking position. Kidson kicked another up and under from the drop-out position and Irvine marked. Irvine missed touch and Luther passed to his scrum-half who kicked diagonally. The Lions were given a scrum after a maul and gained some relief when they were given a penalty kick for offside which Edwards put into touch.

The Lions had been defending their one-point lead for so long that it came as a surprise to see them in their opponents' half. Edwards was so enthused by the prospect that he dropped for goal when Davies turned the ball back from a lineout. The backs were not quite so pleased, because the drop-kick was hooked.

Northerns drove the Lions back with a long penalty kick to touch and although Northerns knocked on the ball in the lineout, the Lions had to put the ball into a scrum near their 25. This is often a position fraught with anxiety and when Edwards ran away from the scrum without the ball, the referee gave Northerns a penalty kick, indicating malpractice in the back row.

Without question, it was the most important kick of Luther's life. It was from close to the 25 and to the left of the posts, and with only injury time remaining there is little doubt that it would have won his side the match. From that range and from that angle, I dare say he would have backed himself to kick the goal nine times out of ten. This, however, was the tenth occasion. The kick faded past the post. It was not really a surprise because Luther had looked fallible under pressure.

Even then, the Northern Transvaal lineout gave their backs another chance. Booyens set off as if at last he meant to run but he had not gone ten yards before he thought better of it. He kicked the ball away for the last time and Milliken counter-attacked up the left wing. Oosthuizen went across and knocked Milliken down with such a dangerous late tackle that McBride gave him a lecture and the referee gave a penalty. Irvine kicked a goal.

The Northern Transvaal coach, Brig. Buurman van Zyl accepted the 16-12 defeat gracefully. He was pleased with the tenacity and the tactical purpose shown by his team. He knew better than anyone that his backs were young and inexperienced and that they were lucky not to be exposed as such, but he said, 'We thought that the key to playing against the Lions was to put as much pressure as possible on Gareth Edwards. He has been doing a lot of kicking and we felt that if we could either deny him possession by our efforts at the lineout, or put his kicking under pressure, we might be able to play enough of the game in the Lions' half of the field to give us a chance of winning.'

Brig. van Zyl was also well pleased by the success of Hans Weber, his tight head prop. 'I thing he gave a good account of himself against McLauchlan,' he said. 'As a result of that, we held our own in the scrums quite well. This was also very important.'

The Lions had less cause for satisfaction. They had relied so heavily upon Gareth Edwards to control their difficult games for them that they had looked lost when he was contained. A detailed analysis of the game showed just how sterile their play had been. Edwards had missed Phil Bennett's ability to take instinctive advantage of those split-field situations where they switch the ball back to the blind side. Consequently, Edwards had become so preoccupied with kicking that he hardly ever passed the ball to his backs. This confined the game to the forwards, which was an area where Northern Transvaal have always been able to play. Northern Transvaal and their coach were properly grateful.

CHAPTER 24

Sling-boks

HOWEVER disappointing their Rugby may have been against Northern Transvaal, the Lions at least had the consolation of winning the match and of knowing that there was then very little to stop them winning all their remaining provincial games in South Africa with something to spare. They also knew that however much they may be fretting about the injury to Phil Bennett, they were 2-0 up in the series and they knew that the Springboks would gladly change places with them.

This was very evident when the Springbok selectors met after the Northern Transvaal game to choose their team for the third test. Their problems were piled high all around them.

The lack of ability of their players in the second test may not have surprised the South African selectors, but they made no attempt to disguise their horror at the way the whole team had capitulated without even putting up a fight. They were not in the least amused by the jokes which were being told all over South Africa about the second test. In one of them, Hannes Marais was supposed to have gone up to Cas de Bruyn in the second half and said, 'Please, can we have a ball to play with?'

The referee said, 'But you've already got one.'

'I know,' said Marais. 'But the Lions are playing with that.'

Losing was bad enough, but when it had got to the stage that the Springbok Rugby team was becoming the butt of as many jokes as the unfortunate Mr. van der Merwe, then something fairly drastic had to be done.

Something drastic was done. The Springbok selectors dropped ten players and made a total of eleven changes in their team. Normally, it is quicker to write about the changes in a side. On this occasion, it was far quicker to write about the five survivors. They were Hannes Marais and Nick Bezuidenhout at prop, Jan Ellis in the back row, and Chris Pope on the wing. Jackie Snyman also survived but was moved from the centre to fly-half.

Tony Roux was chosen at full-back, even though Chris Luther had been preferred to him by Northern Transvaal. Jan Schlebusch and Pete Cronje replaced Peter Whipp and Jackie Snyman in the centre. Gert Muller returned to the wing and Roy McCallum was chosen in place of Paul Bayvel at scrum-half. Gerald Bosch made way for Jackie Snyman at fly-half.

So far, so good. This looked like the back division South Africa should have had all along, with the exception of Roux at full-back and Muller on the wing, although it has to be admitted that in those two positions the Springbok selectors were desperately short of alternatives.

In the pack, Hannes Marais was retained as captain and 'Piston' van Wyk returned as hooker. 'Moaner' van Heerden and Johan de Bruyn replaced J. G. Williams and Kevin de Klerk in the second row, 'Polla' Fourie took over from Morné du Plessis on one flank and Johan Kritzinger came in for Dugald McDonald at number eight.

The pack looked much less convincing. It lacked physical presence in the front row, it lacked leadership and it lacked mobility at number eight. Above all, though, it lacked a lineout jumper.

The Springbok selectors left no one in any doubt that all the forwards they had chosen were considered to be competitors, but it was hard to see how they could compete for anything without the ball. In view of the way J. G. Williams had dominated the lineout for Northern Transvaal that very afternoon, it was an extraordinary piece of selection. It indicated that the Springbok selectors had already made up their minds to drop Williams before they went to Loftus Versfeld. They had decided that he was too soft. They were convinced that anyone as meek and as mild as Williams could never inherit the earth, because he kept allowing himself to be shoved off it.

The omission of Williams was a fatal error. It showed more clearly than any other selection in the series that the Springbok selectors had still not worked out that the way to attack the forward supremacy of the Lions was through the lineout.

Perhaps the Springbok selectors could not believe the evidence of their own eyes in the run-up to the first test. Perhaps they did not want to believe it. But the collapse of the Springbok scrummaging in the test match itself must have made them realise that there was nothing they could do to match the Lions' pack in that phase of the game. They might hope to close the gap a little but they could never hope to close it completely.

After all, propping takes years to learn. It is not something that you can produce in a couple of months, or even in the course of a series. If your props are technically and physically inadequate to cope with the opposition, then you have to write them off for that particular series and think of something else, and the only thing you can do is concentrate on the lineout.

Forward play consists of scrummaging and lineout play and

the mauling and rucking which can be set off one or the other. As the Lions found when they played Western Province, it is essential for a team to dominate at least two of these phases if it is to win at international level with anything like a measure of control. South Africa therefore had no choice but to concentrate on the lineout, just as the All Blacks did when they played the Lions in 1971.

The Lions outscrummaged New Zealand on that tour, too, and with seven world class backs in the side, and another who could not even get into the team, they had just enough options to win the series, but it was a desperately close thing because of the way the All Blacks dominated the lineout.

In that respect, the All Blacks in 1971 were in exactly the same situation as the Springboks were in 1974. The All Blacks based their lineout on Peter Whiting, and the similarity between him and J. G. Williams was remarkable. When Whiting played in the New Zealand trials before the Lions arrived, he was put through the mill by the hard men among the established All Blacks to such an extent that he even thought of giving up the game. He wanted no part of the fisticuffs. Accordingly, Whiting was dismissed as being soft. He was called a cry-baby. Just an English-style jumper (the most disparaging of descriptions) and nothing else.

Fortunately for the All Blacks, someone of influence recognised the value of Whiting. He was chosen for New Zealand and he was surrounded with forwards who not only supported him but made sure that he had room to do all the jumping he wanted, without interference. All the villians who intended to do him a mischief were cleared out of the way and Whiting was left with a nice comfortable vacuum in which to do his work. He alone made sure that the Lions never won more than 40 per cent. of the lineout ball when he was playing, and sometimes it was a whole lot less. Suddenly, this soft man became the most productive forward in the New Zealand pack.

In South Africa in 1974, J. G. Williams was just the same sort of player, except that he was even taller than Whiting, and potentially even more productive. Like Whiting, he was basically a non-combatant. He had no taste for thuggery. The fire of competition did not burn in his belly. But he could have won a lot of ball for South Africa if he had been properly supported and if the Springbok selectors had seen from the beginning that the whole of their forward play had to be built round the lineout.

The strange thing was that they never seemed to rationalise their problems. They never saw until it was far too late that for all his meekness, J. G. Williams could have dominated the Lions in the middle of the lineout. They never saw that for all his looseness, Morné du Plessis would have shown them a far greater profit as a lineout specialist on the flank than Jan Ellis. Even Ellis admitted that he could not get into the game when he was playing test football against the Lions, so with no return from him at all, it would have made much more sense to settle for some ball from du Plessis and to pick two other loose forwards to do the clearing up and the defending. Ellis and du Plessis were of a type in that they were both better in attack than defence and both played best when somebody else found the ball for them and set them up, but it never seemed to occur to anyone to play du Plessis *instead* of Ellis.

The Lions were in no doubt about the Springbok team for the third test.

'How are they going to win the ball in the lineout?' they asked.

No one knew.

One of the old hands among the forwards looked at the names of the Springbok locks. 'Van Heerden won't finish the match,' he said.

The Lions set off for East London in good heart. They were looking forward to the party after the third test at the end of the week.

When they arrived in East London, they were met by a group of Africans from the Xhosa tribe who had bedecked and bedaubed themselves ready to sing and dance a welcome to the team that was going to play against the African team called the Leopards in their new stadium at Mdantsane. The reception on the airport steps went well, and the Lions listened to several encores before they were driven into town to the Carlton Hotel.

East London is a hospitable place, with one of the most readable newspapers in South Africa and a marvellous character called Robbie de Lange firmly installed as Mayor. However, as far as touring Rugby teams are concerned, it seems to be unusually accident prone and especially the Carlton Hotel. I was glad I was staying elsewhere.

The Lions' game against the Africans was to be played on the Tuesday, like all their other midweek games before a test match, to allow an extra day of preparation before the match against South Africa. This meant that they had only one day to look at the stadium at Mdantsane and to train on the ground.

Mdantsane, which is pronounced Oomdoontsarny is some way inland from East London and is uphill all the way. It took about half an hour to drive there and the stadium itself is perched on the top of the highest hill in the area. It dominates the skyline for miles, like some symbol for the future, and workmen were still crawling all over it putting in the finishing touches when the Lions arrived.

The stadium turned out to be even more impressive from close at hand than it was from a distance. Concrete terraces were ramped back from an eight-foot high wall surrounding the pitch and the blue-roofed grandstand was a big new cantilever construction with a magnificent view both of the play and of the sweep of the land back to the sea. The facilities were far better than any of those possessed by the minor provincial unions in South Africa. What was especially ironic was that the stadium at Mdantsane made the Border ground in East London look quite outdated. With protection on all sides, the pitch was a suntrap and as it was a lovely hot day, a big crowd of Africans came to watch the Lions train.

They soon made up their minds that their hero was Andy Ripley. The Lions did a series of 45 yard sprints and each time, Ripley surged away from his group. Each time, the spectators 'Ooohed' and 'Aaahed' in admiration. By the sixth sprint, Ripley was ten yards clear at the end of the 45 yards and every African in the stadium was urging him on.

Dick Milliken and Gordon Brown took things gently. Milliken had been concussed by the late tackle at the end of the match against Northern Transvaal and had been detained overnight in hospital. 'It's the first time I have ever been in a hospital,' he said. Lucky man. Brown jogged along to try to ease the stiffness in his posterior caused by 'Moaner' van Heerden.

Over on the other touch-line, Geoff Evans was also jogging. It was a surprise to see him there at all, considering he had pulled a hamstring only two days before.

Chris Ralston was missing from the practice. He had been having regular dental treatment after having some teeth loosened in the game against the Quaggas the week before and an abscess had formed where a tooth had been crowned. Still, he expected to be fit to play against the Africans the following day. So did Phil Bennett. He looked more spritely than he had for a fortnight and the Lions chose him to test his fitness for the test match at the end of the week.

At the end of the practice, the Lions completed their round of sprints with a series of races between different groups of players along twice the length of the pitch. Both Andy Ripley and Fergus Slattery had to run with the backs rather than the forwards because of their speed and the idea was for the players to run from one end of the pitch to the other and then round the posts at the far end before running back again.

One of the races was quite competitive. John Moloney built up a useful lead on the first leg, with Andy Ripley content just to coast along and stride with the main group, but at the turn, Gareth Edwards cheated a bit by not running round both the posts and he set off for home on the second leg determined to catch Moloney. Ripley started sprinting on that leg, too, and with Edwards closing on Moloney and with Ripley closing on both of them, the last twenty yards looked as if they would be interesting. Just as Moloney reached the last 25, though, he went down as if he had been shot. He had also pulled a hamstring.

The Lions took a surprisingly sanguine view of John Moloney's injury. They even managed to persuade themselves in the early stages that it might not be a hamstring injury at all. This seemed very strange at the time and it seemed even stranger when Moloney was still having trouble with it two months later.

Less than three weeks of the tour remained, including two test matches, and there was little prospect of Moloney being fit for either of them. Certainly, there was no prospect of him being fit enough to act as substitute scrum-half in the third test match at Port Elizabeth five days later. On the other hand, Gareth Edwards had already been heavily overplayed on the tour and was in need of as much rest as possible.

Of all the positions in the team, scrum-half and hooker are the ones which cannot be covered by players other than specialists except with farcical consequences, and yet the Lions made no move to ask for a replacement scrum-half to be flown out from Britain, even though they knew that if Edwards was injured at Port Elizabeth, they would be made to look ridiculous. It seemed a colossal risk to take, particularly when a scrum-half like Jan Webster was available to cover for Edwards and to take some of the load from his shoulders.

CHAPTER 25

Morgan Cushe and the Leopards

I went up to the ground in a specially hired corporation bus, which was filled with Friends of the Springboks, who were mostly Welsh. The other passengers were Brian Rix and myself. The sight of Mr. Rix emerging from the Kennaway Hotel, complete with white jockey cap and with every intention of going to the match, rather took me by surprise. I knew of him as a member of M.C.C. and a keen cricketer, but I had no idea he was interested in Rugby.

As the bus climbed to the ground at Mdantsane, we saw that the gaunt hill of the day before was black with people. The throng was not quite as great as it had been when England had driven seemingly for miles through thousands of African well-wishers on the route to the stadium in Port Elizabeth in 1972, but with our eyes looking upwards all the while, I could not help thinking of Stanley Baker's marvellous film, "Zulu", and the impis gathered on the hills around Rorke's Drift. The only difference was that there were four times as many Africans at Mdantsane.

Brian Rix looked out of the window and said that it reminded him of Bermuda. The same gaiety, and the same involvement in the occasion, even if without quite the same knowledge of the game of Rugby that Bermudans have of cricket.

No sooner had the preliminary game finished than the drums started. They reverberated from the concrete walls of the tunnel under the stand with a rhythm which seemed to embody the history of Africa. Again I thought of 'Zulu', but again there was a considerable difference. Instead of thousands of warriors brandishing spears and shields, there emerged from the tunnel a double line of African girls, with white boots and white mini-skirts and dressed in purple and white cloaks and caps. They carried the batons of drum-majorettes but instead of high-stepping and cartwheeling as they do in America, they moved forward slowly and sinuously, their shoulders and their hips swaying to the rhythm of the drums. For a few moments, several temporarily deprived white men thought some thoughts that would have got them into fearful trouble with South Africa's Immorality Act, and perhaps they understood a little better just how the Republic had come to acquire some of its problems. The drums beat for a quarter of an hour and for the whole of that time, the girls swayed their shoulders and hips and moved their feet with a feline grace to give the rhythm the subtlest of emphasis.

Then they formed up into a double line in front of the players' tunnel, with their batons raised high to form an arch. Alun Thomas, the Lions' manager, emerged with two of the African officials and they walked rather self-consciously underneath the arch and into the sunshine, where they met the two teams.

With proper respect for their visitors, the hosts then played a recording of "God Save the Queen." As far as I can recall that was the only time the National Anthem was played on tour. Unfortunately, it sounded as if it had been torpedoed by a Welsh Nationalist, because after three stirring bars, it crackled into an ignominious silence. There was an embarrassing pause, and the music only emerged again in time to put in a strong finish. The Africans looked politely puzzled. Clearly they thought that the British had a very curious National Anthem.

Their own anthem followed, and it was a much more ambitious affair. It went on for some time, and was very well sung, with lots of reprises, by a mixed choir. Some of the part singing was as good as a Welsh valley choir. The crowd banked high above the seven foot concrete wall listened and watched and waited for the game to start and for Andy Ripley to start running.

As it happened, their own number eight, with his head shaved like Yul Brynner, was the first to make off with the ball, but Burton had knocked on and the Africans were given the doubtful privilege of putting the ball into the first scrum. They were heaved off it unceremoniously, and Brown started a churning movement which peeled the ball along the line to the left.

Four days earlier, the Leopards had been given a crash course in tackling, which apparently had been one of their weaknesses, and they went at it with such determination that they knocked Morley down on the wing, and then when the Lions had regathered and put Morley away again, the Leopards tackled him so hard that he lost possession of the ball.

After a lineout in that corner, which they won, the Lions knocked on again and so for the second time in three minutes, the Leopards put the ball into a scrum. For the second time in three minutes, too, most of which was taken up in repairs to David's eye, the Africans were hurled off the ball in the scrum. Edwards sold a searing dummy and scored a try which Irvine converted.

For the next twenty minutes, the Leopards managed to contain their opponents even though they saw hardly anything of the ball. They did win a lineout, but were in such a defensive situation

34. Bill McBride leads the Lions out against the Leopards.

35. Alan Morley running in to score his only try of the tour.

36. Morgan Cushe, the Leopards' outstanding flanker, challenges Gareth Edwards.

37. Tom David bursts through the middle against the Leopards at Mdantsane.

38. Andy Ripley surfing at Port Elizabeth. He used to be a canoe instructor, too.

39. Stewart McKinney is holding the flippers of the porpoise underwater and "dancing." As the porpoise turned away, it gave him a playful flick with its tail, and broke one of McKinney's teeth!

40. Gordon Brown scores the first try in the third test. Fran Cotton holds off "Piston" van Wyk (No. 2) and Bobby Windsor (left) cackles with glee. Hannes Marais (centre) looks sad.

41. J. J. Williams scores his second try in the third test.

42–44 A sequence of J. J. Williams scoring his first try in the third test.

45. Billy Steele scores against Border, despite the pain of the cracked rib which ended his tour

46. This hat saw a fair bit of training mileage on Gordon Brown. His broken hand had been recently plastered.

47. There he was!

48. Gone! (Phil Bennett, of course, demonstrating the side step against Natal).

49. Ian McGeechan smiles as he runs in to score his only try of the tour against Eastern Transvaal.

50. Andy Ripley celebrating one of his best games of the tour with a try against Eastern Transvaal.

51. Gary Player, Gordon Brown, Mike Gibson and Gareth Edwards enjoying their game of golf.

52. Roger Uttley lunges off the side of the scrum to score as Gareth Edwards spoils Paul Bayvel's pass in the final test.

53. Skrum.

54. Skrum.

55. Skrum. That w
Paul Roos' telegra
to the 1937 Sprin
boks. He would
have shuddered t
see what had
happened to Sout
Africa's scrum-
maging in 1974.

5. Johan Claassen, the
ıairman of the Springbok
lectors, being lifted out
f the front row by Nick
ezuidenhout as the
pringboks practise before
ıe final test.

7. Johan Claassen and
.n Kirkpatrick, who had
.e unenviable task of
ɔaching South Africa in
974.

58. There are not more than about a dozen things wrong with this lineout in the final test as J. G. Williams is lifted by Marais and blocked by Bezuidenhout, van Wyk and van Heerden. Ralston has no chance.

59. Andy Irvine scores in the final test.

60. The Lions' defence falters . . .
61. As Pope goes on the outside . . .
62. and sets up South Africa's only try of the series for Cronje.

63. J. P. R. Williams beats Pope . . .

64. then Snyman . . .

65. then turns outside . . .

66. and into Schlebusch.

67. Williams passes to Slattery, who drives for the line. . .

68. and the referee says, "Five yard scrum."

69. Ellis Park, 1974. Find a gangway or a seat if you can.

70. The ball is over. Bill McBride and Dr. Danie Craven.

that they felt obliged to kick. They missed touch, but so did Irvine and both teams had a further unsuccessful attempt to put the ball away before eventually Mbiko succeeded at scrum-half. The Africans could not win that lineout, or another one that followed, and for a long time, they only touched the ball when the Lions knocked on in the centre. The referee played advantage to allow Mbiko to kick ahead. The referee then penalised the Lions for obstruction and full-back Mnqatu put the ball into touch.

The pronunciation of some of these names had exercised the various broadcasters for some time, but Gerhard Viviers, whose radio commentaries in Afrikaans sound full of poetry and enthusiasm, had all the twanging 'ng' sounds and the clicks in the back of the throat off to perfection. Dewi Griffiths of the B.B.C. also fancied himself as a Bantu linguist. He swears that Welsh and Zulu are so similar that when he delved into his phrase book to ask the way to the ground and fired away in a mixture of clucks and Llanelli, an African bystander said, "Second turning on the right, Boss."

The resilience of the Leopards was remarkable. After Edwards had thrown a reverse pass, the Lions were hustled in midfield and Cushe broke away. He ran with his socks rolled down which accentuated his slightly bandy legs but he certainly produced a surprising turn of speed. He swayed to the left to keep a tackler where he wanted and then did the same with another sway to the right. That done, Cushe blistered through the gap he had preserved and ran so far clear that with two men in support, the Leopards should have scored. Instead, they knocked on and wasted the overlap.

It was a marvellous piece of football by Cushe. It was all the more praiseworthy because his tight forwards were being outplayed so badly that he had hardly touched the ball up to then. Indeed, if you tried to think of the circumstances in which it would be absolutely impossible for a flanker to play well, you would come up with a game very similar to the one the Leopards had to play against the Lions.

The Leopards were so hopelessly outweighted in the tight that the Lions pushed them off every ball they put into the scrum until late in the second half, when it was too late to matter.

In the mauls, the Leopards scarcely had any technique at all and in the lineout they were dwarfed. The consequence was that the Lions won more ball against the Leopards than in any other match they played. Certainly, they won far more ball than they did when the Springbok loose forwards looked so totally anonymous in the first two tests. Jan Ellis complained that "he just could not get into the game," in those matches. So how did Morgan Cushe manage? It must have been because he was a very good player.

Apart from another sortie by Matyeshana, that was the Leopards' ration of attacking in the first half. From then on, they had to go back to defence. To being pushed off the scrums and to losing most of the lineouts. All they had to console them was a few penalty kicks awarded by Steve Strydom. The crowd did have the pleasure of seeing Ripley having a gallop, and the "Ooh" that went round the ground showed that the word had spread since the day before. They cheered even louder when Ripley was stopped.

There was a brief joust between the forwards when Sonjani became cross about something, and Burton pinned his arms to his side while tempers cooled. At that stage, the only way the Africans were getting the ball was when the Lions kicked it to them or knocked it on but by the time they got it, they were so far back in defence they had to kick to touch and start chasing all over again.

Grace was well tackled into touch by the Leopards' full-back Mnqatu, and when the Lions threw the ball crooked into the lineout, the Africans at last started to take lineouts instead of scrums. Ironically, this led to the second Lions' try. McKinney drove to the open side after Ralston had won the ball and then Edwards made an overlap for Grace, who started to run round and would have scored behind the posts if a photographer had not been standing in his way, smack in the middle of the in-goal area. Rather than side-step the photographer, as Tony O'Reilly once did, or risk a nasty collision with a Nikon, Grace put the ball down for a try. The angle was a bit too wide for Irvine to kick the conversion, though, which must have been the first time that a photographer had made such a significant difference to the score. He looked so worried at the prospect of being trampled by Grace that he did not even take the picture.

Two minutes later, Irvine kicked a penalty goal and then Mnqatu had a kick at goal for the Leopards. It was from near the half-way line though, and his kick fell short. The Lions had two more attempts at back row drives when they pushed the Africans off the ball in two more scrums, but each time, the Leopards back row contained them and Grace was forced to kick ahead. When the Africans were penalised in a maul, the Lions took a short kick and might have scored if Burton had not knocked on.

This command of the tight ball enabled Bennett to leave most of the kicking to Edwards. If he did attempt a kick himself, it was with his left foot. However, there was no doubt that the Leopards had defended remarkably well to contain the Lions when they had such a monopoly of the ball, and when the Africans were awarded a penalty kick, the number 8, Nakani, took a tapped kick and wove through with the inevitable Cushe once again at his elbow to kick ahead.

This established a lineout position from which the Africans scored. The Lions were penalised and when Mbiko kicked the goal, the local delight knew no bounds. Unfortunately, the crowd soon came down to earth, because the Lions switched the direction of the kick-off and Grace kicked ahead to set up an identical position in the Africans' left corner. The Lions had to have two attempts at the lineout, but in the end they moved the ball away satisfactorily and Morley scored his first try of the tour. Irvine missed the kick at goal.

The Leopards had another penalty kick at goal themselves before half-time and although Mbiko missed, the Leopards' beautifully built full-back had time to make a bit of room for himself with footwork graceful enough to remind some of us of Josaia Visei, that fine full-back from Fiji.

Nakani began the second half with a couple of flashing dummies and then the Leopards tackled so solidly that McGeechan had the ball knocked out of his hands. David was cut down by Cushe and the Africans spoiled with such determination that Bennett passed into a gap just vacated by McGeechan as the centre cut inside.

As far as injuries were concerned, it had not been one of Ralston's better days and he went back as stiff as a board from a lineout when Maqosha suddenly hit him with a tremendous punch thrown with a roll of his shoulders. Maqosha kept on running in the direction of the punch because his team were so horrified by what he had done that they set off after him. Carmichael brought up an indignant rearguard.

Ralston's right cheek was split right through where the punch had driven the flesh on to his teeth. He lay on the ground unconscious and had to be helped from the field. He said afterwards that he did not recover consciousness until he was in the ambulance taking him to hospital to have 14 stitches in his cheek, and he denied as hotly as he can in that languid drawl of his that he had been pulling Maqosha's jersey. Told that his assailant might have been aiming for someone else, Ralston said, "I do wish then that he would aim his blows a little more accurately."

Whether it was coincidence or not, the Lions suddenly scored

15 points very rapidly indeed. Irvine kicked a penalty goal before Uttley came on as a substitute for Ralston and when Nakani was penalised for obstructing Morley, the Lions called a set move from a penalty in which Burton set off up the blindside touchline, Uttley yelled for the ball in the middle of the field and Ripley sneaked over quietly near the posts. Irvine converted the try and he did the same when Gibson scored after supporting McGeechan as he came inside from a ruck set up by Grace.

The Lions contrived to waste three chances and Mnqatu swayed out of trouble on a fourth occasion before the Lions were penalised in front of their posts and Mbiko kicked another penalty goal. Grace then stormed over and scored a try which Irvine converted before Irvine himself broke out of defence from a scrum and kicked on to regather the ball and score a try which he also converted.

David had another charge from a scrum and was well tackled by Cushe as a prelude to possibly the two most remarkable events of the match. The Leopards won two scrums in succession, not that it did them much good, because after a dummy scissors in the centre, Irvine set up another try for Grace. Irvine was also involved in the movement which led to Gibson's second try. Gibson was then in the fly-half position and after a run by Irvine, Bennett gave a scissors pass to Grace coming infield and the winger passed out to Gibson. Irvine missed both conversions and also had no luck with his kick at goal after the Lions had pushed the Leopards off the ball in another scrum and David had supported an open side thrust by Edwards to score.

The last flourish was made by the Leopards. Ripley went to give a backhand pass to Kennedy and when the ball went astray, Cushe turned and made off with it at such a rate of knots that the Lions defence was left without a hope providing the Leopards made their passes more accurately than they had in the first half. This time they made no mistakes. Magala supported Cushe and sent Mgweba on his way on the left. The winger still had a bit of running to do, because Gibson was covering back desperately, but he leaned in towards Gibson and then went away on the outside and treated himself to an absolutely splendid dive into the corner for his try. Even Ripley never had such a cheer and the Leopards' substitutes were so overjoyed that one of them ran on the pitch to embrace Mgweba.

But it was the performance of Morgan Cushe on the flank that was most significant. It was a complete vindication of the Four Home Unions' decision that the Lions should play the Coloureds and the Africans because for the first time, those two communities had produced a Rugby player who was clearly good enough to be considered for one of the flank forward positions if South Africa were to hold mixed trials.

The Springbok selectors traditionally pick four teams for their trials, which means that they choose eight flankers. I certainly had not seen eight better flankers than Cushe on the tour, and for that reason, the whole concept of non-White sport in South Africa shot forward as fast as he did when he first cut through the middle of the field against the Lions at Mdantsane. Basil Kenyon, the former Springbok captain, said afterwards that he thought that Cushe, "was one of the outstanding players on the field." High praise from a man who was a great Springbok loose forward himself.

When the Quaggas had tried to pick a couple of the Proteas to play against the Lions, I felt that they were rushing their fences. In all honesty, I did not think that any of the Proteas were really good enough to be chosen. Nothing would have done their cause more harm than pushing them into a bracket beyond their capabilities simply because they were non-white. The important thing was to wait for an African or a Coloured player to emerge who was good enough to make the sort of impact on South African Rugby that Basil D'Oliveira had made indirectly on South African cricket. It may be that Morgan Cushe could turn out to be that player. The Springboks had arranged a tour to France later in the year, and they had other touring contacts with Argentina. Obviously, it would be easier for the South African Rugby Board to approach their government with a view to taking a player like Cushe and maybe another like the full-back Mnqatu on a tour abroad than it would be to introduce the principle in their own country.

After the Lions' game against the Leopards, there was every hope that these possibilities would be examined by both the South African Rugby Board and by their government. That in itself represented a solid advance for the African and Coloured sporting communities. As Albert Agar, the secretary of the Four Home Unions, said before ever the tour started, "We believe that more will be achieved by maintaining contact with the different Rugby communities in South Africa than it will by isolating them." The proof that what he said was right was there to be seen at Mdantsane.

CHAPTER 26

The Third Test

THE greatest relief to the Lions was that Gareth Edwards survived the match against the Leopards unscathed, but as the touring party made the short flight back along the coast to Port Elizabeth, Alun Thomas announced that the selection of the team to play South Africa in the third test was being delayed for 24 hours because of various injuries.

Phil Bennett had just about managed to get through the game against the Leopards but he had done it on such restricted terms as far as his kicking was concerned that it was clear that he was still being troubled both by his bruised cartilage and by his injured foot. The Lions had to decide whether to risk playing him despite the fact that he had not felt fit enough to risk himself much either in the way of kicking or of physical contact.

Gordon Brown was also suffering from two injuries he had sustained against Northern Transvaal. He had twisted his left knee when he was spread-eagled awkwardly in a collapsed maul and the base of his spine had been severely jarred when van Heerden had stuck his knee into it. Brown confined himself to limited activity with the semi-invalids like Geoff Evans when the Lions trained at Boet Erasmus in the afternoon.

The problem was that Chris Ralston was unlikely to be fit because the stitches in his torn cheek were not due to be removed before the weekend, and Roger Uttley was already in the team on the flank. Brown was optimistic about recovering in time to play so the Lions decided to give him the chance.

However, there was not much that they could do about a reserve scrum-half. It seemed doubtful whether John Moloney would be fit to play again on tour, and as Alan Old was no longer available, the Lions had to decide whether to use Tony Neary or Mike Gibson as an emergency substitute for the match itself. Neary had stood by as substitute for the Leopards game, but after playing fly-half with him in the morning, Mervyn Davies was not sure whether Gareth Edwards or Phil Bennet would be first off the field in the event of Edwards being injured and Neary emerging as substitute.

The Springboks had problems at scrum-half themselves. Roy McCallum had been forced to withdraw from the team with a broken finger and Paul Bayvel was not available either because of a pulled hamstring. Accordingly, an emergency call was sent out by the Springbok selectors, as a result of which, scrum-halves began to descend on Port Elizabeth from all over South Africa.

Gerrie Sonnekus came down from the Free State, Gert Schutte came down from Kimberley and Barry Wolmarans flew up from Boland. The Lions would have settled for any of them as a substitute, even one of the cast-offs, but if they had been given a choice, I imagine that they would have chosen Wolmarans. He would have had Tom David's vote, at least.

The Springboks practised at Boet Erasmus stadium on Thursday afternoon after the Lions had practised there in the morning. They did it rather coyly, because they sneaked off to a pitch away from the main ground to do their preliminary work, but after the fiasco of their prison wall performance at Pretoria, there was no question of them doing it privately. Then they took a deep breath and ventured to appear on the main ground itself, before the eyes of the watching world and before the eyes of those few nosey souls who had already detected them training in the outback.

The Lions sent an emissary to watch both performances and he found the proceedings as difficult to believe as the rest of us, because despite their extended warm-up elsewhere, the Springboks found it almost impossible to get even their kick-offs right, no matter how hard they tried. They also subjected their three scrum-halves to a little test, in which they were required to throw a few passes first off one hand and then the other. It was for all the world like a schoolmaster examining an intake of 11-year-olds. It seemed inconceivable that it could have any bearing on who would be asked to play for South Africa in a test match. As it turned out, of course, it did not, because Johan Claassen and his selectors chose Sonnekus, and he was comfortably the worst passer of the three. No wonder. He had been a number eight until about two months before.

By then, the Lions had already decided to risk choosing Phil Bennett at fly-half but they made up their minds that they would also have to choose Andy Irvine on the right wing as what Alun Thomas called 'an insurance policy' in case Bennett was injured again. Bennett had taken a fitness test in the morning, sidestepping along a line of stationary forwards like a skier doing a slalom run round marker posts. He also did a series of 25 yard and 45 yard sprints and these convinced the selectors that he was fit to play. Gordon Brown had also recovered enough to be chosen. He did his training without difficulty.

The Lions even nominated John Moloney as substitute scrum-half. It was hard to be sure who they thought they were kidding, because there was no possibility of it being a serious selection, but at least it diverted the attention of the South African newspapers from a very obvious weakness and stopped any speculation until the battle had been won. Not that the Springboks would have derived much comfort from it. They were too busy trying to work out how they could win the match without the ball.

The nervous tension in the Springbok team could be seen as they ran out on to the pitch. The main stand of the Boet Erasmus Stadium is built on a hill at the side of the ground and the dressing rooms underneath are high above the playing surface. To reach the pitch, the players have to run down a long steep tunnel and by the time they reached the sunlight, Hannes Marais and his men were running faster than they did at any time in the series. They went past in a flicker of green and white and overwrought faces. By comparison, the Lions sauntered forth, with Mervyn Davies carefully observing his own personal superstition of coming out last.

South Africa kicked off with the sun and the breeze behind them and won the first maul but Sonnekus threw a terrible pass at his fly-half and all Snyman could do was clear up the mess. This did nothing either for his confidence or for that of the Springbok forwards. However, they kept going, and even though the Lions won the next ruck, they put enough pressure on Edwards to charge down his kick.

The Springboks worked the ball back from the Lions in the next lineout, too, but again the pass from Sonnekus was too high for Snyman and again the Springbok forwards had to rush back with their dustpans and brushes. They retrieved the situation and Roux put the ball into touch on the left.

Brown won the lineout, but Edwards' kick was charged down again, this time by van Heerden, and the Springbok forwards surged in support to drive de Bruyn over the line. They all thought he had scored, and it was hard to see how he could have failed to do so, but the referee was apparently unsighted and gave the Springboks a five yard scrum. Windsor won this against the head and Bennett kicked the ball safely to touch.

The Springboks called a short lineout, and threw the ball deep for Ellis. He lost the ball in a maul but again Edwards had his kick charged down and South Africa scrambled the ball into touch. At that lineout, the Lions were penalised for lifting Brown and Snyman kicked a penalty goal. It had been an eventful five minutes.

The Lions were accidentally offside at the maul following the kick-off. It did not matter much, because it gave Cotton the opportunity to force Bezuidenhout to scrummage at a most uncomfortably low altitude. The repercussions of this had their effect on the Springbok hooker, who was penalised for foot-up. Irvine could not get the distance with a long kick at goal and Ellis found touch.

The Lions won that lineout with a deep throw, and although they had to withstand a lot of positional pressure for another 25 minutes, they began to restrict South Africa's supply of the ball by gradually taking their expected command of the lineout. As the Lions also exercised their usual control of the scrummage, the Springboks had to rely more and more for their possession on what they could scrape up from the loose or on what the Lions gave them in the way of missed kicks. In this respect, South Africa did quite well, because Edwards had persistent trouble first in getting his kicks in at all, or alternatively, in finding touch.

For a while, McGeechan and Bennett found the most effective touches for the Lions and the Springboks decided to use Bezuidenhout as a jumper at the front to try to break the grip being established by Brown and Davies in the middle and at the back of the lineout. Bezuidenhout had won a lot of short ball for Northern Transvaal against England two years before and he looked distinctly unamused when he brought off a splendid leap and then turned to see Snyman knocking on another bad pass by Sonnekus. Windsor did not look pleased, either, when the referee indicated that he was penalising him for heading the ball back in a scrum.

The Springboks put that penalty kick away to touch, but the Lions' forwards' increasing control of the set play won them three balls and a penalty kick in a row. First they won the lineout, then they won a scrum against the head after Milliken had knocked on, then they won a scrum of their own, and after they had helped to retrieve another kick of Edwards which was charged down, they settled into a scrum in which Sonnekus was penalised for putting the ball in crooked. Irvine kicked a penalty goal from 45 yards.

Snyman kicked off too deep for South Africa and Davies set up a maul in which the Lions held the ball securely enough to be given a scrum. Edwards dummied to run away from the scrum and pointed out the Springboks he thought were offside. When Edwards eventually called for the ball Bennett kicked a long diagonal which Roux caught and kicked into touch on the full.

The Springboks made another mistake in that lineout, which gave the Lions another scrum, but Edwards missed touch again and Roux kicked another up and under. Once more, the Lions' mauling saved them and Bennett got the ball away. South Africa were given a penalty kick in the lineout and found a deep touch. For once, they won a lineout from their opponents, too, and the Lions were grateful when Muller knocked on at the end of a Springbok threequarter movement in which they missed out a man in attack. Still, South Africa won that scrum against the head, and launched a blind side drive which Davies did well to frustrate with an interception.

Davies could afford to be fairly sanguine when he was pushed into touch because the Lions were winning South Africa's throws as often as they were winning their own and they duly won the ball on that occasion. Edwards was still having no luck with his kicking and when he missed touch again, Roux had an unsuccessful drop for goal which J. P. R. Williams fielded and cleared.

The Springboks maintained their attacking position, and they built up their best sequence of attacks since the first ten minutes of the match. Snyman pulled a drop at goal, Irvine had to make a solid tackle on Muller, then Irvine was harassed into touch. On the other side of the field, J. J. Williams also had to kick out in a hurry. Pope was held after a dummy scissors from a lineout and Kritzinger, Ellis and Snyman launched an attack which ended with Kritzinger being stopped only three yards short of the line.

The Springbok forwards ran up that ruck in their desperation to win the ball, just as Alex Wyllie had run up a ruck at Christchurch in the Lions match against Canterbury in 1971. The reaction was just as explosive. A fight started, with Van Heerden the chief target of the Lions' outrage. McBride was busy slinging punches, and J. P. R. Williams ran quite a long way to pick out a spot and hit it as hard as he could. He then stood with his feet braced and his fists raised, ready for all-comers.

From that moment, the Springboks' brave early effort subsided and the Lions took control. Not much more than five minutes remained before half-time, but in that time, McGeechan had a drop at goal and the Lions broke out of defence and delivered an absolutely mortal thrust by scoring in the last minute of the half.

McGeechan suddenly straightened the direction of the attack by cutting infield as the Lions moved the ball from inside their own half and he put a deep kick to the right. This decoy move, to leave the blind side with an almost empty field, had been used from time to time by the Lions with varying degrees of success and this time it left Irvine with a 40-60 chance as he set off in pursuit. He was not able to reach the ball either to pick it up or to drive it over the line, but he did bustle it into touch very close to the Springboks' left corner flag. It was the first time the Lions had been in their opponents' 25.

Anticipating that the Springboks would throw the ball short, Brown came up to the front of the lineout and bent down with his hands on his knees to make himself look as inconspicuous as possible. This was no easy task, but fortunately for him, the Springbok winger who had the onerous task of throwing in the ball seemed to be preoccupied with sorting out the signals. It was Muller who had to make the throw and he frowned in concentration as he tried to hear what was being said. From the hunted look on his face, he was not too clear about what he was supposed to do even then, and after a moment's pause for deliberation, he threw a nice short lob straight to Brown, who leapt like one of the dolphins at the oceanarium just down the road to catch the ball and plunge over for a try. Brown had the same sort of smile on his face as the dolphins, too, because, at the end of their enormous leap out of the water is a juicy fish. The only man who might have stopped Brown was van Wyk, the Springbok hooker, but as soon as the ball was thrown, Cotton wrapped him in his arms as if he had been some particularly delectable young lady on the dance floor. Van Wyk peered over the top of this bear hug in some surprise. He was just in time to see the cackle of glee on Windsor's face as Brown thudded to the ground.

Even though Bennett could not convert it, the try could not have come at a more demoralising moment for South Africa. They had done nearly all the attacking in the first half and yet when they arrived at half-time and had five minutes to reflect on what they had achieved, they had to adjust their minds to the fact that they were losing 7-3 and would have to face both the sun and the breeze in the second half. The opportunities had been there, and they had not taken them.

South Africa knew that their forwards had such a restricted ball-winning capacity that they could not afford to waste anything. They had succeeded in putting pressure on Edwards and they had forced him to make an uncharacteristic number of mistakes but they had nothing to show for it. Above all, they had needed to be crisp and accurate at half-back and they had to make the right choice of play. Instead they had been soggy and inaccurate in those key positions. Sonnekus had passed badly and he had passed short. He had not trusted himself to use any of the range of kicks that ought to be at the command of an international scrum-half either and he had never run at the opposition to test the Lions' back row defence. This had restricted South Africa's range of play in mid-field to such an extent that Slattery had been able to rush at Snyman, waving his arms about and snarling over his gum shield and had harassed him so much that he had reduced the options open to his opponents even further.

The Springboks' oranges must have tasted like lemons as they sucked them and glumly contemplated the half to come. They must have known that if the Lions could reach half-time winning 7-3 when the conditions were against them, they were likely to do very much better when the conditions were in their favour in the second half and when fatigue produced its inevitable lowering of resistance.

Those apprehensions were soon confirmed. Irvine kicked the dead ball down the wind from the kick-off so that South Africa had to drop out from their 25. The Springboks were given a penalty kick in the maul from the drop-out and although they forced Bennett to find touch, it was something he could afford to do with impunity because by then, Brown and Davies had established themselves in the lineout to such an extent that the Lions stood just as much chance of winning South Africa's throws as they did their own. Once more, the ball came back on the Lions' side and Bennett fired a long diagonal kick to the open side wing. The Lions' midfield backs were obstructed as they went to follow up and the referee gave them a penalty kick which Irvine took and pulled to the left of the posts.

South Africa did not escape. They won the maul from the 25 drop-out but kicked into touch on the full and Davies turned the ball back from the lineout to Edwards who kicked the ball dead again. Once more, South Africa had to drop out from their 25. This put pressure on their kicking and their catching, and once more, they were given a penalty kick in the maul. They found touch in midfield and although once again, South Africa lost the lineout, they caught the Lions' backs in possession in midfield. However, instead of concentrating on the ball, the Springboks stupidly kicked a man on the ground and the referee gave the Lions a penalty kick. It was from well inside their own half, and from the better part of 70 yards, but Irvine hit it beautifully down the wind to kick a goal.

That was effectively the end of the match, and any doubts were dispelled when Snyman began a lamentable run in which either he or his forwards made mistakes with four kick-offs in succession.

It is true that on the first occasion, Edwards had his kick charged down yet again and the ball rebounded to the Springboks, but J. P. R. Williams marked Snyman's kick and returned it with an up and under which Pope was glad to get into touch. The Lions were therefore able to resume the pressure they were exerting from the lineout and Edwards had the pleasure of putting a kick where he intended and driving the Springboks back to their line.

The ball eventually went into touch from the 25, and when the Lions won the lineout, Edwards fired the ball over the top. He received some interference as he did so which raised his ire to such an extent that he went steaming after the ball and flattened the Springbok catching the ball near the touchline. Running the shortest route from the front of the lineout, Windsor was up too, and although Edwards' tackle looked perfectly fair, another fight started. Windsor threw a punch in response to something that happened on the ground, and in no time the fight esculated into a full 99 affair. Brown leapt in to hit Fourie and Van Heerden and Kritzinger waded in and McBride went bobbing and weaving for what looked like 10 yards, throwing a succession of short lefts and rights while keeping his head prudently tucked in his shoulders much after the style of Joe Frazier. The further McBride advanced, the more isolated he became from his troops. On the following Monday morning, in practice, McLauchlan and McBride smilingly did an action re-play and it looked just as unlikely then as it did on the field. The final shot of the real battle was fired by Kritzinger, who caught Brown with a very good punch indeed as the Lions' captain went bobbing and weaving off into the sunset. Quite a few eyes then turned to the referee. He thought for a while, and gave the Springboks a mark. In a way, it was the richest moment of the whole drama. Those schoolboys present must have been as mystified as everyone else that the referee had not seen anything violent to penalise in the two preceding minutes.

The Lions quickly tightened their control. Irvine had to put the ball into touch on the full when South Africa kicked the ball high from the mark, but his forwards won the ball back and Bennett rifled a long diagonal kick across the field. Roux was late tackled as he went to kick the ball and was given a penalty kick which he put well away to touch. Again Brown won the lineout and after the Lions' forwards had driven the ball, the backs did a scissors from a scrum and Milliken set up a maul which eventually resolved into another scrum for the Lions.

This was another leisurely affair, because as long as the referees were prepared to allow it, the Lions were never in too much of a hurry to get the ball into the scrums. They preferred to let their opponents feel the weight and force them to work for as long as possible. When eventually Edwards did put in the ball, he threw a dive pass from the scrum and Bennett dropped a goal. Whatever misfortunes were befalling Edwards' kicking, no criticism could be directed at his passing. It remained superb throughout.

Snyman's kick-offs were in the same sort of groove as Edwards' tactical kicking. They were either too short or too long. This one pitched straight into touch and again the Springboks had to come back to a scrum. Again they were reprieved by a penalty kick.

The Lions won two Springboks lineout throws in succession, and from the second of them, Edwards missed a drop at goal. Davies worked the ball back from the 25 drop-out and Edwards put up a kick which Roux caught and tucked away to touch. Roux's kicking was never long enough to give his forwards much encouragement and even though this was one of those rare occasions when they won the ball in the lineout, Sonnekus passed the ball badly and the Springboks had to kick in the centre.

J. P. R. Williams put the ball away with an open side diagonal kick to touch and was probably surprised to see the Springboks win the ball in the lineout and to see them pass it along the line to their left wing. The strength and the thrust which had made Muller such a dangerous winger against the All Blacks four years earlier had gone with the years. He never looked remotely likely to beat Irvine. He had to struggle even to reach the advantage line, and was pushed into touch.

The Lions' throw into the lineout was not straight but they succeeded in wheeling the Springboks' scrum into touch so that they could start again. That time, everything went perfectly. Brown caught the ball at number five, J. P. R. Williams dummied to come into the line in the centre but instead backed up J. J. Williams and took a pass from the wing on the inside. The Lions' full-back then used his strength to take a tackle and swivel to give a scissors pass to J. J. Williams coming infield. The lack of mobility of the Springbok back row was there for all to see as Williams was left with a clear field to run through to score by the posts. Irvine converted.

As he did so, van Heerden was helped off the field. He had suffered a rib and a shoulder injury as he collided with an opponent in chasing vainly after the ball from one of Snyman's kick-offs. Some damage to a nerve made the injury appear to be more serious than it turned out to be. De Klerk came on as substitute.

With 20 minutes to go, therefore, the Lions led by 19 points to 3 and only the formalities remained to be completed. Slattery was given offside at a maul and Snyman kicked a penalty goal but the Springboks were so demoralised that even when Cronje went through the middle from a lineout, he passed straight to Milliken.

Bennet was so relaxed when he put in a little chip to touch from a lineout that he looked as if he was helping himself to a cool drink while sunbathing and Davies once more helped himself to the ball when Ellis took a pass from Snyman and tried to carry it one-handed.

Another bad kick by Edwards gave the Springboks the chance to win their best lineout of the match, but another dreadful pass by Sonnekus gave the Lions the chance to recover the lost ground. They did not take it, because the referee penalised Windsor for foot-up in the scrum and Snyman kicked another penalty goal from forty yards.

Irvine again used the wind to kick the ball over the dead-ball line. When Snyman took the drop-out from the 25, one of his forwards ran in front of the kick so that the Springboks had to scrummage back in midfield again. This was a dangerous position and they did not escape from it, even though they had three chances to do so.

They won the ball in a maul and found touch as the Lions went away to the right from the first scrum. The Lions' throw was crooked but South Africa lost that scrum against the head. Even then, they recovered the ball and Muller came in off the left wing from a 3-2 split of the backs with various possibilities opening in front of him. He chose to kick, which ought to have been the last thing in his mind after watching J. P. R. Williams catch everything for three matches. Inevitably, the ball went straight to Williams, who called for a mark.

Whether the referee was unsighted as Williams turned side on to catch the ball or whether he did not hear the call or whether he just did not give the mark was impossible to tell. Anyway, Williams turned and spun-passed the ball casually infield and the Lions moved it quickly to J. J. Williams on the left wing. He indulged himself in his favourite kick ahead, which he judged nicely and then picked up the most perfect bounce to race away and score. The cover went over with him. The bounce of the ball had been such that there was nothing they could do to stop Williams' momentum. Bennett missed the conversion.

The Lions returned to the attack almost at once. Milliken was forced into touch near the line and although South Africa won the lineout, they won the ball so badly that they had to concede a five yard scrum. It was then Edwards' turn to enjoy himself. He dodged this way and that while the Lions controlled the ball and eventually ran off to the left, to the short side. Most of the defence went with him and so were left stranded when Edwards fired a colossal reverse pass right across the back of the scrum to Bennett in the middle of the field.

It was such a devastating delivery that it left Bennett with an almost embarrassing range of choice. He could have either taken a dropped goal or taken advantage of a 4-2 overlap on his right. He even had time to take a leisurely bath. Having set his mind on the dropped goal, he took it, though the unmarked Irvine looked a bit disconsolate on the right wing.

The Lions' victory by 26 points to 9 gave them the series by three matches to nil. In the course of it, they had scored 66 points from three goals, five tries, six penalty goals and four dropped goals. South Africa had scored 21 points from five penalty goals and two dropped goals. Eight tries to nil was conclusive enough, but even that did not truly represent the poverty of the Springbok play.

Ian Robertson, the former Scottish international fly-half, had travelled down from Rhodesia to join his B.B.C. colleague Nigel Starmer-Smith. Robertson, who is a very amusing man, had been touring with a team from Cambridge known as the Light Blue Travellers but he felt that he just had to make the effort to see the test. Nodding in the direction of Snyman and Sonnekus, as they dragged themselves wearily off the pitch, he said, 'They must be the worst pair of half-backs to play international Rugby since Starmer-Smith and I stopped playing!'

Dr. Danie Craven, the president of the South African Board, had become philosophical about it all by the time he came to present their caps and blazers to the latest queue of new Springboks later that evening. 'I don't know what we will do for the fourth test,' he smiled. 'I think the tailor is running out of material.'

It was not only the tailor who had run out of material. Dr. Craven said bravely, 'I believe we have the players, but perhaps we are neglecting our talents. We will have to build. You went into everything very carefully a few years ago, and it worked. We must do the same.'

By that stage of the tour, it was hard to see on what grounds Dr. Craven could justify his belief that South Africa had the players. The barrel looked empty. The chief preliminary game before the test match had revealed this as unkindly as any game on tour. It was a match between the Junior Springboks and South African Universities. If ever a game should have revealed the potential of the country, this was it, but it turned out to be a non-tackling game of almost total irrelevance in which the lack of technique and organisation were brutally reflected in the score, which was 44-23. If the present of South African Rugby was nil, the future looked to be a minus quantity.

In the clear light of the following morning, Dr. Craven seemed to have moved some way towards accepting this himself. 'We make no excuses,' he said. 'We were beaten by a better team, but we made the Lions look better than they are.'

While he was saying that, most of the Lions were off up the coast at Sardinia Bay, relaxing on the sands in the sunshine with a few beers and a braai.

Some of them were catching up on some sleep, too. It had been a busy night. The Marine was one of those hotels which was not fitted out with an automatic sprinkler system in case of fire. It still relied on those splendid reels of hosepipe, complete with brass nozzles, to contain any conflagration, but unfortunately, these have always had a fatal fascination for touring Rugby teams, particularly when they are celebrating. The 1974 Lions had formed a Firemens' Union especially to take advantage of these facilities, and that night, a lot of people and a lot of carpet got very wet indeed. The hotel management was not pleased.

CHAPTER 27

Border

GORDON BROWN went to have a hand injury examined while the Lions were training at the Boet Erasmus stadium for the last time on the way to catch a mid-day flight to East London. It was a gentle session, but even in that, the Lions looked as if they were about to run out of scrum-halves. John Moloney jogged cautiously on his own and Gareth Edwards was so full of aches and bruises in his buttocks and legs that he almost creaked as he tried to run.

Still, Edwards knew that at the very least, he would have to play in the next match against Border and in the following game against Natal, so he tried to run some of the stiffness out of his muscles. Ian McGeechan was more fortunate, or at any rate, he thought he was. He had just finished a run in which he had played seven of the last eight games so the selectors decided to give him a rest and they chose Phil Bennett again. This meant that the Lions were due to go into their game against Border with their test half-backs, and even though Natal seemed unlikely to provide a really serious challenge in the following game, they were enough of a threat to commit the Lions to playing Edwards and Bennett again. This would have meant them playing three matches in succession, which was the last thing the Lions wanted to do at that stage of the tour, particularly as Border were struggling with one of their weakest teams ever.

A couple of hours later, a few of the Lions found themselves thinking that they might be lucky to go in against Border with anyone, never mind their test half-backs, because a bird flew into the port engine of their Boeing 727 as it took off for East London. Port Elizabeth is not the best place for tricky take-offs and landings, because it is not over-endowed with runway, and the 727 was well past the point of no return on its take-off run when those of us sitting level with the two engines felt a distinct thump. Eastern Province officials watching the flight leave saw smoke and sparks coming out of the engine.

The aircraft lifted off but climbed much less quickly than usual and inside the aircraft there was an unnatural quiet as it limped out over the sea on one engine. The aircraft then turned and manoeuvred cautiously back into position to land again. The captain switched on his microphone and said, 'Sorry about that.

We are just going back to have a look to see what happened.' By then, the 727 had only one engine, which did not provide the greatest of safety margins, but the captain managed to get the aircraft down very close to the end of the runway and without too much of a bump.

Fergus Slattery, who had been reading a newspaper, looked out of the window and said brightly to Gordon Brown sitting next to him, 'Is this East London already? That was a short flight. Hey, East London airport looks just like Port Elizabeth.'

Brown, his knuckles showing white, told him it was Port Elizabeth. He also explained what had happened.

'Why didn't you tell me before?' asked Slattery indignantly.

Brown did not like to say that it was because he could hardly speak.

'Probably a bird flew into the engine,' said the senior steward in a matter-of-fact way. 'We'll just have a look at the rotor blades, and if there is not too much damage, they'll just scrape the meat out and we'll get on our way.'

As soon as they climbed out of the aircraft, the Lions inspected the engine, which was conveniently low slung, and saw enough damage to the rotor blades to make them realise that the engineers would be most unlikely to get it working again simply by scraping out the meat. And so it proved. The party went back into the airport to have lunch and it was announced that the flight would be delayed for four or five hours while a replacement aircraft was flown down from Johannesburg. Some of the Lions and at least one of the broadcasters had already made up their minds that they had done enough flying for one day and they arranged for cars to take them on to East London. Chris Ralston's vocal delivery just does not lend itself to emphatic pronouncements, but he said very firmly, 'I'm not getting back in that thing,' and he found himself quickly joined by Stewart McKinney and Bobby Windsor. It was a four-hour journey by road and almost certainly more rewarding than any flight. One of the Lions preferred to use the time in another way, and returned to Port Elizabeth to complete some urgent unfinished business. Others fortified themselves in the bar, so that it was a depleted and slightly less coherent party which took off in the fading light of the late afternoon.

Gordon Brown re-appeared at training the next day. He emerged in his floppy sun-hat and with his broken right hand in plaster. He was doggedly hopeful of being fit to play in the fourth test, despite the misfortune which had befallen Clive Rees with exactly the same fracture of the metacarpal bone. Brown would not accept, either, that the injury would necessarily stop his playing a golf match against Gary Player that had been arranged for the last week of the tour. The thought of playing the British Open and U.S. Masters champion would have been enough to give qualms to most people even in the best of health, never mind about a broken hand. The Broons of Troon are made of sterner stuff.

He was not able to scrummage at the training session. Mervyn Davies moved up into his place at lock and J. P. R. Williams dropped back from his customary emergency position at prop and filled in enthusiastically at number eight. Phil Bennett, meanwhile, looked to be favouring his injured leg which did not augur well for Ian McGeechan's prospects of a day off.

Brown argued that donkeys, which is a generic term applied to forwards ever since the 1959 tour of New Zealand, were less in need of unbroken hands than backs and in most cases, there is no doubt that was true. Tony O'Reilly often recounted how Tom Reid confessed that as an international lock forward, his greatest dread was to be discovered 'with the ball in me hands in the middle of Twickenham.' Brown's case, however, was rather different. He had won most of the Lions' lineout ball in the tests and he had had the ball in his hands on such an indecent number of occasions that he had managed to score eight tries. At that stage, only J. J. Williams and Tom Grace had done better among even the backs so that Brown was the third highest try scorer in the team. He was lucky to escape expulsion from the donkeys' union.

That afternoon, some of the touring party took advantage of a trip up into the Transkei to see the industrial development taking place for the Africans in their homelands. With only ten days of the tour remaining, these outings had a limited appeal but Fergus Slattery was as game as ever to go and have a look. An added bonus for him was the fact that late starters were flown up in a light aircraft to join those who had gone on earlier by car and the pilot let him fly the aircraft for a fair part of the way.

Enthusiasm was a commodity which took a good deal of finding when the Lions played Border the next day. A strong wind blew down the pitch, which is the most disruptive of all the elements, and it soon became apparent that the Lions were not going to run up the huge score which the Border officials had feared when they read the result of the Lions' match against S.W. Districts at Mossel Bay.

The Lions chose to play into the wind in the first half and the photographers who had set up camp behind the Border goal-line soon saw that they were going to be relatively unemployed if they stayed there. The Border half-backs had only to kick the ball hard downfield for it to run and run until it reached either the dead-ball line or a deep touch. Ground gained into the wind was hard won and easily lost, as the Lions discovered when the advance made from two drives by Ripley and a scrummage penalty kicked to touch by Edwards was swept away when Border were awarded a penalty kick in the lineout which Steenekamp, the Border fly-half, punted over the dead-ball line from far, far away.

That morning, it had been confirmed that McGeechan was not going to have his rest after all, because Bennett withdrew from the team and McGeechan went in at fly-half. It did not take him long to realise that it was not going to be an easy game, from the point of view of either kicking or passing. Border were able to maintain a positional pressure simply by kicking and hustling.

The Lions scored first after they had won a scrum against the head. The Border backs ran offside as Gibson kicked and when the referee saw that no advantage would accrue to the Lions, he gave them a penalty which Irvine kicked into a goal.

Border put the kick-off over the Lions' dead-ball line so that they had to drop out from their 25 and start defending again. The Border scrum-half Gendall, who rejoiced in the nick-name of 'Chicken', broke away from the maul after the drop-out and might have made a score if he had been better supported.

As it turned out, perhaps the most significant event of the first half occurred when van der Linde picked up a loose ball and bundled through the middle in such a spirit of chunky determination that he handed off Gibson backwards. Even van der Linde would have been surprised by the repercussions of his achievement.

It was one of those games where the wind was very much worse on the pitch than it appeared to those watching in the stand, and the crowd's understandable disappointment with the quality of the play was only relieved when Burton had to change his shorts. He came across to the main stand to fetch a new pair and as he pulled them on, he turned away and turned both cheeks, as it were, by flipping up the tail of his jersey and exposing the full width of the scrummaging platform available to the Lions' locks. Only Burton would have done a thing like that, and it raised the biggest cheer of the day.

Whether by coincidence or not, the Lions were inspired to produce their best-rounded move to date. They forced Venter and Kotze into finding touch near their line, and when Ralston won the lineout, Gibson broke through to set up a try for Steele on the left wing. Irvine could not convert.

Border had obviously given some thought to the various ways in which they might break up the scrummaging and lineout superiority of the Lions and apart from short lineouts, they also tried a couple of three-man scrums.

Border did not really need to do this because the wind was a sufficiently disruptive force by itself and they did not pursue the three-man scrum tactic long enough for it to become effective. Still, it earned marks for originality and when fighting broke out after one of these abbreviated scrums, Border were awarded a penalty from which Steenekamp kicked a goal. Steenekamp also had a drop at goal from the halfway line, but as in the Rhodesia match, Border's variations were not controlled well enough with the result that they confused themselves even more than the opposition.

Just before half-time, Steele was late tackled as the Lions spun the ball across from a lineout. The Lions were awarded a penalty kick but Steele looked very much the worse for wear. Irvine's kick at goal fell short and Border ran the ball out to Stephenson on their right wing. However, he had such an unfortunate day with his handling that he did not begin to live up to the promise he had showed when playing for the Quaggas. His knock-on gave the Lions a scrum from which they set up a second phase situation and when Vos went into the ruck offside, Irvine kicked a penalty goal. The Lions therefore led 10-3 at half-time.

Irvine started the second half by doing exactly the same unto Border as Border had done unto the Lions. He kicked the ball over the dead-ball line from the kickoff, and for ten minutes it looked as if the Lions would run away with the match. Steele scored a try after Border had missed touch under pressure and Irvine kicked a penalty goal after a lineout.

The Lions scored only one more try, and that came initially from another ball taken against the head in a scrum. The Lions drove that and held it until they were given the ball at a scrum themselves, and then Edwards scored on the open side. Irvine converted.

Steele had to go off before the end, holding his ribs, and before J. P. R. Williams came on as substitute, ten minutes from the end, McKinney went on to the wing. When Williams came on, he went to full-back and Irvine moved forward to the wing.

Irvine had no sooner done so than he might have been faced with having to make an awkward tackle against the burly Stephenson but again the Border right wing could not hold an excruciating pass. Border were given a penalty kick in the scrum, but Neale-May was held as they tried to set up a passing move and a fly-kick by Edwards led to a scrummage position at which the Lions were awarded a penalty kick when Edwards was obstructed. Irvine kicked the goal.

The only other score came two minutes from the end, when Border produced their best passing of the match. First they attacked to the left and then van der Linde cut back to the right before passing to Stephenson. The Lions were penalised from the maul, and Steenekamp kicked a penalty goal.

It was not much of a game and there was not much worth celebrating particularly when it was learned that Billy Steele had cracked a rib. However, some jollifications started and somewhere in the course of the evening, Tom David's bed was thrown out of his bedroom window. Fortunately, he was not in it at the time, and it came to rest on a stone ledge before it could hit the ground, so at least there was no danger to passers-by or to parked motor-cars.

The correspondent of one of the Afrikaans newspapers also reported that he had seen some Lions scrummaging in the nude against some girls in a similar state of undress in one of the corridors. It was the sort of Rugby scene which might have appealed to Rubens and it conjured up a vision so striking that it was hard to believe that the man who saw it was imagining things.

It prompted a most amusing article in one of the English language newspapers in which the writer explained the Lions' superiority in the scrums by saying 'When you scrummage against nude women, you really know you are up against something.'

Sadly, things like this seem to have an unhappy knack of happening in East London. The 1968 Lions had various arguments with doors there, the stems of wine glasses had suffered horribly and then there had been the ceremonial burning of the bill for champagne in a night club. The 1970 All Blacks were involved in a rumpus there, too.

The only conclusion to be reached was that it was a mistake to go to East London twice on the tour. Men like Basil Kenyon and Doug Orr make the Border Union one of the most hospitable in South Africa, and whatever the strength of the local team, the match against Border is always an enjoyable occasion. However, it would have been better to play the game against the Africans either out of Port Elizabeth, or better still, out of Durban. The Lions were due to stay a week in Port Elizabeth in any event, and they would have been glad of the opportunity to spend the same amount of time in Durban. Of all the cities in South Africa, Durban is the best equipped to keep a touring team thoroughly diverted.

CHAPTER 28

Natal

THIS was evident as soon as the Lions arrived. The rickshaw boys had been moved from their old place just along from the Edward Hotel, which rather spoiled the impact as the buses from the airport turned along the sea front, but at least the sun was warm enough and the beach was colourful enough to add a zest of expectation to even those players who felt that they were coming to the end of a long, hard road and would be glad to get home Durban is the Riviera of South Africa, with the sun and the sand and the sea available on the instant and with gardens and tasteful amusements stretched along the front. The sea can be dangerous, as Andy Ripley discovered the next day when he got into difficulties with the big surf and the strong undertow, but for the Lions who did not want to take the risk of such aquatic adventures there were the delights at the Country Club out by the Rugby ground at Kings Park and there were enough night clubs for every member of the party to have one to himself.

The Lions went down to Kings Park to train as soon as they arrived and Billy Steele stood watching them sadly. He said that he hoped to be fit for consideration for the Lions' match against Eastern Transvaal in five days' time, but in his heart of hearts, he knew that he was kidding himself. That much was evident when he reflected how ironic it was that his tour should have been stopped by a rib injury when almost everyone, including himself, had expected that he would have a recurrence of the leg injuries that had troubled him for so long.

The Lions had chosen all but three of their test team for the match against Natal. This was a tribute to the mystique of Tommy Bedford more than anything, because it was hard to see how a team which had lost to Rhodesia, as Natal had, could possibly beat any combination fielded by the Lions.

Tommy Bedford obviously thought the same. Peter Ripley-Evans, who had captained Natal against the British Lions in 1962 and in 1968, took me over to see Tommy Bedford that lunch-time and it was fascinating to hear someone as articulate as Bedford expand on the ills which had befallen South African Rugby. 'I think it's ironic that Natal are now being put forward as South Africa's last hope,' he said. 'The last outpost of the British Empire is the last hope for South Africa.' Bedford laughed.

The whole of South Africa was aching for someone to beat the Lions. Even the Transvaal would have offered a small cheer if Natal could have succeeded where all the other provinces had failed. 'I have had calls from all over the country from people who want to wish us well,' said Bedford. 'I have had to leave the office just to get away from the telephone.

'We haven't got any magic formula for beating the Lions,' he said. 'We shall play in the way that we have always played. The way that the Springbok selectors say is no good. We shall run the ball and we shall pass it. We shall try a few things. The selectors say "That's no good. You've got to play up front." I argue that we must have certain basic skills to play and to pass as we do.

'But I don't want to talk about Natal's game against the Lions. I would rather talk about South African Rugby, and where it has gone wrong.'

'We went to Britain in 1969-70, and we got the chop. We did not win one of the four tests. In the beginning, we thought it was the demonstrations that upset us. I must admit that I thought that too. But after about five matches, the authorities got on top of the demonstration problem and yet still we did not produce the Rugby of which we should have been capable.

'After all, we had the players. Frik du Preez was on that tour. Mof Myburgh, Hannes Marais, Piet Greyling, Jan Ellis, Dawie de Villiers, Syd Nomis—they were all there. But we did not achieve the results and I think that it was because too many of us had the wrong approach.

'Things were happening in Rugby in Britain. The Welsh had developed squad training and it was spreading to other countries. The forwards were developing their organisation. The backs were developing their moves, and they were putting it all together as a team. They were beginning to play a game we had never even heard of.

'I remember talking to Avril Malan at Porthcawl. Avril saw the way ahead, and he wanted to make changes. He could see the way the game was developing in Europe, and he knew that if we did not change our own game, we would be left behind. I must admit I was surprised that Avril should be thinking so progressively as a coach. He had never been like that as a captain, and I asked him what had changed him.

'He said, "As a captain, I never used to think. I just used to go out and play. It's only since I've been a selector and a coach that I have really started thinking about the game. And I can see we must change."

'But Avril was resisted. Some of the players did not want to carry out his ideas. Take the simple business of the hooker throwing the ball into the lineout, instead of the winger. It is a small enough example, but Frik du Preez would not have it. I am not breaking any confidences, because he wrote it in his book, but he said, "What does a hooker like Charlie Cockrell know about throwing in the ball?" So we went on playing the same way. The Lions have used their hooker to throw in the ball throughout this tour, whereas the Springboks have used their wingers.

'Avril must have prepared a report on that tour. It would be interesting to know what happened to it. I don't suppose anyone was interested. People were saying, "Oh, that tour is over. We've got the All Blacks coming. We've got to beat them."

'So we went on doing the same things. We went back into the past for a few players and we beat the All Blacks, and everybody thought that that was the end of all our problems. Then we went to Australia, and we won all our matches there, and everybody thought that was great, too. In the first two matches in Western Australia, we were playing the blind school. The Rugby was meaningless. Then we played Victoria in Adelaide and they were even more blind. Victories like that meant nothing, but we took them seriously and believed that we had achieved something great when we came back from Australia unbeaten. They were false values. They told us nothing about either the players, or the coaching or the captaincy.

'While we were in Australia, the Lions were winning in New Zealand. Now that really WAS something, but we took no notice. Then the French came here, and although they had finished bottom of the championship in Europe, we only just scraped away with a draw in the last match to beat them.

'Then England came here and we lost. They came here and played their last match in Durban and they beat us 19-0. I said then that I could not imagine any province in South Africa doing that, or anything like it. That England team played seven matches in this country and they went through unbeaten and they finished up by beating South Africa at Ellis Park. They beat us because their forwards were better organised and because they all knew what pattern of game they were playing

'I said before this tour started that the Lions would win all four Test matches. I could see it coming. I have seen it coming for years. There are none so blind as those who will not see. There are none so deaf as those who will not hear.'

Tommy Bedford said what he did both in sorrow and in anger. It grieved him that South Africa should have been so insufferably complacent for so long about their Rugby but it also angered him that the Springbok selectors had ignored both the Natal players and any contribution that Natal Rugby might make.

There is not much doubt, either, that there was a personal element of frustration for Tommy Bedford in all this, not only as a player, but as a captain, too. He had watched as the Springbok selectors had ignored his own much more obvious claims to the captaincy of South Africa and had gone to a great deal of trouble to persuade a reluctant Hannes Marais to come out of retirement.

What made the pill even harder for Bedford to swallow was that Marais had no pretentions to blinding genius as a captain. Marais was an immensely likeable fellow, with a wry sense of humour, but Eastern Province had already preferred George Barnard to him as captain and Marais' captaincy in the first three tests had not been exactly been the stuff of which Caesars are made. Bedford, on the other hand, had experience of captaincy going back for nearly ten years.

He also had the capacity to organise a loose forward effort which, as Carwyn James had said at the beginning of the tour, was the area where the Springboks ought to have been most dangerous and where they ought to have been trying their hardest to succeed. Bedford was far too shrewd not to know these things. Hence his sorrow and his anger.

Alun Thomas was feeling much the same. He had called a team meeting to discuss the damage done to the hotels in Port Elizabeth and East London. The Lions' manager told the players that all touring parties were allowed a certain sum of money, either to spend on damage of this sort or to disburse on something which would be to the mutual benefit of everyone at the end of the tour. Quite apart from the bad image which was created, he said, it was manifestly stupid to spend that money paying for avoidable damage. By then, however, Alun Thomas had some strong critics among the players, and so they did not take as much notice as they would have done if the lecture had been delivered by either Syd Millar or Bill McBride.

It never is possible to undo fully the damage which is done when stories of this nature appear, even if they are either untrue or exaggerated, but in this case the Lions did what they could to demonstrate that the stories had been exaggerated. They talked about one of the players going along a corridor with a towel round him and the manager of the hotel in East London wrote a letter in which he revealed that the bill for the damage done was really quite small.

The Lions had a fair amount to discuss as they crossed the road in front of their hotel to sunbathe on the beach or as they went along to the Country Club to play a round of golf on that most attractive of courses. Jack Ward, one of the members of the Natal committee looking after the Lions, was delighted to see that at least one of the members of the touring party had improved his driving since his previous visit, when he had smashed two drives in succession straight up the middle of the adjoining motorway, much to the consternation of a medley of Mercedes.

The Natal Rugby team also had a fair amount to discuss as they practised that evening at the University club. Tommy Bedford knew quite well that Natal had nothing like the strength at tight forward to hold the Lions in the scrums, and so he devised a series of lineout variations in the hope that they would break up the established pattern of the Lions' game of scrummaging and kicking for pressure positions. Natal wanted as much broken play as possible so that they could win enough loose ball to play a game. Rhodesia had tried something of the same thing, but had found that unless the variations were so thoroughly practised as to be second nature to the players, they usually led to so many mistakes that the innovators would have been better off playing an orthodox game.

Natal discovered that for themselves when they played the Lions at King's Park. They subtracted forwards from lineouts. They added forwards to lineouts. They used short lineout. They tried split lineouts. They tried advancing and retiring from lineouts. They threw the ball over the top of lineouts. They took lineouts instead of scrums.

More often than not, they either threw the ball crooked, or knocked it on, or lost it, or were penalised, or were beaten to the ball when they threw it over the top by the sheer speed of Fergus Slattery and Tony Neary. Sometimes, they just confused themselves. Each time Natal made a mistake, the game returned to the point of the Lions' greatest strength, which was the scrum, and Natal took another fearful pounding. Ian McLauchlan lifted Derek van den Berg out of Natal's first scrum, and although the Natal tight head kept his feet well back from that moment on, the Natal scrummage was so lacking in strength and technique that it was in the most terrible trouble.

The situation was no better for Natal when the Lions threw the ball into the lineout. Bill McBride had far and away his best game at the front of the lineout since the first test, and with Chris Ralston and Mervyn Davies firmly in command further back, the Lions won more than 70 per cent. of the set ball.

Fortunately for Natal, the Lions did not use that ball at all well. Once again, they played far more cautiously than they need have done and with fifty or sixty points there for the taking, they trudged through the game with such a lack of enterprise and Gareth Edwards kicked so much that with ten minutes to go they were leading by only nine points to six. Just after half-time, the Lions backs almost exploded with despair when Edwards was given a loose ball in front of the Natal posts and he had a drop at goal which missed. The photographers on the touch-line were startled to hear some of the words used by men not normally given to using strong language.

It was hard to blame Edwards. Scrum-half is a position which puts intense mental and physical pressure on a player, especially when he has to do much of the kicking and is responsible for the tactical direction of the team. This was the style adopted by the Lions, and Edwards had been playing in so many matches because of the injuries to John Moloney that he was even finding it hard to sleep. Barry John would have walked off the field in disgust if he had been playing and Gareth Edwards had kicked away as much of the ball as he did against Natal but Edwards had become so conditioned by the policy of keeping the ball in front of his forwards to avoid mistakes and he had perfected the deep rolling kick to the blind-side touch-line to such an extent that by the later stages of the tour, his first thought almost invariably was to kick. A child at school could have predicted that the Lions would scrummage Natal to pull in their loose forwards and that initially the Lions would kick to eliminate Tommy Bedford even further from the game, but that child at school would not have been much entertained when the Lions went on doing that long, long after it was necessary.

The Lions could not have been given a more accommodating start. Basson was penalised in the second ruck and the third minute of the match after Davies had won a lineout and Bennett popped over a 40-yard penalty goal from the left touch-line. Edwards hit the corner flag with a kick from the back of the first scrum of the match and with van den Berg taking off in the scrum after that, Natal were soon looking harassed. Davies won successive lineouts and Edwards concentrated on kicking for position.

However, Natal had a chance to draw level when they were given a penalty kick on the Lions' 10 yard line. Pitcher came across from the left wing to take it, and he lined up the ball with those familiar twin towers of C. W. Ralston and T. M. Davies standing underneath the proposed flight path of the ball. Just as Pitcher ran up to take the kick, those twin towers moved solemnly to their right, and whether by accident or not, the ball followed them and sailed past the left post.

Natal had already seen enough of the Lions' scrummaging to choose to take a lineout when the Lions threw the ball in crooked, but Natal threw it crooked themselves when they went to project the ball over the top and into the midfield. So the Lions still had a scrum and Natal had to tackle solidly to hold up Edwards just short of the line.

Shortly after, Holmes lost the ball in a ruck on his right touch-line, and Bennett put a kick in front of the Natal posts which Swanby caught and marked. The Lions won the lineout after Swanby had kicked to touch, and although Morley lost the ball as he came infield, Natal were shoved so hard in the scrum that their back row was penalised as the ball emerged. That gave Bennett the chance to kick his second penalty goal.

Natal were also given a second chance to kick a penalty goal, and it looked very much as if Windsor was being penalised again for heading the ball. Once again Pitcher advanced to take the kick, a rather easier one this time. Once again those twin towers shuffled sideways, and once again Pitcher pulled the ball to the left of the posts.

Bennett worked the Lions away from defence with a very good penalty kick, and after Natal had thrown in crookedly once again, Edwards took the ball from the scrum and sent a grub kick down the left which Slattery pursued into touch. The referee then caused a howl of indignation because after Natal had started with a short lineout, they went to add some forwards to it and were penalised. Natal argued that the lineout had not been formed and that it was a ploy they had used most successfully against Northern Transvaal. The referee was not impressed. He gave the Lions a penalty and Bennett kicked his third goal.

Not content with that, Natal tried splitting a lineout, which ended in an even greater shambles, and not long after, their lock, 'Binkie' Kapp, left the field with a leg injury. He could have been forgiven for pleading that he had pulled a muscle trying to keep up with the lineout ploys. Brocklehurst came on as sus-stitute.

The first half was three minutes into injury time when Natal were awarded their third penalty kick at goal. Swanby came up to take it, but by then, Ralston and Davies were going so well that they would have fancied their chances against Don Clarke. Sure enough, Swanby pulled the kick to the left, and the self-satisfaction on the faces of Ralston and Davies as they sauntered across to partake of their oranges at half-time had to be seen to be believed.

The Lions' backs were not so pleased. Too much ball had been kicked away by Edwards for their liking, and when he began the second half by taking a ball from a ruck near the Natal 25 and having a drop at goal charged down, they spoke their minds in no uncertain terms.

A crashing tackle by Gibson on van der Watt made a loose ball which J. J. Williams kicked ahead and Bedford had to make a desperate save by the corner flag to stop a score. Natal worked away from their 25 with a long drop out followed by a kick to the blind side corner after the referee had wrongly judged that J. J. Williams had thrown a forward pass, but they could not keep their attacking position by winning controlled ball from the short lineouts they called. Davies took the ball at the back of one of them and the ball from another was bundled straight back into touch. Both van der Watt and Morley were injured almost simultaneously and left the field within a few minutes of each other. Before they went, Edwards nearly scored when the Lions pushed Natal off the ball in a scrum with contemptuous ease. The referee ruled that Edwards had lost the ball over the line in a boiling scrimmage of bodies.

Hannaford came on as substitute for the injured van der Watt and could scarcely have provided a greater contrast. Instead of the lean dark sprinter lurking on the wing, there emerged this slightly Falstaffian figure who was thoroughly suited by his nickname of Tubby. It did not take him long to make his presence felt.

He it was who supported Holmes on a blind side break from a scrum and turned the ball inside for McKenzie to kick ahead. J. P. R. Williams was caught near the right touch-line as he picked up the ball and Bedford, as the second man up, whirled him into touch. Williams thought Bedford had kicked him deliberately and he punched him more than once. Bedford sprawled across with his head near the concrete surround and he lay inert in the foetal position as the crowd restrained Williams.

Natal took the lineout and the ball went across to the other side of the field into another lineout. In that, Bedford was flattened again, this time by Cotton, and the crowd became so incensed that it hurled such a fusillade of oranges and coke tins at the Lions that McBride led his players into the middle of the field to take refuge until the police had restored order. This took a long time, and at the end of it, the referee gave Natal a penalty kick which Hannaford took.

From the moment he stepped forward, Hannaford made his preparations with such a solid air of confidence that Ralston and

Davies were hypnotised into almost complete immobility and Hannaford kicked the goal from 30 yards as if he could do that sort of thing all afternoon.

This encouraged Natal to produce their best Rugby of the match. Holmes, Ferguson, Healey and de Lange worked Natal into a lineout position from which Bedford found a long touch and when Natal won the lineout again, the Lions were fortunate that the referee did not see that they had encroached well within the ten yard limit. Hannaford could have kicked that goal with his eyes shut as he demonstrated very forcibly three minutes later when Edwards was penalised for dummying the ball into a scrum just inside his own half. The kick was from 50 yards, but off a very short run, Hannaford struck it the most beautiful blow to kick a soaring goal. Ralston and Davies tried their little shuffle and their leaning tower of Pisa act, but you could see that their hearts were not in it.

With less than ten minutes to go, and the Lions leading only 9-6, it was interesting to speculate on what might have happened if Hannaford had come on sooner. On kicks alone, Natal could have been in the lead even though they had won considerably less than 30 per cent. of the ball. It was a ridiculous state of affairs but the Lions had no one to blame for it but themselves.

This soon became very apparent, because although the Lions were settled into a pattern of kicking, they did see the chance that was offered when Slattery stopped Holmes and set up a winning ruck. Edwards immediately attacked the blind side and Irvine squeezed in to score on the right. He hit the corner flag, and Natal protested that he had been tackled into touch in goal, but the referee awarded the try. Bennett hit the near post with his kick at goal from the touch-line.

As the match went into injury time, the Natal scrummaging effort finally collapsed and the Lions' forwards, by their adventure in the loose, showed their backs just what they might have achieved if they had started running the ball earlier.

McLauchlan led the first sortie, after Natal had made a mess of yet another short lineout, and reached a position from which the Lions pushed Natal off the ball at a scrum in their 25. Davies drove from the back of the scrum, safe in the knowledge that even if the ball was killed in the ruck, the Lions would have the put-in at the next scrum, five yards from the Natal line. That was exactly what happened, and the Lions pushed the Natal forwards over their line before turning the scrum so that the ball was in the best position for Davies to pick it up and score. Bennett converted.

Bennett then started side-stepping people both in the Natal team and in his own like a shuttle on a loom. He dropped the ball when the Lions again pushed Natal off the ball in a scrum, but did not knock it forward and put up a kick into the box from which the Lions were able to force an attacking lineout position. The Lions called a peel but Natal were penalised before it could develop and Bennett kicked a penalty goal.

Bedford tried to switch the direction of the kick-off but Gibson saw it coming and caught the ball on the full before taking off on a bewildering run in which he sold two dummies to everyone in the stand as well as to the whole Natal team. He cut right through and McLauchlan supported him to create the position for an attacking scrum from which Edwards kicked for the corner. Bedford managed to reach the ball but had been stretched so much that he was rushed into trying to be too ambitious with his kick for touch. Davies had also done a magnificent piece of anticipatory covering at number eight for the Lions and he fielded Bedford's kick near the Natal 25. More than that, he turned and rolled a beautiful pass infield and with the Natal back row spread all over the place, Bennett ran through the broken field like a master. His side-stepping reduced the Natal defence to such a tangled mass of wreckage that Irvine was able to run round and score behind the posts. Again Bennett converted.

As the match went on and on, people kept looking at their watches, scarcely able to believe that the referee could be allowing so much extra time. To add to Natal's misfortunes, they made a mess of their last kick-off and Bennett cut through again. He looked as if he might have scored if he had really gone for the line, but he checked and set up a maul which again dissolved into a scrum with the Lions putting in the ball. Again, they pushed the Natal forwards over the line and Slattery touched the ball down for a try. Again Bennett converted, and as the players came off the field, McLauchlan raised his arms in the gladiator's salute of triumph.

Long before the game against Natal, it had been clear that the Lions would break almost every scoring record in South Africa, but in scoring 21 points in what is commonly known as injury time, they surely set one of the most bizarre records in the history of the game. The referee added 11 minutes of extra time for the various stoppages.

The Springbok selectors had turned up in force to watch the Lions play Natal, and at the reception afterwards, Tommy Bedford said how delighted he was that they had all managed to catch the plane to Durban at long, long last. He smiled and welcomed them by lifting two fingers, not in the way Winston Churchill used to signal his hopes for victory, but with that derisive reversal of the hand to which there is no adequate reply.

Unfortunately, such a gesture usually results in complete alienation. It is much, much worse than being cuffed across the face by a velvet glove in the days when gentlemen duelled over their honour, because at least there was a way out of that confrontation. Giving someone the fingers merely shuts the door.

Perhaps Tommy Bedford thought that the door was shut already, and had been shut for years, and that he was only replying in kind. Perhaps he was right. It was easy to sympathise with his personal frustration, but to a visitor, it seemed that the protest could have been made with much more style and therefore with much more point.

Bedford apologised to the Lions for the behaviour of the crowd and said, 'I never thought I would see a thing like that at King's Park.' He congratulated the Lions on their win and said that for weeks, South Africans had been trying to work out why the Lions were so good in the scrums.

'Now we know,' he said, and held up a newspaper poster which said, 'LIONS AND GIRLS IN NUDE SCRUM.' To a roar of laughter, he added, 'We have been doing the wrong training all the way along!'

At the end of his speech, Bedford referred to the clash with J. P. R. Williams and the incident which had led to the crowd throwing tins and oranges at the Lions. He said, 'In my years at Oxford, I played some of the most enjoyable Rugby of my career. But today I saw another side of British Rugby—and I know which I prefer.'

J. P. R. Williams had apologised to Bedford after the match, but said that he thought Bedford had kicked him deliberately and that in any case, he had not hit Bedford hard enough to knock him out. Bedford said that he disagreed with that version of what happened, but that he did not want to go into the matter any further.

Alun Thomas, the Lions' manager, also made a wry reference to it. 'J. P. R. is coming back to Durban in a week's time when the tour is over,' he said, 'but perhaps it is as well that he is only coming to coach tennis!'

A former policeman, who was among the crowd who helped to restrain Williams, said afterwards that the Lions' full-back had been kicked, but that he thought that the kick was accidental. Either way, it was an unsavoury incident, and it was unworthy of the players involved. J. P. R. Williams himself had once said that every match should contain at least one moment when the players could laugh. The Lions did not play too many of those in South Africa. More snarls than smiles came over the gumshields and the abiding memory of J. P. R. Williams was with his fists clenched and his feet braced for all eventualities in the third test at Port Elizabeth.

The Lions had established weeks before that they were better than the South Africans at Rugby and that they were better than the South Africans at fighting, and this had tended to breed a certain arrogance in some of the players that was unbecoming. In all respects, it was so much a case of the men playing the boys that it was not necessary for the Lions to over-react as they did. It would have been much better for them to take the philosophical attitude of a former England flanker, one of the hardest men in the history of the game, who was confronted by a stroppy young undergraduate in a club game against Oxford University. In the next lineout, he said conversationally, 'Now look, son. Do you want to play in the Varsity match or don't you?' There was no more trouble.

J. P. R. Williams did very much better when he went with his wife to the party that night and was confronted with an extremely embarrassing scene when a lady harangued him for his part in the altercation with Bedford.

He said nothing, and eventually, she burst into tears, and was led away.

CHAPTER 29

Eastern Transvaal

BOTH Billy Steele and Geoff Evans were still hoping to be chosen for the Lions team to play Eastern Transvaal in Springs in the last provincial match of the tour but in Steele's case, it looked a vain hope. Evans, too, had started to run on his injured hamstring much too soon after the damage had been done to give it much chance of healing. However, they both had fitness tests when the Lions went to Ellis Park to begin their last week of training and at least they were able to run in warm and pleasant conditions.

Steele was the first to accept that his tour had come to an end. As soon as his injured ribs were jarred, he realised that there was no possibility of him being fit for what might turn out to be a contentious game at Springs the following day, and he walked sadly off the field.

Evans lasted longer. He went through the warm-up and started to take part in the team practice, but when the backs called a couple of moves and he tried to stretch out at full pace to make up ground on the outside, he tweaked the injured hamstring again and pulled up. Ian McGeechan and Roy Bergiers finished the practice in the centre, with Tom Grace on the right wing and Andy Irvine trying another positional venture on the left. J. P. R. Williams played full-back and it was announced that he would captain the team. This revealed that the Lions judged John Moloney fit enough to give Gareth Edwards a rest at scrum-half.

Williams had climbed such a pinnacle of performance on tour that it was mildly surprising that he had not been asked to captain the team before. He had been the most consistent of all the backs, even including Gareth Edwards, and that consistency had been pitched at such a high level of perfection for so long that it towered above every other personal performance in the team. J. P. R. Williams never had a bad game. It is true that not many teams in South Africa were able to win enough ball even to extend him, but it was hard to imagine that any full-back of recent times had ever played better anywhere in the world. Even on the practice field, Williams was almost infallible, and watching him go through the routines day after day with undiminished enthusiasm and listening to his perceptive comment on the positioning and the angles of running and the ball-watching of the backs around him made one realise that for sheer ability and involvement in the game of Rugby football, there were few players better qualified to lead by example.

There are times when Williams is shut so tightly in his own world of concentration that he can seem remote, but on the face of it, his claim for consideration as a captain was much stronger than was generally accepted. Indeed, very few people even thought of him as a possibility as captain. Perhaps that stemmed from the fact that his career in the Welsh team had developed slightly behind that of Gareth Edwards. One recalled a disagreement between the two on the subject of a kick at goal in a match between Ireland and Wales in Dublin. A small thing, maybe, but perhaps that was a contributory factor.

The choice of Williams as captain for the match against Eastern Transvaal was intriguing on two counts. First, of course, it followed the match in Durban where he had been involved in an unseemly scuffle with Tommy Bedford, and second, it put him in command of the team on the one ground in South Africa which seemed to be associated with trouble more than any other.

The Pam Brink stadium at Springs sounds innocuous enough for ladies' hockey but even the scholars of St. Trinian's would have blanched at some of the goings on there. John O'Shea, the Lions prop, was sent off the field after a running fight in 1968, and as he made the long, sad walk across the wide running track which surrounds the pitch and made his way towards the players' tunnel, he was attacked by a spectator. The Lions jumped over the fence and went to his rescue and they in turn attacked the spectator.

Then on the All Blacks' tour of 1970, Colin Meads had his arm broken in what many New Zealanders believe was a deliberate attack on their most formidable player. Until that match, Meads had been playing the best Rugby of even his astonishing career, but as a result of that injury, he missed the first two tests and was really only approaching full fitness again by the end of the tour. It has been argued that that injury alone cost New Zealand the series.

There were also scenes of considerable carnage in matches against both the Wallabies and the French at Springs, and two months before the Lions went to play there, the referee Cas de Bruyn abandoned the match between Tarbes, the French club champions, and Eastern Transvaal, because of fighting. Tarbes were much depleted for their tour but whoever was to blame for the misdemeanours, both Tarbes as a club and the French Federation took so serious a view of what had happened that they slapped suspensions on their players wholesale. The track record of the Pam Brink stadium could scarcely have been less encouraging as J. P. R. Williams contemplated the beginning of his career as a captain, and before the inhabitants of Springs write to me to tell me that their stadium is named after a benefactor named P. A. M. Brink, I should say that I know that perfectly well, but they are the ones who have left out the full stops.

Apart from the fact that it seems to be so accident prone, the ground at Springs is also the least congenial in the whole of South Africa. The playing surface has the brightest and the yellowest glare of all the frost-killed pitches in the Transvaal and the width of the running track and the distance from the pitch makes the dark of the low-roofed stand even gloomier by comparison.

As it turned out, J. P. R. Williams did not have to act as mediator, or diplomat, or even as soother of aggrieved parties in his first venture at captaincy. The proceedings could not have been conducted with more decorum if indeed the match had been played in a ladies' hockey stadium. The Lions won the match very easily, which surprised no one, but the fact that they won it without a punch being thrown surprised almost the entire southern hemisphere.

The Lions owed this state of affairs to the intervention of one of the senior officials of the Eastern Transvaal union. He went into the dressing room before the match and told his players that his committee did not want to see a repetition of the brawl against Tarbes. He probably knew that with South African Rugby safely buried for the series, some of the Sunday newspaper correspondents had only gone to the match on the off-chance of seeing a punch-up. The Rugby had ceased to have any value, but the possibility of a news story like that was too important to be ignored. The wishes of the Eastern Transvaal committee were respected. The players in their team who had been identified as meanies went through the match so circumspectly that the 400 millimetre photographic lenses which had been following their every movement with such fidelity eventually wavered and drooped and were put on the ground while the photographers tried to keep warm.

Eastern Transvaal took the lead after only three minutes when they won a lineout and the Lions were caught offside. The kick at goal was from 53 yards, and McKinney and Ripley tried to distract Salt by solemnly leaning sideways like Ralston and Davies, but Salt did not seem in the least disturbed and gave the ball such a good clip with his right foot that he kicked the goal. Two minutes later, Irvine had a chance to do the same thing, and he aimed off sufficiently to allow the cross wind to pull the ball into the posts. It was a well-judged kick.

The Lions followed that by pushing Eastern Transvaal off the ball in a scrum, and Ripley launched himself to the blind side with more determination than he had shown for a long time. He sustained this throughout the match, and from the Lions' point of view, the pity was that Moloney was so badly handicapped by his injury that he could only go through the motions of passing the ball. He could not run or defend or threaten the opposing back row in the way that was necessary to make Ripley and the other loose forwards even more effective. Eastern Transvaal soon saw the extent to which Moloney was handicapped and their scrum-half Petersen took the opportunity to probe the blind-side and play a busy and effective game.

For some time, too, Moloney did not have the best of ball to work with. Most of his forwards knew that it was the last match they would play on tour, and almost inevitably, their effort was beginning to wane. The result was that it took them nearly 20 minutes to control the ball well enough to arouse any enthusiasm among their backs.

In that time, Irvine bounced over another penalty goal off the right post after the Lions had drawn one of the opposing flankers offside by holding the ball in the back of their scrum. Salt also kicked another penalty goal for Eastern Transvaal. His captain rather surprisingly offered it to van Rensburg first when the referee Steve Strydom penalised the Lions for closing the one yard gap in a lineout. The full-back declined with thanks and indicated that Salt should be given the kick. He was right.

The Lions then raised their game. Ripley, Burton, David and Carmichael set up a ruck and Bergiers made a break which led to Williams going into touch near the Eastern Transvaal line. Eastern Transvaal knocked on the ball in the lineout but the referee played advantage and Ralston set up a ruck on the open side with enough room for Gibson to go back to the short side and float a pass to Grace. The winger juggled with the ball before gathering it and even then had to take care that he did not fall into touch but he managed both and scored in the corner. Irvine could not convert.

For the rest of the half, the Lions' forwards played their most controlled Rugby. They won possession almost without interruption and it took some solid defending by Eastern Transvaal to restrict their opponents to one more score. Ripley made the try with a drive from the back of a lineout and although he was held short of the line, he released the ball for Tom David to pick it up and score. Irvine converted.

The Lions began the second half with an equally peremptory demonstration of forward domination. They forced a scrum five yards from the Eastern Transvaal line, and although it was not their ball, they pushed their opponents off it so far and so fast that Ripley was able to score easily. Again Irvine converted.

In the first quarter of an hour of the second half, the Lions scored 17 points. McGeechan scored a try after a drive through the middle by David had been supported by Ripley, J. P. R. Williams and Uttley, and although Irvine could not convert, he did kick a penalty goal from the halfway line. That gave him 13 points in the match and brought his total for the tour to 139.

Almost at once, Uttley led another fierce drive to set up a ruck and when the Lions moved the ball through their backs, Grace scored easily on the right. At that point, with 25 minutes to play and Irvine beginning to run dangerously on the left wing, another score of 50 or 60 points looked likely.

However, Moloney was showing signs of greater and greater discomfort, and the Lions' impetus gradually faded. It was almost as if the midweek team suddenly reached a collective conclusion that they had done enough for the tour, and decided to declare.

Eastern Transvaal attacked Moloney and built up a series of drives on the short side which enabled them to scrummage away busily near the Lions' line. The radio commentator who suggested that Eastern Transvaal were hoping for a push-over try at that stage was generally thought to have provided the gem of the tour, because no pack anywhere had succeed in moving the Lions' scrummage more than a foot. Eastern Transvaal had more to hope for in quick-witted use of the ball, and after two minutes of injury time, Petersen took a tapped penalty kick and was supported by his number eight to make a try for Fourie on the flank.

Ripley celebrated his emphatic return to form by appearing at the reception in a very free interpretation of the Lions' number two rig. He sat on the steps in a black leather jacket as various Eastern Transvaal speakers heaved a succession of sighs of relief that the game had been so free of strife and Alun Thomas cleared his throat as apologetically as ever as he projected his line of Afrikaans, 'Dames en Heeren,' at a South African provincial audience for the last time. The Lions were soon away and the quickest movers were into dinner in their alcove at the Landdrost Hotel long before eight o'clock.

CHAPTER 30

Golf with Gary Player

THE Lions announced the next morning that they had accepted that Gordon Brown would not be fit to play in the last test and that Chris Ralston had been chosen to play at lock instead. Ralston himself had been injured against Eastern Transvaal and his running in training at Ellis Park the next day was much impaired, but he was able to scrummage and he recovered enough to play, even though he was not able to prepare as well as he should have done.

The selection of Ralston instead of the injured Brown was the only change from the team which had beaten South Africa in the third test. It was the only change expected, too, even though Mike Gibson had shown the form against Natal to warrant selection if the team had been using its platform of forward domination to play a style of Rugby based on exploring the possibilities of attacking threequarter play.

However, it was not playing that style of Rugby in the important games and it never had. It's prime objectives were to make no mistakes behind the advantage line and to keep the ball in front of the forwards either by kicking or by having enough physical presence in midfield either to set up a ruck or to tackle. Tom David could just as easily have fulfilled the function required of the centres except that, like Gibson, he was judged to be 'not a good first-time tackler.' Remembering the way the Lions' backs had played in New Zealand in 1971, and the breath-taking vision of the game they had revealed against the All Blacks in Cardiff in 1973, it all seemed scarcely credible. None of the other threequarters had ever tasted the delights of playing in a Lions' team determined to fulfil every scrap of its attacking potential, but even they knew enough to be embarrassed. Of course, Gibson had missed that tackle against Border. It was like saying to Jack Nicklaus, 'You missed that green with an 8-iron. I know you hit the previous 302 greens with your 8-iron, but you did miss that one, so you're out of the Ryder Cup team.'

Ian McGeechan was not able to train on the day the team was announced. He had scored his first try of the tour before and had then gone down with a stomach upset. He must have felt that it was a poor way to celebrate.

Gordon Brown was determined to salvage something from the

week and even if he could not play in the test match, he had made up his mind that a little thing like a broken hand was not going to stop him taking on Gary Player at golf. The match had been arranged to take place at Killarney the following day, so Gordon took his team of Mike Gibson and Gareth Edwards up to look at the course that afternoon and to play 18 holes of practice.

While the Lions' golf team was pacing out yardages and working out club selection, the Springbok Rugby team was assembling at a hotel on the other side of the city. It was still only Wednesday, so it meant that for the third time in four matches, the Springboks had broken the International Board regulation which decrees that international teams other than touring teams must not assemble more than 48 hours before a game.

The Springboks went out to practice at the Transvaal Rugby Union's huge acreage of sports pitches at Springfield, which is only ten minutes' drive from the centre of Johannesburg. The sight of these facilities and a dizzy estimate of the noughts involved in the value of the land made one realise that both from the point of view of income and capital assets, the Transvaal Rugby Union must be one of the richest sports organisations in the world. Even though the series was over, every ticket for the last test match had been sold and there was even a vigorous black market. At that very moment, the Transvaal Rugby Union officials were busy in their counting houses counting out their money, and when they had finished they announced that the gate receipts for the fourth test match alone were more than 520,000 rand, which is more than £300,000. Another world record, and no wonder, with unreachable seats in various ricketty crows' nests priced at £5 each.

The Springboks, trained for two hours in the late afternoon and on into the chill of the early dusk. They had not gone to the trouble of organising an effective group of players to be used as really determined opposition, so the scrummaging practice they did was mostly against a scrummaging machine. For the most part, the Springboks concentrated on lineouts, which was about three tests matches too late, and they tried hard to get their kick-offs right. It was all very orthodox, and not very relevant to a game situation. After all, a scrummaging machine is depressingly static, and not at all susceptible to being wheeled. The Springboks also needed not only opposed practice in lineout support play, but fiercely opposed practice, so that they could get some idea of what they would have to do to make sure that J. G. Williams could jump for the ball. They also needed to develop their scrum-half and back row drives from the scrum but they showed no signs of doing so

The Springboks practised at Springfield the next morning, too. Their full-back, Tony Roux, had injured himself in practice the night before and dropped out of the match team. His place was taken by Malcolm Swanby. A former Springbok contemplated the possible change in the team with glum resignation. 'It makes no difference,' he said.

There were two or three other things that were interesting about the practice. The first and most obvious was that they played the whole of it on one side of the field. This was really intriguing. We all knew that Johan Claassen did not really like outsiders to watch Springboks practices, and having watched three, I could understand why. But playing the whole of the practice on the far side of the field was another thing. There they were jammed up against the back of a corrugated iron stand which faced out on to an adjoining pitch, tucked safely away from prying ears. Unfortunately, it meant that they did all their lineout practice with the sun behind them, which might have been convenient, but was unrealistic. It inspired the thought that perhaps they intended to dig up half the pitch in front of the Glasshouse at Ellis Park and do something useful with it, like sow it with cabbages. Certainly, it would have made the task of defending against the Lions a whole lot easier. I must confess I had never even thought of it.

Two other things stood out a mile. Ian Kirkpatrick was far and away the best kicker in the Springbok squad and Johan Claassen will never make a tight head prop. Kirkpatrick was the selector in charge of the backs, and even though he finished playing years before, he was the one kicker who could put the ball where the opposing full-back did not want it and he was the one kicker who could take a kick-off and put the ball exactly where his forwards DID want it.

The lack of an opposition pack meant that the selectors had to rake up a few reserves to scrummage against the Springboks in their semi-opposed practice, and Mr. Claassen himself scrummaged at tight-head prop. Nick Bezuidenhout lifted him out of the scrum and hung him up to dry with his feet dangling in the air. Cuts do not come unkinder than that. Even more important, it did not help the Springbok cause much, either. They could have done with twenty or thirty good solid scrums against a ten-man pack.

The Lions trained again at Ellis Park, and Ian McGeechan had recovered sufficiently to train with them. Chris Ralston moved rather better than he had the day before, but still looked in some discomfort. Gordon Brown watched anxiously in case the members of his golf team came to any harm.

They survived the session and set off at once to the Killarney Golf Club, where Gary Player met them and took them in to lunch. He could not have been a kinder or more generous host, and the Lions found him fascinating company. He had just returned from winning the British Open championship, which followed his success in the U.S. Masters earlier in the year. This meant that he had won eight major titles in his career. For most of that time, Gary Player had been conducting an indefatigable public relations exercise both for his country and for his country's sporting image, and although he must have needed every second of relaxation and family privacy he could find in his crowded schedule, he was so grateful to the Lions for their decision to tour South Africa in the face of political pressure that he went out of his way to make a day available when he heard that Gordon Brown wanted to meet him and to play a round of golf with him.

'We are greatly in their debt,' he said. 'I hear they have had trouble with accommodation in some of their hotels. Well, I think that they are each entitled to a suite.'

A gallery of two or three hundred people had gathered near the first tee when they emerged from the clubhouse and while Mike Gibson wondered about which nervous twitch he should use to hit the ball, Gary Player smilingly posed for pictures with the Lions in the sunshine. He barely came up to Gordon Brown's shoulder but the intensity of his personality and his immaculate choice of clothes dominated the whole group.

While they were waiting, Gary Player ascertained that both Gordon Brown and Mike Gibson played off somewhere near ten handicap, and that Gareth Edwards would cheerfully count himself lucky to break a hundred on any golf course at any time. 'Gareth and I will play you two,' he said. 'Better ball. Gareth gets a shot on every hole and you get shots according to handicap.' That suited everyone, and with many a nervous swallow, the Lions walked across to the first tee.

Gordon Brown drove first, and despite the splint on his right hand, he hit a nice easy ball a very long way down the middle. The crowd burst into rapturous applause, though having seen Brown play elsewhere, I knew it was not a particularly long drive by his standards. When he can really get his right hand into the ball, he can hit it a country mile.

Mike Gibson went next and hit a most uncharacteristic shot, skying the ball about 200 yards into the short rough on the right of the fairway. 'Oh Michael,!' he said in justified self-reproach, because after a session with Harry Middleton, a fellow-Ulsterman now professional at the Walmer Country Club in Port Elizabeth, Gibson had started to take the club away straighter and had been hitting his drives like rifle bullets.

Then it was Gareth Edwards' turn. Like Sean Lynch on the 1971 tour and like that unforgettable character from P. G. Woodhouse, Gareth Edwards is a golfer who never spares himself in his efforts to do the ball a violent injury. He is tremendously strong, with such power in his chest and arms and legs that when he does make contact properly he can hit a six iron as far as most people can hit a drive, but at that stage he had not learned how to swing easily and most of that ferocious power was used in doing a violent injury to the ground just behind the ball. He had two unavailing attempts to advance the ball materially, and then shouted, to the vast amusement of the crowd, 'Let's get on out of here.'

Gary Player smiled with them and then stood up and gave everyone present the equivalent of six lessons with nothing more than his practice swing. The unwind of his hips and the drive from his legs before his hands even moved from the top of his backswing, and the grace and the rhythm of it all made an unforgettable visual impression. He then drove his ball, the big American ball, about 260 yards into position alpha double plus in the middle of the fairway. Still, Gordon Brown made a par four, which gave him a nett birdie, and as Gary Player's own birdie putt hit the hole and lipped out, not for the last time, the Lions went one up.

The Lions lost that lead, but they had a chance to go one up again at the seventh, where Mike Gibson had two putts from twelve feet to win the hole. Normally, his short game is soundness itself, but he put his first putt a long way past and missed the return. Gary Player made only a couple of birdies on the first nine holes but his approach putting was so accurate that his score could have been something ridiculous. After watching yet another putt stop about an inch and a half from the hole, Mike Gibson looked at it and said, with a perfectly straight face, 'We'll give you that.'

By the turn, it was obvious that the Lions' decision to play Chris Ralston in the test match was the right one, because Gordon Brown was in such pain from his injured hand that he could not begin to do himself justice on the golf course. His shots sprayed all over the place.

This left Mike Gibson to do battle against Gary Player on his own and inevitably, he could not match his opponent's consistency, even with his handicap allowance. To cap it all, Gareth Edwards stepped in to improve his partner's score on one hole with a nett birdie. First he smashed a six iron about twenty yards short of where Mike Gibson had put his drive and then he projected another iron shot on the green. With Albert Agar and John Hart joining the gallery and smiling with approval, Edwards stalked off jauntily to the next tee and Brown and Gibson looked at him as if they had been nurturing a viper in their bosom.

By then, Gary Player had persuaded his partner to swing more easily at the ball, but although this brought about a considerable improvement, it was not enough to persuade Gareth Edwards that the British Open and U.S. Masters champion could afford to relax his efforts for a moment. At one beautiful short hole to a diagonal green across a lake, a hole which Gary Player insisted was the best short hole in South Africa, Edwards was visibly alarmed to see his partner proving to Gibson that a four iron was plenty of club to reach the green. 'I could get there with a six,' said Player, and proceeded to do so. 'I could even get there with a seven,' he said, and reached into his bag.

Edwards leapt to restrain him. 'Don't strain yourself partner,' he said in a very Welsh accent. 'Yew're doing all right as it is.'

The Lions caused a fair amount of consternation on the nearby motorway when one of their shots went bounding down the centre lane, but they did have one moment of glory. That was when Gibson outdrove Player. As they came to where their drives had stopped, and Gibson saw that his ball was indeed 10 yards in front of his opponent's, Gary Player said, 'Great shot, Mike. Man, what a beautiful swing.' Gibson, standing in the middle of a group of delighted spectators, had a grin on his face which went right round to the back of his neck. 'I can go home now,' he said.

The match ended at the fifteenth but Gary Player happily completed the course in 67 shots and even though it was nearly dark, he gave an exhibition of bunker play at the 17th which delighted the Lions. He also invited them to his home for dinner with his family afterwards and kept them absorbed for hours with talk about golf and the theory of the game. When it was all over, and the Lions were on their way back to their hotel, they looked at each other in disbelief. 'What a day,' they said. 'What a day!'

CHAPTER 31

The Final Test

THE same thing might have been said after the Lions had played South Africa in the last test, though for rather different reasons. It was a drawn match which either side could have won, and it ended with a steaming controversy about the refereeing without which no British Lions tour of South Africa would be complete.

Before the match, there were signs that some of the Lions were not in the right frame of mind to play well. They had not prepared for the match as thoroughly as they had for the first three tests and there was a natural feeling of reaction and tour weariness. In addition to that, the stomach upset which had troubled McGeechan earlier in the week had spread to Bennett, Milliken and Windsor, and although all of them recovered in time to play, their physical well-being must have been lowered. Bennett in particular looked much out of sorts. Windsor had his troubles, too, but these were aggravated by a nasty head injury he received in the first ten minutes of the match.

This had its origins in a scrum. As the forwards formed up, there was an altercation which provoked Windsor to throw a punch before the front rows went down and the referee gave South Africa a penalty kick which Snyman took accurately from 45 yards to give the Springboks the lead.

South Africa soon exacted further retribution for Windsor's punch because after McLauchlan had burst away from Bennett's kick-off to set up a ruck, Windsor was kicked on the head by Kritzinger and was cut so badly that he had to have a huge bandage wrapped around it. Even then, he looked as if he might have been concussed, because his subsequent performance was unusually laboured.

When Windsor had been repaired, he threw the ball into a lineout on the left. The Springboks made a mistake and conceded a scrum which the Lions won and Bennett had an unsuccessful drop for goal. The Springboks dropped out from their 25 and once again Irvine using the Lions' tactic of kicking the ball dead for another 25 drop-out if they became isolated behind their support.

Roux, who had recovered from the ankle injury he received in practice, found a short touch the second time but the Lions retained control of the ball first in a ruck following the lineout and then in a scrum. Davies took the ball to the right and Edwards threw a huge reverse pass to Bennett on the other side. J. P. R. Williams came into the line and J. J. Williams chipped the ball into the corner. With J. P. R. Williams committed to coming into the line, Roux tried to find touch but missed and Bennett went back to collect the ball.

When he turned, the Lions' fly-half put up a high kick in front of the posts. The Lions won the maul and Edwards grub-kicked towards the left corner where Pope had to push the ball into touch. Windsor threw the ball crooked into the lineout, and the Springboks were given a scrum but by then they were defending uncomfortably close to their line, and sure enough, the Lions squeezed a score out of it.

The Lions wheeled the scrum as Bayvel put in the ball and the Springboks lost control of their channelling. Instead of moving the ball across to the far side of the scrum to protect their scrum-half, the Springbok forwards let it come out on the left and as Bayvel picked it up and went to pass, Edwards just managed to knock his right arm. The ball went loose in the Springbok goal and Uttley came off the left of the Lions' scrum and dived for it with Pope, the Springbok right wing. The referee had positioned himself in goal, well ahead of the players, and was in no doubt that Uttley had beaten Pope to the touch and gave him a try.

Bennett converted the try, though not very convincingly. It was not a difficult kick but he topped it and it only just skated over the bar. That seemed to disturb Bennett's confidence because his place kicking afterwards had none of its usual authority.

The Springboks were just as unsure of themselves. J. G. Williams retrieved the kick-off, only to see his backs knock on in midfield and when the Springboks won a scrum after a crooked lineout throw by Windsor a few minutes later, Bayvel fumbled the ball and Kritzinger compounded the error by picking up the ball from an offside position. That gave Irvine a kick at goal from 50 yards. He pushed it to the right of the posts.

Both sides went on making mistakes. South Africa knocked on from the 25 drop-out and the Lions were penalised in the subsequent scrum. The referee indicated to Edwards that he should not take so much time to put the ball in, which showed that at least one referee in South Africa had noted this tactic of the Lions. He then gave a penalty kick for picking the ball out of the scrum. South Africa knocked on in the lineout after Snyman had found touch but were then given another chance because Bennett kicked to touch after the Lions had won the scrum. Uttley was penalised for being offside in that lineout and Snyman kicked for goal from rather more than 50 yards. Snyman built a noticeably high tee with the sand from the bucket brought on by the ball-boy and ended up by kicking more of the sand than he did of the ball. Exactly the same thing happened five minutes later when Davies was penalised in a maul following a drop-out from the Lions' 25. That kick was only 35 yards from the posts.

Cronje had a wild drop-kick at goal from a lineout and although the Lions were given a scrum at the maul after the drop-out from the 25, Ellis caught Edwards for almost the first time in the series and really dumped him. The Lions scraped the ball into touch deep in defence and when J. G. Williams caught the ball in the lineout, their midfield players were caught offside and Snyman kicked his second penalty goal.

Neither side could achieve any continuity. J. G. Williams broke through after Ralston had made the first take at a lineout and turned to see the ball knocked on. McGeechan missed touch and Roux, for his part, caught a ball one yard outside his 25 and rather deliberately kicked the ball straight into touch on the full. This must have depressed his forwards no end, because even though Windsor threw the ball crooked into the lineout, he won the scrum against the head and Edwards kicked for a pressure position which only just missed the corner flag.

South Africa had a chance to work their way out of defence when Milliken threw a pass behind J. J. Williams but their control of the scrummage was not good enough to assure them of quality possession and they gave the ball away to the Lions again. Davies, Edwards and Bennett attacked from one scrum, and J. P. R. Williams surged contemptuously past Bayvel and Snyman from another. The Lions' full-back made so much ground up the right touch-line that he set up a scoring position.

He was forced into touch near the Springbok line where Muller, perhaps with awful memories of the fiasco in Port Elizabeth uppermost in his mind, threw the ball crooked and gave the Lions a scrum. The Lions won this comfortably enough, and Edwards went to the right to the blind side. It was a perfectly orthodox situation but Ellis stayed on the side of the Springbok scrum as if he was nailed to it and Muller had to make up his mind whether to come in for Edwards or stay on his wing and mark Irvine.

Most of the top wingers in Europe are firmly of the opinion that the defending winger in this situation must stay out and mark his opponent and leave the man inside to the cover. Admittedly, Ellis was so unbelievably slow in moving off the side of the scrum that Grobler was away first but Muller clearly thought that neither was likely to stop Edwards so he came inside and made a desperate lunge for man and ball. As Muller came at him, Edwards squeezed a pass away to Irvine on the right wing and left him a clear run to score halfway in to the posts. Roux, the Springbok full-back, was nowhere in sight, either. Again, it was not a difficult conversion, but Bennett kicked that one even worse than he did the first.

South Africa tried hard to repair the damage in the five minutes before half-time and had three chances to do so. Roux knocked on in a dummy scissors move after J. G. Williams had won a lineout in the Lions' half, and then Grobler knocked on a few yards from the line when Bayvel broke to the blind side with a heel against the head. Finally, in the last minute of the half, Edwards was penalised for taking too long to put the ball into a scrum and Snyman took a kick at goal which he missed.

Bezuidenhout had been showing signs of distress and at half-time he went off for treatment to a back injury. He returned for the beginning of the second half and was just in time to see a confrontation between McBride and van Heerden. McBride also took strong exception to the second of two penalty kicks awarded to South Africa by the referee and he wagged his finger at Max Baise so forbiddingly that it looked as if the Lions might be penalised a further ten yards for arguing. It was noticeable in this game that both captains had plenty of advice to offer to the referee, and it was something about which Marais made a joke afterwards.

The Springboks gained a lot of ground with the second kick, forcing the Lions to put the ball into touch with no appreciable advance, and although Bayvel was in difficulties from the lineout and knocked on, the Springboks won the scrum against the head and drove past Uttley before setting up a good maul on the blind side. They won the second phase sweetly, too, and it was only when the ball was moved across to the backs on the open side that the attack was spoiled by yet another mistake. Cronje knocked on.

This could have cost South Africa a score, because Edwards made 50 yards down the right with a kick from the back of the scrum. Muller threw in the ball crookedly again and the Lions were given a penalty kick in the scrum. Irvine took it instead of Bennett, even though it was from the 25, but he too kicked badly and pushed the ball out to the right.

The only thing decisive about the play at that particular time was the medical opinion passed by the doctor on Bezuidenhout's back injury when he finally retired from the field. Snyman had caught the ball from Irvine's kick ahead as Bezuidenhout departed and the Springbok fly-half duly found touch. At that stage, Bezuidenhout was only in the mouth of the players' tunnel, and it is quite a long way up to the dressing rooms at Ellis Park, but the Lions only had time to throw the ball into the lineout and begin to form themselves into a scrum as South Africa knocked it on before 'Rampie' Stander appeared on the field as a substitute to win his first cap for his country.

Coming fresh into the game after a quarter of an hour of the second half, Stander was able to make the Springbok scrummage look more comfortable than it did at any time in the series. Ever since the Transvaal game, Bayvel had fancied his chance as a kicker against the Lions and the tourists must have been glad to see him indulging himself as much as he did. He wasted some good ball and never more so than when his forwards gave him a strike against the head and he kicked it away for Irvine to make a mark. Bayvel was lucky indeed to see South Africa make a try from that lineout after Irvine had kicked through the mark to touch.

The Springboks threw the ball long and Grobler judged his movement backwards as neatly as a tennis player under a smash to deflect the ball to Ellis. The Springbok flanker ran across field at his centres but Schlebusch straightened the line of attack with a powerful run through the middle and passed to Pope on the right. For the first time in the series, Pope was really able to run with the ball and the Lions' defence on the left was notably less than resolute as the Springbok right wing burst deep across the advantage line before passing inside. Schlebusch missed the ball but Cronje was close behind in support and he picked it up off the ground before ploughing over the line to score. Even though Snyman missed the conversion, the Springboks were delighted with themselves. It was their first try of the series.

For the next quarter of an hour, the Springboks looked as if they would win. Ellis led a furious drive to the left and Slattery twice had to hasten back from offside positions as J. G. Williams caught the ball and controlled it from lineouts. Bayvel broke a long way past Uttley from a scrum on the right and J. J. Williams had to scramble the ball into touch as the Springbok scrum-half kicked ahead. Snyman and Muller attacked on the left and then the Springboks brought off a good dummy scissors from a lineout. They spoiled it at the end with a lobbed pass, though, and McGeechan was able to intercept. Still, McGeechan had to find touch under pressure, and when J. G. Williams caught the ball in the lineout again, Davies was offside in midfield and Snyman kicked another penalty goal to give his side the lead at 13-10.

South Africa then made two mistakes from lineouts which cost them valuable ground and they had to scrummage back on their 25. The Lions put the ball into the scrum out on the right, and Edwards ran away to the blind side without the ball. By that time, South Africa had seen the move so often that they ought to have been prepared for it, but both Bayvel and Roux took the bait and moved forward offside. The referee pointed first at Bayvel but when he saw that no advantage would accrue to the Lions, he turned and penalised Roux in front of his posts. Irvine kicked the goal, but placed the ball so close inside the left post that the touch-judge on the other post waited for his colleague to raise his flag before he raised his own. Five minutes to go, and the score was 13-13.

Even then, both teams had further chances to win the match. South Africa made their first with a lovely old-fashioned break by Snyman at fly-half. He ran out of defence and changed pace to cut clean through to J. P. R. Williams with Muller overlapping in support to his left. Snyman was in position 'A' and Williams was in position 'Z' and there was nothing that the Lions' full-back could do about it. All Snyman had to do was draw Williams and time his pass to Muller and all Muller had to do was catch it and make sure that he did not over-run the ball. Snyman did his part beautifully. Muller fell down on his job from start to finish.

It looked very much as if Muller was nervous about his lack of speed, because in his anxiety to get on his way, he first overran the ball, which forced Snyman to pass it behind his shoulder, and then knocked it on. It was the cleanest opening South Africa had made in four test matches and the only time they had a chance to run in a try between the posts.

South Africa still pressed forward. They took a tapped kick when Uttley was penalised for being offside at the second of two more lineouts won by J. G. Williams. The Lions were penalised again for encroaching within ten yards of that kick and Snyman found touch deep in the Lions' half. It was a good position and South Africa held it long enough to have the chance of improving it. They won a lineout which would have enabled them to do that, but instead of initiating a close-passing rush, Grobler astonished friend and foe alike by kicking the ball straight to J. P. R. Williams.

The Lions' full-back kicked the ball as deep as he could and Roux touched it down for a drop-out from the Springbok 25. South Africa knocked on from the drop-out and the Lions won a scrum which Edwards kicked over his forwards. Roux could have let it run over the line for another 25 but instead raised just as many eyebrows as Grobler had by catching the ball and kicking for touch so badly that he gave the Lions a throw on the Springbok 25.

This was a position from which the Lions had a real hope of achieving something, and when Ralston won the lineout, J. P. R. Williams came into the threequarter line and broke through the middle of the field. Williams had shown such spectacularly successful footwork in three long runs in the match, as well as in several minor instances where he had to make enough room to kick, that he looked more capable than any of the Lions' backs of breaking clean through to score, particularly as he had the strength to supplement his recently developed skill as a runner.

However, he was held just short of the line but he managed to keep on his feet and turn so that he could release the ball to Slattery coming up in support. Slattery drove for the line and crossed it to the left of the posts. He was tackled head on by Cronje who fell backwards in a sitting position with Slattery on top of him and Marais driving in from Slattery's right.

The referee was positioned in goal, beyond the players, just as he had been for Uttley's try, and for an instant the ball was trapped on the top of Cronje's leg. Slattery forced the ball down backwards, beyond Cronje's leg, but by the time he had pushed it to the ground, the referee had blown his whistle for a five yard scrum.

There was much talk at the time that the referee was in error to award the Lions a five yard scrum, but this was the only decision possible if he had made up his mind that the attacking side could not ground the ball. The Lions won the scrum and J. J. Williams was held short of the line. As soon as that happened, the referee blew his whistle for the end of the match and ran off the pitch.

The Lions were clearly disgusted that the referee had not given them a try, and Bennett ran across to pass a very emphatic opinion as Max Baise ran past him, but both the television film and various photographs vindicate the referee, and he did not have the opportunity of looking at either. The photographs show that the ball emerging underneath Cronje's body had apparently been dropped and the television film shows that the referee's view was obscured when he made his decision to give a five yard scrum. There is no doubt that Slattery did get the ball down, but equally, there is no doubt that for a second or two, it was stopped.

Max Baise himself said afterwards, 'Mauls in that sort of situation can be dangerous, and I don't like to let them develop. The ball was stopped and other players were arriving quickly. I gave a five yard scrum. I don't know whether Slattery got the ball down afterwards or not. I had blown my whistle by then.'

The referee said that the Lions had been quite happy to accept his decision when he gave Uttley his try, even though the Springboks had protested. 'I was in the same position both times,' he said, 'and that was the way I saw it.'

Max Baise admitted that he had been under constant pressure from both captains almost throughout the game. 'Hannes Marais was right when he said what he did after the match,' he said. 'Hannes made a joke of it, but it is not so funny if you happen to be the referee in the middle. Other players hear what is being said and it undermines your authority. It's something I don't like at all.'

This development will be familiar to those who watch Association football on television in Europe. Dissent and the rejection of authority have become so widespread that it constitutes one of the biggest problems in the game, especially as the close-up cameras lovingly portray every detail and every syllable of the foul-mouthed wrangling. It would be regrettable indeed if that spread into Rugby football.

There had been talk that the Lions would have asked Max Baise to referee all four tests if the South African Board had put him on the international panel each time. He referred to that wryly, and asked, 'Do you think they would have asked me again if this match had been the second test?'

I said that I doubted it very much. 'Touring teams almost invariably choose the referee they think will do them most good,' I said, 'but they will only go on choosing him as long as he keeps his nose clean.'

Max Baise nodded. I explained that in Europe, the practice of allowing the teams involved to have any say in the choice of referee had been abandoned for international matches, because it is obviously invidious and because the first principle of law has always been that it has to be above the interests of the parties involved.

Unfortunately, this system does not yet apply to touring teams, because South Africa, Australia and New Zealand have not yet accepted the principle of appointing neutral referees, but there are indications that even this obstacle may soon be demolished.

Dr. Danie Craven, who is now the most influential figure in the world of Rugby, has changed his own view on the subject. He always opposed the idea of neutral referees but now that he has seen how effectively the principle has worked in South Africa's domestic Rugby, he is prepared to accept them in international matches.

South Africa's new stance on the question of neutral referees opens up a whole new world for referees like Max Baise. He is an international class referee by anyone's standards, and if Australia and New Zealand can agree with South Africa that it is time neutral referees were appointed to all International Board matches, men like Max Baise and John Pring of New Zealand can look forward to a valuable widening of their experiences.

After their indignation had died down, the Lions accepted that a draw was probably a fair result, even though it had denied them the pleasure of winning all 22 of their matches in South Africa. The Lions knew that they had not played well and that their back row had not taken command in the way it might have done. Mervyn Davies especially was nothing like the force he had been in the first three matches of the series and Roger Uttley had a distinctly uncomfortable time in defence against Paul Bayvel in the second half.

The Lions could not blame their inertia on lack of possession. They put the ball into 31 scrums in the match, whereas the Springboks only put it into ten. It is true that the Springboks did appreciably better than the Lions in the lineout, and that J. G. Williams achieved the sort of return that he should have achieved throughout the series, but the breakdown of the scrummage ball indicated clearer than anything just what the Springboks were doing with the lineout ball Williams won.

Most of the time, they were making mistakes with it. They were knocking it on, or losing control of it when driving, or losing it in mauls, or throwing it away with bad passes and bad kicks. Admittedly, the Lions lost the strikes against the head 4-1, and they had four penalty kicks awarded against them in the scrums whereas the Springboks had none, but even so, the Lions still finished up with a healthy balance of scrummage possession. The difference was that in this match, the Lions' use of that ball simply to achieve pressure positions was not as rewarding as it should have been having regard to the amount of ball won and to the quality of the opposition. The Lions had no-one to blame but themselves for failing to win a very poor match.

CHAPTER 32

There WAS a Lot of Kicking

THE 1974 British Lions played 22 matches in South Africa. They won 21 of them and drew the other and so remained unbeaten. They scored 729 points on tour and had 207 scored against them. They were seriously challenged in only seven of their matches and in three of those, they eventually won by more than a single score. They were seriously challenged in only one of the four test matches. That was the last game of the tour, by which time they had already won the series 3-0. They scored ten tries against South Africa in the series and had only one scored against them. In eight consecutive Saturday games from the first test to the end of the tour, they had only one try scored against them and that was in the last match.

Nothing like this record had ever been achieved by a British Isles Rugby Union team in South Africa since 1896, when the team captained by John Hammond won 19 of its 21 matches and lost only one in winning the test series 3-1.

The top scorer on that tour had been the full-back, J. F. Byrne, with 123 points. Andy Irvine finished the 1974 tour with 156 points, even though he scored only eight points in the first six games.

There were other individual records, too. J. J. Williams scored six tries against S.W. Districts at Mossel Bay to beat the record of five set by W. Wallace in 1924, and in the same game, Alan Old scored 37 points. This was not only a record for a British Lion but it was also a record for any tourist in South Africa.

Alun Thomas, the manager of the 1974 Lions, was in no doubt about what all this meant. Speaking in the jubilation of victory after the Lions had won the series 3-0 in Port Elizabeth, he described his team as, 'the greatest Lions team in history.'

Such enthusiasm was understandable. England felt just the same after they had finished their tour of South Africa unbeaten and had defeated South Africa 18-9 at Ellis Park in 1972. England felt just the same after they had beaten New Zealand in Auckland in 1973.

On the first occasion, England had just lost all four matches in the championship in Europe. On the second occasion, they went home and finished at the bottom of the international championship. England discovered then that all things are relative.

Of course, all winning teams like to think that they are 'the greatest' just as all losing teams like to think theat they have lost to 'the greatest,' because that makes the pain of losing so much easier to bear. However, British Rugby would be just as unwise to draw false conclusions from the 1974 Lions' tour of South Africa as the Springboks were when they came back from Australia in a glow of euphoria after winning all their matches in 1971. This tour persuaded the Springboks to form completely false estimates of their playing strength, their captaincy and their coaching. They ignored the Lions' win in New Zealand in 1971. They dismissed the England tour of South Africa in 1972 as, 'just one of those things.' They thought that it could not happen again, even though they had lost three of their best players from that 1972 team. Piet Greyling and Syd Nomis had retired and 'Joggie' Jansen was not available because of injury, and what was even more damaging, Africa did not have players of anything like the same class to replace them.

That tour by England revealed the true poverty of South African Rugby. It showed that judged by the standards of the Barbarians' game against the All Blacks in 1973, which represented what the Lions had achieved in New Zealand in 1971, the true measure of superiority for any self-respecting Lions team against South Africa in 1974 ought to have been at least forty points a match.

After all, England had played seven of the Lions' fixtures, which represented a third of a full Lions' tour, and no market research organisation anywhere in the world would need to take a sample as big as 33 per cent. to provide an accurate analysis of the subject being examined. The strange thing was that British Rugby ignored the implications of the England tour almost as completely as the South Africans. It never seemed to occur to them that for the time being, at any rate, South Africa might have ceased to be a major power in the world of Rugby. Even when the Lions' tour was over, they did not look back and compare what they had done with what England had done and ask themselves whether, with all their extra resources, they should not have done better.

As the Lions were preparing to start their tour, the Lancashire county team played in Rhodesia and flew down to Port Elizabeth for a match against Eastern Province. Lancashire were considerably under strength when they left London and by the time they played Eastern Province they included seven or eight players who were not first choices, yet the Lancashire forwards had the better of their opponents in all phases of possession.

South Africans knew that John Burgess, the Lancashire coach, had just been appointed coach of England for the coming season, so they asked him what he thought of it all. 'Well,' he said, 'if what we have seen here is at all representative of South African forward play, then the Lions will win the series very easily.' It turned out to be an accurate assessment. It was the great good fortune of Alun Thomas, Syd Millar and Bill McBride to reap the benefits of all the hard work done in British Rugby in the previous eight years and to feast off some of the fruits of that labour while touring through a barren land.

With that pool of forwards established in 1971, and with world class players in the key positions of half-back and full-back, the Lions could afford to make an indifferent team selection and to leave three world class backs at home as well as three of their best forwards and still beat South Africa with something to spare.

Indeed, granted the same pool of props, the same half-backs, the same full-back and possibly the same number eight, British Rugby could have permutated any nine or ten players from forty and still have beaten South Africa. It was not even a contest. It was the men versus the boys.

Yet even with that sort of an advantage, the Lions played such a desperately unambitious game that many of the hundreds of supporters who had flocked out to see the second half of the tour were so bored with the football that they did not even bother to watch the midweek games. It was a forwards' tour. The backs were there just to make up the number. They had no significant influence in the councils of war and the team was the poorer for it.

This was the inevitable consequence of appointing a coach and a captain who were both tight forwards and who both came from the same club and the same country. Their vision of the game was restricted to the scrummage and to the tighter aspects of forward play. The work they did in this area was both thorough and effective and they sustained it until the end of the tour, but scrummaging ought to be a means to an end, and not an end in itself. Their view of the contribution of the backs was strongly influenced by their desire to keep the ball close to the forwards and they did not have the flexibility to expand their approach when they saw that such a cautious approach was no longer necessary. It was miserly stuff compared with the visions of grandeur of the 1971 tour, visions which were realised on that unforgettable day in Cardiff when the Barbarians played the All Backs in 1973. The 1971 tour embraced the aspirations and the philosophies of Llanelli, London Welsh and Wales at that time. They were the clubs and the national team of Carwyn James, the coach, and John Dawes, the captain. The 1974 tour embraced the aspirations and the philosophies of Ballymena, Ballymena and Ireland. There was a world of difference between the two concepts of the game.

South Africa will never know how lucky they were. Had the Lions played them on their merits or had the Lions used their backs with the confidence of the 1971 team, the Springboks would have suffered at least two defeats even bigger than the 44-0 thrashing they gave Scotland in 1951.

Unfortunately, the Lions' management went to South Africa thinking that the task of winning would be much more difficult than it turned out to be. They had suffered in South Africa as players themselves and they went there with the traditional tin-hat and slit-trench mentality of British teams in that country. None of them had been in South Africa since 1968 and they could not believe that the whole situation had been transformed and that the Springboks no longer stood supreme in their own country.

Accordingly, for those games that threatened to be difficult, the 1974 Lions set out to scrummage and to kick, just as Syd Millar said they would. They set out to peel the ball from lineouts or to drive it; to keep it tight or to keep it in front of the forwards. Above all, they set out to make no mistakes behind the advantage line. J. P. R. Williams stayed back as almost an orthodox full-back, despite his unrivalled ability as a counter-attacker, and Gareth Edwards developed the rolling kick to the blind side. The chief requirement of the centres was enough physical presence to take a tackle and set up a maul.

The Lions almost never used their set ball to attack. They kicked for position instead. They never sought to counter-attack from their own 25. They kicked for touch instead. They preferred to wait until they were in their opponents' half of the field before they attempted anything. Better still, they preferred to wait until they were five yards from their opponents' line.

That was the way that the All Blacks used to play, with centres like Ian MacRae to take the tackles and to set up the mauls, and for twenty years we in Britain jeered at it. 'No wonder you never have any backs,' we said. 'You never give them the ball, even though your forwards are winning it all the time.'

That was the style of football that the Lions rejected so emphatically in 1971, and the fact that the Lions succeeded with it in South Africa in 1974 was simply an indictment of South Africa.

Above all, though, it was a betrayal of the traditions of British Rugby with its great heritage of back play. There was indeed a lot of kicking.

For years, British Rugby had worked to improve its forward organisation so that it could release the skills of its backs. The pot of gold at the end of the rainbow was always 50 per cent of the ball. 'If only we can win 50 per cent of the ball.' Our coaches said it so many times, and they said it so wistfully.

In South Africa in 1974, the British Lions won more than 70 per cent of the ball. And what did they do with it? They played like the 1963 All Blacks, but you cannot possibly criticise the All Blacks and the Springboks for playing that sort of game and then say that it is all right for the Lions to play it.

The sad thing was that it was all so unnecessary. It was no good arguing that the Lions had to play as they did because their leading backs were not available to tour. The backs who went in their place may not have been the greatest defenders in the world and some of them may not have been the greatest footballers either but they were all a lot better than anything in South Africa.

In any case, the Lions' forwards were so much in command that the backs never had to do much defending anyway, and on the wings, they had runners in Andy Irvine and J. J. Williams who could have cut South Africa to pieces if J. P. R. Williams had been encouraged to set them up.

To some people, the end justified the means. They did not care how the Lions won, just as long as they *did* win. They did not stop to think of the implications for the future of British back play contained in the way the Lions played the game. They shut their minds to the fact that British back play would have no future if that style of play was adopted. They were not remotely concerned about the battle for the hearts and the minds of the young, and of the enthusiasm of all those selfless people who teach the young how to play. Winning was all that mattered.

John Dawes went to New Zealand as captain of the Lions in 1971 convinced that he was leading a missionary expedition to save a whole country from the burning. He said then, 'Look at the changes we have seen since we were here two years ago with Wales. Soccer is on the increase everywhere. Look at what is happening in the schools.

'Everywhere we go, our players see the same thing—more and more soccer and less and less Rugby. Schoolmasters are not supporting Rugby in the way they did, and who can blame them? Rugby in this country is no fun for a schoolboy. He has no freedom of expression. He has to conform to a pattern, the same dull pattern which you see right through the game. It is efficient, I grant you, but because it is so dull it contains the seeds of its own destruction.

'Look at the teams we have played so far. They all play in the same way and they all train in the same way. Who would want to be a back in New Zealand? He is only there to stop the other side and return the ball to the forwards. They all look as if they have come out of a machine.

'We must show them here that our way is so much more interesting than theirs. I really do believe that if the All Blacks win this series playing ten man Rugby, it will do irreparable damage to the game in New Zealand. It is for their own good that we must win.'

John Dawes needed to continued his missionary work in South Africa in 1974—with the British Lions. That was exactly the way the Lions played and only a hypocrite or someone very ignorant of Rugby football would have pretended otherwise.

Of course, if you are playing against a team which is beating you consistently for possession, as the Lions were in 1971, then you have to live off your wits as John Dawes and Barry John did, but if you are playing against a team which has nothing to offer either fore or aft, as the Lions were in 1974, then you can play the game on any terms you choose.

The Lions chose to use their backs to stop the other side and to return the ball to the forwards. It was efficient, I grant you, but it was dull, and because it was so dull it contained the seeds of its own destruction, or at any rate, the destruction of British back play.

Fortunately, those seeds are unlikely to flower, because each of the four home countries which make up a Lions team has its own way of playing the game. No doubt Ireland will go on playing the same sort of Rugby as that played by the Lions in 1974, and perhaps Scotland will be tempted to do the same, but it is hard to imagine Wales or England presiding over the demise of the threequarter. Most of the supporters who watched the second half of the Lions tour were Welsh, and those who had also been in New Zealand in 1971 had no doubt of their preference.

Syd Millar justified his choice of tactics by saying, 'It's winning Rugby.'

Indeed it was, but England had played winning Rugby in 1972, and they had played it with infinitely more style. In that respect, a comparison of results is interesting, particularly if you adjust the Lions' scores to the points values applying in 1972.

Here is a table of those results:—

	England	Lions
Natal	19- 0	30- 6
Western Province	9- 6	15- 6
Proteas	11- 6	32- 6
Leopards	36- 3	46- 9
Northern Transvaal	13-13	14-12
Griqualand West	60-21	57-12
South Africa	18- 9	17- 8 (average score of four matches)

The similarity between the achievements of England and the Lions is truly remarkable. In only one of the games, that against the Proteas, is there a significant difference in the scores.

However, there were considerable differences in the touring progarmmes. England's was far more intensive. England had to start their tour with successive matches against two of South Africa's strongest provinces, they went with 27 players instead of the 30 allowed to the Lions, they went without David Duckham, Peter Dixon and Roger Uttley, they had nothing like the luxury of a training camp in which to spend ten days to prepare, and they had a quarter of the Lions' playing resources.

Despite all that, and despite the fact they they had just lost all four matches in the international championship for the first time in their history, and despite the fact that they were playing a better Springbok team, they achieved the same results as the Lions. This would elevate the England team of 1972, complete with its wooden spoon, to quite unexpected heights if the Lions team of 1974 was indeed, 'the greatest team in history.'

In fact, of course, the 1974 Lions were nothing like as good as the 1971 Lions and they, in turn, would probably bow the knee, at least as far as individual ability is concerned, to the 1959 team. The 1974 Lions were not even as good as the Welsh national team of 1970 and 1971.

The 1974 forwards were admirable. Syd Millar had technically one of the best equipped packs ever to go on tour from the British Isles and he used it to produce a top-class scrummage which outplayed the Springboks from first to last. Fran Cotton broke through into the highest class as a tight head prop and on the loose head, Ian McLauchlan took on all-comers with a rasping disdain which never allowed him to accept defeat even on those rare occasions when he was in difficulty. Behind them, Bill McBride and Gordon Brown locked the scrum with unfailing power.

The lineout was more vulnerable because of McBride's lack of ball-winning ability, but thanks to the development of Brown as an all-round forward and thanks to the inadequacies of the South Africans' team analysis, this potential weakness was hidden until the last match, and even then it was not fully exploited.

The loose forwards played their part, too. Mervyn Davies gathered himself to make another great contribution at number eight. He made nonsense of the opinions of his own countrymen that he was past his best and that he would lose his place to Andy Ripley. Roger Uttley took the chance that was offered on one flank and provided invaluable support in the lineout and in the tight-loose. On the other flank, Fergus Slattery played with an urgency and a committment which made it seem as if Jan Ellis was doodling.

The 1974 forwards were about on a par with those of the 1971 team. The pool of props was roughly the same, although no one in 1974 matched the technical excellence or the knowledge of the game of Ray McLoughlin at loose head in 1971. The locks were probably better because of the greater depth and because of the considerable advance made by Gordon Brown. The Lions' masseur Dave Goddess, gave Andy Irvine a shirt for being the most improved player on tour, but he was only comparing Irvine's dismal form in the first few games with what he achieved later. The most improved player from the British season to the one in South Africa was unquestionably Brown.

On the other hand, the loose forwards in 1971 were better than those in South Africa. John Taylor succeeded in keeping Fergus Slattery out of the test team in New Zealand, which was something Tony Neary could not do in South Africa, and Peter Dixon and Derek Quinnell operated at a higher level than their rivals three years later.

Behind the scrum, there was no comparison between the teams. The Lions in New Zealand had seven world class backs, and one who could not even get into the team, whereas the Lions in South Africa had only three. J. P. R. Williams was an even better player in South Africa than he was in New Zealand, and without an adversary as formidable as Sid Going against him, Gareth Edwards was able to do much as he liked at scrum-half, but I doubt whether even Phil Bennett would suggest that he was as good a player as Barry John. Above all, the 1974 backs were not encouraged to make full use of their ability.

The pity was that Alun Thomas did not consider that there was an imbalance between the backs and the forwards. Admittedly, the definition of the areas of managerial responsibility makes it more difficult now for a manager to have as much influence on the way a Lions team plays as he did in the years before 1962, but the backs needed a voice and they did not have one.

Part of the trouble was that Alun Thomas never overcame the lack of confidence he showed at the beginning of the tour when he was so apprehensive of the media. He was overconscious of the poor behaviour of the 1968 Lions and found it so hard to relax in this respect that he did not establish a good relationship with his players. He came to rely more and more on Syd Millar and Bill McBride and they in turn had to shoulder more and more of the work of management-player relations.

Millar and McBride did this work very well. However fortunate McBride may have been to captain the side, and however limited Millar's vision of the game may have been as a coach, they were both respected as men by the players. They knew which players needed encouragement and they knew when they needed it and they were careful to provide that encouragement. They were also able to provide calm and good sense in moments of stress. It was fortunate that the team was winning, otherwise it would have been much more difficult for Millar and McBride to keep the internal dissensions below the surface. Chute Visser, the Lions' liaison officer, sat at the side and watched it all with a shrewd eye. The South African Board must have been well informed about the inside workings of the touring party.

If there was no comparison between the 1971 and the 1974 teams, there was no comparison between the respective tours, either. Apart from four test matches in which they were battling against the odds almost every yard of the way, the Lions in New Zealand had to play Saturday games against Canterbury, Otago, Wellington, Hawke's Bay, Auckland, North Auckland and Taranaki and they had to play midweek games against the Maoris and Kign Country. All except one of those games were more difficult than any the Lions had to play in South Africa. The quality of the opposition was entirely different, too, at both provincial and national level. In New Zealand in 1971, the pressure never ceased. In South Africa in 1974, it never even started. Most of the Lions' matches in South Africa were little more than fitness runs of slightly varying severity.

The result was that the series had been won and lost before any of the new Lions even realised what it was like to play in a test match. In the first two tests, they were not under pressure of any sort and in the third game, the pressure only lasted half an hour. At no time were they faced with the problem of making decisions and sorting out options under pressure for 80 minutes, which is what test match Rugby should be about.

As Billy Steele said wonderingly after the first test at Newlands, 'It was like playing in a practice game.'

He was right. Until they arrived at Ellis Park, the Springboks had not played a test match. They had played three very loose, untidy and unsatisfactory Springbok trials in which the team looked like a combination of the Highly Improbables and the Totally Impossibles.

While all this was going on, the selection and the coaching of the Springbok team almost passed belief. Admittedly, South Africa had never had fewer good players in living memory but the way they moved players in and out of the team and the way they jumped from one concept of playing the game to another gave them no chance whatever of making the best use of the material available.

In the first three test matches alone, South Africa used 32 players. Whether out of mischief or not, the programme for the third test included a photographic gallery of Springboks who had played test Rugby against the Lions in 1974 but who were not then in the team. There were as many players in that gallery as there were in the team.

While they were losing the series, the Springboks were not able to match the Lions in the scrummage and at no time did they assemble either an effective lineout or an effective back row. They used six different half-backs in three matches while becoming progressively worse and they did not produce one back of genuine international class. Any one of those deficiencies would have been a severe embarrassment. Together they represented a situation of complete despair.

In the first test, the Springbok selectors ignored the rain in the Cape and chose a team to run the ball. They did that because Western Province had played well against the Lions the week before. In the mud and the rain of the test, however, it took South Africa more than an hour to pass the ball as far as the outside centre and when he presented Chris Pope with his Springbok blazer after the match, Dr. Danie Craven said that it must be the first time a Springbok had ever won a cap without touching the ball.

As it happened, the theory behind that Springbok selection was right. On the day, they should have used their loose forwards far more to try to drive the ball through the middle of the field but it was not their fault that the weather turned out to be so impossibly unsuited to the style of play they had in mind. At least they could look forward to three dry grounds in the rest of the series. All they had to do was sit tight, and repair the obvious weaknesses.

Above all, they had to stick to the same style of play, because there was no way that they could beat the Lions at nine-man Rugby.

Instead of that they dropped half their team and changed their style of play as well. They picked Gerald Bosch and Paul Bayvel at half-back, which was like shutting the stable door after the horse had gone. The day for kicking the ball was in the first test at Newlands. That was history. Now the Springboks had to run, run, run and drive, drive, drive. Not a bit of it. They decided to kick, kick, kick instead, and they did that because Transvaal had played well for an hour against the Lions the week before.

To make the whole venture even more incomprehensible, they chose two runners in the centre. Having picked a kicker like Bosch at fly-half, the only requirement from the centres was defence, because they were never going to be given the ball to run anyway. Some centres, of course, can both run and tackle conclusively but the two centres chosen by the Springboks for the second test were not among that number, and neither was the fly-half.

That being the case, it would have been logical to choose a loose forward combination of great strength in defence. The Springboks did not do that, either. They chose an attacking number eight who was out of his depth in defence and they flanked him with two players who made absolutely certain that his defensive limitations would be exposed. They also dropped Roy McCallum, who was by far the strongest defensive scrum-half who played against the Lions. The result was almost certainly the worst performance by a Springbok team in this century.

With their team 2-0 down in the series, the Springboks selectors either ignored or did not recognise the most important lesson to be learned from the first two games, and that was that with their scrummage under so much pressure, they had to concentrate on the lineout. If they were in any doubt of this, Northern Transvaal proved it for them on the afternoon before they sat down to pick their team for the third test. It could not have been a more timely demonstration of South Africa's last hope of salvation, but again, they ignored it. Far from attacking the Lions' comparative weakness in the lineout, the Springboks chose to play the third test with a lineout which had no capability at all. By the side of an error of that magnitude, the lapses which had allowed Roger Uttley and J. J. Williams to escape for two tests without being attacked from scrums on the right of the field were simply forgotten. This suited Uttley and Williams down to the ground.

The coaching of the Springboks was just as illogical as the

selection. In the first test, the great ploy was for Morné du Plessis to rush backwards from the scrums and the lineouts as if his life depended on it. He did this despite the fact that his scrum was being pushed all over the field, and he went on doing it. He seemed to be intent on covering Gareth Edwards' kicks to the corners rather than take the much more effective course of putting pressure on Edwards at source, as Northern Transvaal did.

What made the theory even more difficult to follow was that du Plessis had shown himself to be such an indifferent kicker. Almost every time he kicked the ball in his various games against the Lions, he either did something irresponsible or set up J. P. R. Williams.

In the second test, the Springboks first picked a horribly vulnerable midfield defence, and then denuded it further by moving Jan Ellis up to the front of the lineout. They then spent the afternoon kicking the ball away so that Phil Bennett could run back and pick it up and enjoy himself by counter-attacking through the middle of an empty field.

Bennett is really very good at this, even when there are a few people about, and for some time teams in Britain have gone to no end of trouble to make sure that they give him no ball to run back at them. They all try to force him to play with set ball only, because he does not use that with such confidence.

The Springbok selectors said that they had studied the "fillums" of all the international matches played in Britain in recent years. Therefore, they must have seen the Barbarians' match against the All Blacks in 1973, when Bennett went back to his own line at the beginning of the match and set off on a counter-attack which led to that unforgettable try by Gareth Edwards at the other end of the field. There was Bennett's counter-attacking ability in black and white, the black and white of the Barbarians' shirts. It ought to have been obvious that the Springboks had to avoid that at all costs. However, they not only gave him the ball, they even went to almost endless pains to remove the defence in front of him.

This was all a bit complicated, of course, and in the third test the Springbok selectors decided to make the whole thing much simpler. They decided that they could get along without the ball at all. At least that way they would not be giving it to Bennett. Edwards would. It was an extraordinary saga of incompetence.

Whether it was lack of practice in selection and match preparation, or whether it was simply because they were years out of date, the Springbok selectors never looked like coming to terms with the problems they faced, or even rationalising them. They lunged about in a series of desperate permutations which revealed with ever increasing clarity their lack of playing talent, their lack of forward organisation, and their lack of a viable coaching structure.

The lack of a coaching structure was the thing which hurt them most, because they did not have an established progression of checks on playing ability and on technique and they did not have a pool of technical analysts. Their complacency in this respect did irreparable damage.

The South African Board had ignored the warnings sounded by Avril Malan and Tommy Bedford in 1970. They had done nothing to appoint a coaching organiser and to set up a coaching structure which might have had some hope of bringing South African Rugby into the second half of the twentieth century and to close the gap which was being opened by the organisation of coaching in Britain. In 1972, Dr. Danie Craven said that South Africa was three years behind Wales. He qualified that later by saying that they were three years behind Wales in the appointment of a coaching organiser. It amounted to the same thing. By 1974, South Africa were five years behind.

Across the world in Australia, Ray Williams, the Welsh coaching organiser who has done so much for British Rugby, was touring the country with Dick Marks, who had just been appointed as Australia's first national coaching organiser. The Australian Rugby Union is not a wealthy organisation, but with the help of a tobacco company, it was able to make the appointment. South African Rugby made well over a million pounds out of the Lions' tour alone, yet as their 1974 season drew to an end, they still had not made a similar appointment.

Part of this inertia stemmed from the unique position of Dr. Craven himself. When Sir William Ramsay died, Dr. Craven became the biggest man in the world of Rugby but he always liked to maintain his contact with the dressing room. The smell of sweat and embrocation remained in his nostrils. He retained an identification with players which was unusual for an administrator of his generation. I think he always saw himself as South Africa's national coaching organiser. The trouble was that he did not have the time to do it.

No man could possibly do what Dr. Craven does in Rugby football and still have time to climb into a track suit and go up and down South Africa selecting regional coaches and instructing them in a common approach to the game. In any case, that is a young man's job, and in 1974, Dr. Craven was no longer a young man. He had turned 60.

What is more, Dr. Craven had set himself a far greater task. He saw that the international future of sport in South Africa depended on the introduction of multi-racial sport within the country, not only in Rugby football, but in every other sport as well. He concluded, quite rightly, that Rugby football could make this adjustment more easily than most other sports in South Africa and that he was one of the few sporting personalities in the whole country with sufficient stature to have any chance of persuading the South Africa government to make the change.

Now this is the sort of work which wins Nobel Prizes. A national Rugby coach can never work himself into that league. Certainly, no man could possibly do both.

This reluctance of Dr. Danie Craven and the South African Board to come to grips with the realities of what was happening in Rugby in Britain cost South Africa dear. When the British Lions played them in 1974, South Africa had lost all their traditional status as one of the world's great Rugby powers. They were no longer capable of dealing with a composite team drawn from the four home countries. They were a second class power, not even as strong as the individual countries which made up the British Lions' team.

And indeed, why should they have been? There has never been any reason why South Africa should be stronger than England, Scotland, Ireland or Wales individually, or even as strong as some of them. South Africa were only allowed to enjoy a false position for threequarters of a century because of the shortcomings of British Rugby. The wheel has come full circle. British Rugby is shaking the sleep out of its eyes, and South Africa are back where they were in 1896. It will be interesting to see whether this turns out to be a lasting state of affairs, and whether Lions teams go on winning just as inevitably and just as easily as they lost in the years between 1896 and 1968.

In terms of match results, the Springboks can count themselves lucky that they did not go to New Zealand in 1973. They would have been hard pressed to win more than three or four Saturday games on the whole of the tour. With backs as dangerous as Sid Going, Grant Batty, Bryan Williams and Joe Karam against them behind a typically competent New Zealand pack, they would have stood little chance of winning any of the test matches. Indeed, they could have ended up losing nearly as many matches as they won. Whether this situation will be allowed to continue remains to be seen. It may be that South Africa will react to the defeat by the British Lions in 1974 in the same way that British Rugby reacted to the 4-0 annihilation by the All Blacks in 1966. The playing of the game in Britain was rebuilt from the ground upwards as a result of that tour and although the administration has not kept pace with it, at least the playing attitudes which had been accepted for the previous seventy years were thrown overboard.

South Africa should remember that only one of their players in 1974 could have got into the British Lions team, and even that was by no means certain. He was J. G. Williams in the second row. What is more, Williams was the only player in South Africa in 1974 who might have got into *any* of the teams of England, Scotland, Ireland and Wales. South Africa had fallen that low.

This in itself helped to establish a sense of proportion about what the Lions had achieved. To borrow Tommy Bedford's analogy, they were playing the blind school.

When Alun Thomas called the 1974 Lions, 'The greatest Lions team in history', it is as well to remember that he did not have the pleasure of touring New Zealand in 1971 and hearing the clash of the steel. If he had he would have seen that playing against Colin Meads and Sid Going was a rather different proposition from playing against Johan de Bruyn and Gerrie Sonnekus.

APPENDICES

Appendix 1 Tour Results

MATCH 1

W. Transvaal 13 pts., British Lions 59
Played at Potchefstroom on Wednesday, May 15, 1974

SCORERS: W. TRANSVAAL
Penalty goal: de Bruyn.
Tries: Stoffberg, Schaap.
Conversion: de Bruyn.

BRITISH LIONS
Tries: Edwards (2), David (2), Brown, Steele, Rees, Moloney, Ripley.
Conversions: Bennett (7).
Penalty goals: Bennett (3).

W. Transvaal:

W. de Bruyn; J. van der Merwe, P. Roodt, T. van der Berg, I. Schip; C. Taylor, M. Benade; S. Raath, P. de Wet, J. Burger, J. Tromp, P. Brand, R. Owen (*capt.*), J. Stoffberg, T. Jacobs.

British Lions:

J. P. R. Williams; W. C. C. Steele, I. R. McGeechan, R. T. E. Bergiers, C. F. W. Rees; P. Bennett, J. J. Moloney; J. McLauchlan, R. W. Windsor, I. Carmichael, W. J. McBride (*capt.*), G. L. Brown, T. David, A. Neary, A. G. Ripley.
Substitutes: G. O. Edwards for Moloney, F. Cotton for Carmichael.
Referee: P. Robbertse (*E. Transvaal*).

MATCH 2

South-West Africa 16 pts., British Lions 23
Played at Windhoek on Saturday, May 18, 1974

SCORERS: SOUTH-WEST AFRICA
Tries: Ellis, Prinsloo.
Conversion: Karg.
Penalty goals: Karg (2).

BRITISH LIONS
Tries: Milliken, Edwards, Rees.
Conversion: Irvine.
Penalty goals: Irvine (2), Old.

South-West Africa:

J. Smuts; M. Smith, K. Germishuys, B. Meyer, W. Prinsloo; D. Karg, T. van Zyl; H. Coetzee, P. van de Merwe, B. de Jong, J. Coetzee, T. van Rensburg, J. Ellis (*capt*), H. Schroder, G. Parker.

British Lions:

A. R. Irvine; C. F. W. Rees, G. W. Evans, R. A. Milliken, J. J. Williams; A. G. B. Old, G. O. Edwards (*capt.*); I. McLauchlan; K. W. Kennedy, F. E. Cotton, C. W. Ralston, R. M. Uttley, T. David, J. F. Slattery, T. M. Davies.
Referee: C. de Bruyn (*Transvaal*).

MATCH 3

Boland 6 pts., British Lions 33
Played at Wellington on Wednesday, May 23, 1974

SCORERS: BOLAND

Penalty goals: Thiart (2).

BRITISH LIONS
Tries: Milliken (2), Edwards, Grace, McBride.
Conversions: Old (2).
Penalty goals: Old (3).

Boland:

D. Visser; J. van der Merwe, D. Mostert, V. Odendaal, R. le Rous; J. Thiart, B. Wolmarans; N. Rossouw, H. Reynecke, D. van der Merwe, J. du Toit (*capt.*), M. Craven, D. de Plessis, D. Shroeder, U. de Jager.

British Lions:

J. P. R. Williams; T. O. Grace, I. R. McGeechan, R. A. Milliken, J. J. Williams; A. G. B. Old, G. O. Edwards; F. E. Cotton, R. W. Windsor, A. B. Carmichael, W. J. McBride (*capt.*), G. L. Brown, T. P. David, A. Neary, A. G. Ripley.

Substitute: R. M. Uttley for David.

Referee: G. Bezuidenhout (*Transvaal*).

MATCH 4

Eastern Province 14 pts., British Lions 28
Played at Port Elizabeth on Saturday, May 26, 1974

SCORERS: EASTERN PROVINCE

Tries: Erasmus, Marais, Campher.
Conversion: Erasmus.

BRITISH LIONS

Tries: Davies (2), Steele.
Conversions: Bennett (2).
Penalty goals: Bennett (4).

Eastern Province:

H. van Vuuren; C. Fourie, G. Cowley, D. Campher, F. Meyer; K. Erasmus, F. de Villiers; R. Parker, B. de Coning, H. Marais (*capt.*), T. van der Westhuizen, H. Olwage, K. van Eyck, G. Barnard, P. Clarke.

British Lions:

A. R. Irvine; W. C. C. Steele, R. T. E. Bergiers, G. W. Evans, C. F. W. Rees; P. Bennett, G. O. Edwards (*capt.*); J. McLauchlan, R. W. Windsor, M. A. Burton, G. L. Brown, R. M. Uttley, J. F. Slattery, S. A. McKinney, T. M. Davies.
Referee: F. van der Vyver (*N. Transvaal*).

MATCH 5

South West Districts 0 pts., British Lions 97

Played at Mossel Bay on Wednesday, May 29, 1974

SCORERS: BRITISH LIONS

Tries: J. J. Williams (6), Evans (3), J. P. R. Williams (2), Davies, Grace, Moloney, Slattery, Old.
Conversions: Old (15).
Penalty goal: Old.

South West Districts:

D. Pienaar; A. du Toit, S. de Lange, J. Botes, A. van Tonder; M. van der Westhuizen, J. Taljaart; L. Swart (*capt.*), J. Blom, J. Gerber, D. du Toit, S. van der Merwe, J. le Grange, H. du Toit, S. Jonker.

British Lions:

A. R. Irvine; T. O. Grace, G. W. Evans, R. A. Milliken, J. J. Williams; A. G. B. Old, J. J. Moloney; M. A. Burton, K. W. Kennedy, F. E. Cotton, W. J. McBride (*capt.*), C. W. Ralston, S. A. McKinney, J. F. Slattery, T. M. Davies.
Substitute: J. P. R. Williams for Grace.
Referee: Max Baise (*Cape Town*).

MATCH 6

Western Province 8 pts., British Lions 17
Played at Cape Town on Saturday, June 1, 1974

SCORERS: WESTERN PROVINCE
Tries: Read (2)
BRITISH LIONS;
Tries: Brown, Rees.
Penalty goals: Bennett (3).

Western Province:

J. Brink; A. Read, J. Oosthuizen, P. Whipp, C. Pope; D. Snyman, R. McCallum; R. Bryant, R. Cockrell, C. Claxton, K. Immelman, P. du Plessis, J. Coetzee, M. du Plessis (*capt.*), D. McDonald.

British Lions:

J. P. R. Williams; C. F. W. Rees, I. R. McGeechan, R. T. E. Bergiers, W. C. C. Steele; P. Bennett, G. O. Edwards; J. McLauchlan, R. W. Windsor, A. B. Carmichael, W. J. McBride (*capt.*), G. L. Brown, A Neary, S. A. McKinney, A. G. Ripley.
Referee: I. Gourlay (*Natal*).

MATCH 7

Proteas 6 pts., British Lions 37
Played at Cape Town on Tuesday, June 4, 1974

SCORERS: PROTEAS
Penalty goal: Tobias.
Dropped goal: Tobias.
BRITISH LIONS
Tries: Brown, Slattery, Milliken, Bergiers, J. J. Williams.
Conversion: Irvine.
Penalty goals: Irvine (3), Old (2).

Proteas:

E. Frans; E. Wildermans, C. Cupido, H. Shields, J. Noble; E. Tobias, A. Lategan; T. Shields, C. Davids, D. Dyers (*capt.*), T. Petersen, J. Smith, J. J. Meyer, R. Mason, J. Juries.

British Lions:

A. R. Irvine; T. O. Grace, G. W. Evans, R. A. Milliken, J. J. Williams; A. G. B. Old, J. J. Moloney; M. J. Burton, K. W. Kennedy, F. E. Cotton, G. L. Brown, C. W. Ralston, R. M. Uttley, J. F. Slattery (*capt.*), T. M. Davies.
Substitute: R. T. E. Bergiers for Old.
Referee: D. Katzenellenbogen (*Western Province*).

MATCH 8

South Africa 3 pts., British Lions 12
Played at Cape Town on Saturday, June 8, 1974

SCORERS: SOUTH AFRICA
Dropped goal: Snyman.
BRITISH LIONS
Penalty goals: Bennett (3).
Dropped goal: Edwards.

South Africa:

I. D. McCallum; G. H. Muller, P. J. M. Whipp, J. J. Oosthuizen, C. F. Pope; D. S. L. Snyman, R. J. McCallum; J. T. Sauermann, J. E. B. van Wyk, J. F. K. Marais (*capt.*), K. B. H. de Klerk, J. G. Williams, J. H. Ellis, J. H. H. Coetzee, M. du Plessis.

British Lions:

J. P. R. Williams; W. C. C. Steele, I. R. McGeechan, R. A. Milliken, J. J. Williams; P. Bennett, G. O. Edwards; F. E. Cotton, R. W. Windsor, J. McLauchlan, W. J. McBride (*capt.*), G. L. Brown, R. M. Uttley, J. F. Slattery, T. M. Davies.
Referee: Max Baise (*Cape Town*).

MATCH 9

Southern Universities 4 pts., British Lions 26
Played at Cape Town on Tuesday, June 11, 1974

SCORER: S. UNIVERSITIES
Try: McDonald.

BRITISH LIONS
Tries: Brown, Bergiers, Uttley, Kennedy.
Conversions: Irvine (2).
Penalty goals: Irvine (2).

Southern Universities:

J. Brink; A. Read, P. J. M. Whipp, P. Goosen, L. Oosthuizen; D. S. L. Snyman, C. Wait; R. Bryant, P. Ingwersen, D. Claxton, F. Burger, H. Muller, M. du Plessis (*capt.*), D. McDonald, J. H. H. Coetzee.

British Lions:

A. R. Irvine; T. O. Grace, R. T. E. Bergiers, G. W. Evans, C. F. W. Rees; P. Bennett, J. J. Moloney; A. B. Carmichael, K. W. Kennedy, J. McLauchlan (*capt.*), G. L. Brown, C. W. Ralston, T. P. David, A. Neary, R. M. Uttley.
Referee: Dr. J. de J. Moolman (*Eastern Province*).

MATCH 10

Transvaal 15 pts., British Lions 23

Played at Johannesburg on Saturday, June 15, 1974

SCORERS: TRANSVAAL

Penalty goals: Bosch (3).
Dropped goals: Bosch (2).

BRITISH LIONS

Tries: J. P. R. Williams, Milliken, Neary.
Conversion: Bennett.
Penalty goals: Bennett (3).

Transvaal:

J. Coetser; J. van Wyngaardt, T. Symons, P. Cronje, G. H. Muller; G. Bosch, P. Bayvel; T. Sauermann, D. Frederickson, J. Strauss, S. du Randt, K. de Klerk, C. Pypers, A. Oberholzer (*capt.*), J. Kritzinger.

British Lions:

J. P. R. Williams; T. O. Grace, R. A. Milliken, R. T. E. Bergiers, J. J. Williams; P. Bennett, J. J. Moloney; J. McLauchlan, R. W. Windsor, W. J. McBride (*capt.*), G. L. Brown, R. M. Uttley, A. Neary, A. G. Ripley.

Referee: P. Robbertse (*E. Transvaal*).

MATCH 11

Rhodesia 6 pts., British Lions 42

Played at Salisbury on Tuesday, June 18, 1974

SCORERS: RHODESIA

Penalty goals: Robertson (2).

BRITISH LIONS

Tries: Grace (2), Irvine, Edwards, Slattery, Steele.
Conversions: Irvine (3).
Penalty goals: Irvine (3).
Dropped goal: Irvine.

Rhodesia:

I. Robertson; E. Barrett, P. Semple, L. Lloyd-Evans, J. Harris; I. Lendrum, D. Christian (*capt.*); A. van Zyl, T. Chamney, R. Coleshaw, G. Hodgson, M. Jakobi, R. Woodman, P. Chalmers, B. Murphy.

British Lions:

A. R. Irvine; T. O. Grace, R. T. E. Bergiers, G. W. Evans, W. C. C. Steele; I. R. McGeechan, G. O. Edwards (*capt.*); A. B. Carmichael, K. W. Kennedy, F. E. Cotton, R. M. Uttley, C. W. Ralston, S. A. McKinney, J. F. Slattery, T. M. Davies.

Referee: S. Strydom (*Orange Free State*).

MATCH 12

South Africa 9 pts., British Lions 28

Played at Pretoria on Saturday, June 22, 1974

SCORERS: SOUTH AFRICA

Penalty goals: Bosch (2).
Dropped goal: Bosch.

BRITISH LIONS

Tries: J. J. Williams (2), Brown, Bennett, Milliken.
Conversion: Bennett.
Penalty goal: Bennett.
Dropped goal: McGeechan.

South Africa:

I. D. McCallum; C. F. Pope, J. Snyman, P. J. M. Whipp, G. Germishuys; G. Bosch, P. Bayvel; N. Bezuidenhout, D. Frederickson, J. F. K. Marais (*capt.*), K. B. H. de Klerk, J. G. Williams, J. H. Ellis, M. du Plessis, D. McDonald.

Substitutes: D. Snyman for McCallum; L. Vogel for D. Snyman.

British Lions:

J. P. R. Williams; W. C. C. Steele, I. R. McGeechan, R. A. Milliken, J. J. Williams; P. Bennett, G. O. Edwards; J. McLauchlan, R. W. Windsor, F. E. Cotton, G. L. Brown, W. J. McBride (*capt.*), J. F. Slattery, R. M. Uttley, T. M. Davies.

Referee: C. de Bruyn (*Transvaal*).

MATCH 13

Quaggas 16 pts., British Lions 20

Played in Johannesburg on Thursday, June 27, 1974

SCORERS: QUAGGAS

Try: Stephenson.
Penalty goals: Kirsten (4).

BRITISH LIONS

Tries: Brown (2), Ripley.
Conversion: Irvine.
Penalty goals: Irvine (2).

Quaggas:

J. C. Coetser; K. Thoressen, G. Cowley, P. Cronje, A. Stephenson; P. Kirsten, P. Bayvel (*capt.*); D. van den Berg, G. Strydom, J. Strauss, S. U. Rand, S. Kapp, P. Fourie, C. Pypers, A. Kritzinger. *Substitute:* G. Schutte for Bayvel.

British Lions:

A. R. Irvine; C. F. W. Rees, R. T. E. Bergiers, C. M. H. Gibson, T. O. Grace; I. R. McGeechan, J. J. Moloney; F. E. Cotton (*capt.*), K. W. Kennedy, M. A. Burton, G. L. Brown, C. W. Ralston, T. P. David, A. Neary, A. G. Ripley.

Substitute: J. P. R. Williams for Rees.

Referee: I. Gourlay (*Natal*).

MATCH 14

Orange Free State 9 pts., British Lions 11

Played at Bloemfontein on Saturday, June 29, 1974

SCORERS: ORANGE FREE STATE
Dropped goal: Snyman.
Penalty goals: Snyman (2).

BRITISH LIONS
Tries: Davies, J. J. Williams.
Penalty goal: McKinney.

Orange Free State:

P. Strydom; J. S. Germishuys, J. Schlebusch, P. Du Toit, B. Swartz; J. C. P. Snyman, G. Sonnekus; R. Stander, A. Bestbier, M. le Roux, S. Botha, J. de Bruyn, J. Swart (*capt.*), H. Verster, C. Grobler.

British Lions:

J. P. R. Williams; W. C. C. Steele, R. A. Milliken, G. W. Evans, J. J. Williams; I. R. McGeechan, G. O. Edwards; A. B. Carmichael, R. W. Windsor, J. McLauchlan, W. J. McBride (*capt.*), C. W. Ralston, S. A. McKinney, J. F. Slattery, T. M. Davies.

Referee: G. Bezuidenhout (*Transvaal*).

MATCH 15

Griqualand West 16 pts., British Lions 69
Played at Kimberley on Wednesday, July 3, 1974

SCORERS: GRIQUALAND WEST
Tries: Wiese (2).
Conversion: Wiese.
Penalty goals: Van Eck, Wiese.

BRITISH LIONS
Tries: Grace (4), Steele (2), David, Evans, Slattery, Ripley, Kennedy, Moloney
Conversions: Irvine (8), Gibson.
Penalty goal: Irvine.

Griqualand West:

S. Smith; O. Fourie, J. van Der Walt, J. Lategan, D. Wiese; J. van Eck, G. Schutte; J. Harrison, D. Slabbert, K. Mulder, J. Young, K. Esterhuizen, J. Lochner, K. Bester, van as Jordaan (*capt.*).

British Lions:

A. R. Irvine; T. O. Grace, G. W. Evans, R. A. Milliken, W. C. C. Steele; C. M. H. Gibson, J. J. Moloney; A. B. Carmichael, K. W. Kennedy, M. A. Burton, R. M. Uttley, C. W. Ralston, J. F. Slattery (*capt.*), T. P. David, A. G. Ripley.

Referee: Cas de Bruyn (*Transvaal*).

MATCH 16

Northern Transvaal 12 pts., British Lions 16
Played at Pretoria on Saturday, July 6, 1974

SCORERS: NORTHERN TRANSVAAL
Penalty goals: Luther (4).

BRITISH LIONS
Tries: Neary, Davies.
Conversion: Irvine.
Penalty goals: Irvine (2).

Northern Transvaal:

C. Luther; F. Aucamp, J. Knox, K. Kidson, H. Jacobs; V. Booyens, B. van Wyk; N. Bezuidenhout, P. van Wyk, H. Weber, J. G. Williams, J. L. van Heerden, T. Lourens, G. Eloff, C. Oosthuizen.

British Lions:

J. P. R. Williams; A. R. Irvine, C. M. H. Gibson, R. A. Milliken, J. J. Williams; I. R. McGeechan, G. O. Edwards; J. McLauchlan, R. W. Windsor, F. E. Cotton, W. J. McBride (*capt.*), G. L. Brown, R. M. Uttley, A. Neary, T. M. Davies.

Referee: P. Robbertse (*E. Transvaal*).

MATCH 17

South Africa Leopards 10 pts., British Lions 56

Played at East London on Tuesday, July 9, 1974

SCORERS: S.A. LEOPARDS
Try: Mgweba.
Penalty goals: Mbiko (2).

BRITISH LIONS
Tries: Grace (3), Gibson (2), David, Morley, Irvine, Ripley, Edwards.
Conversions: Irvine (5).
Penalty goals: Irvine (2).

S.A. Leopards:

V. Mnqatu; T. Tsotsobe, B. Mnyazi, M. Matomela, C. Ngweba; P. Swartz, N. Mbiko; M. Maqosha, T. Magxala, B. Sonjani, L. Ntshongwana, S. Ttakayi, P. Matyeshana, M. Cushe, V. Makani.

British Lions:

A. R. Irvine; T. O. Grace, C. M. H. Gibson, I. R. McGeechan, A. J. Morley; P. Bennett, G. O. Edwards; A. B. Carmichael, K. W. Kennedy, M. A. Burton, W. J. McBride (*capt.*), C. W. Ralston, S. A. McKinney, T. P. David, A. G. Ripley.

Substitute: R. M. Uttley for Ralston.

Referee: S. Strydom (*Orange Free State*).

MATCH 18

South Africa 9 pts., British Lions 26

Played at Port Elizabeth on Saturday, July 13, 1974

SCORERS: SOUTH AFRICA
Penalty goals: Snyman (3).

BRITISH LIONS
Tries: Brown, J. J. Williams (2).
Conversion: Irvine.
Dropped goals: Bennett (2).
Penalty goals: Irvine (2).

South Africa:

O. A. Roux; C. F. Pope, J. J. Schlebusch, P. A. Cronje, G. H. Muller; J. C. P. Snyman, G. Sonnekus; N. S. E. Bezuidenhout, J. F. B. van Wyk, J. F. K. Marais (*capt.*), J. L. van Heerden, J. de Bruyn, J. H. Ellis, T. T. Fourie, J. L. Kritzinger.

Substitute: K. B. H. de Klerk for van Heerden.

British Lions:

J. P. R. Williams; A. R. Irvine, I. R. McGeechan, R. A. Milliken, J. J. Williams; P. Bennett, G. O. Edwards; J. McLauchlan, R. W. Windsor, F. E. Cotton, W. J. McBride (*capt.*), G. L. Brown, R. M. Uttley, J. F. Slattery, T. M. Davies.

Referee: Cas de Bruyn (*Transvaal*).

MATCH 19

Border 6 pts., British Lions 26

Played at East London on Wednesday, July 17, 1974

SCORERS: BORDER

Penalty goal: Steenekamp.
Dropped goal: Steenekamp.

BRITISH LIONS

Tries: Steele (2), Edwards.
Conversion: Irvine.
Penalty goals: Irvine (4).

Border:

P. Venter; T. Kotze, N. Harper, E. van der Linde, A. Stephenson; J. Steenekamp, C. Gendell; J. Vos, W. Hattingh, P. Schutte, S. Wood, G. Barter, K. Watt (*capt.*), D. Neal-May, G. Wilson.

British Lions:

A. R. Irvine; T. O. Grace, C. M. H. Gibson, R. T. E. Bergiers, W. C. C. Steele; I. R. McGeechan, G. O. Edwards (*capt.*); A. B. Carmichael, K. W. Kennedy, M. A. Burton, R. M. Uttley, C. W. Ralston, T. P. David, S. A. McKinney, A. G. Ripley.

Substitute: J. P. R. Williams for Steele.

Referee: G. Bezuidenhout (*Transvaal*).

MATCH 20

Natal 6 pts., British Lions 34

Played at Durban on Saturday, July 20, 1974

SCORERS: NATAL

Penalty goals: Hannaford (2).

BRITISH LIONS

Tries: Irvine (2), Davies, Slattery.
Conversions: Bennett (3).
Penalty goals: Bennett (4).

Natal:

M. R. Swanby; R. J. Pitcher, R. I. Ferguson, P. de Lange, A. E. van der Watt; I. Healey, S. A. Holmes; T. G. Basson, J. W. Trollope, D. S. van den Berg, J. A. Kapp, J. de Kock, M. McKenzie, H. G. Norton, T. P. Bedford (*capt.*).

Substitutes: K. Hannaford for van der Watt; E. Brocklehurst for Kapp.

British Lions:

J. P. R. Williams; J. J. Williams, C. M. H. Gibson, R. A. Milliken, A. J. Morley; P. Bennett, G. O. Edwards; J. McLauchlan, R. W. Windsor, F. E. Cotton, W. J. McBride (*capt.*), C. W. Ralston, J. F. Slattery, A. Neary, T. M. Davies.

Substitute: A. R. Irvine for Morley.

Referee: P. Robbertse (*E. Transvaal*).

MATCH 21

Eastern Transvaal 10 pts., British Lions 33

Played at Springs on Tuesday, July 23, 1974

SCORERS: E. TRANSVAAL

Try: Fourie.
Penalty goals: Salt (2).

BRITISH LIONS

Tries: Grace (2), David, Ripley, McGeechan.
Conversions: Irvine (2).
Penalty goals: Irvine (3).

Eastern Transvaal:

D. van Rensburg; G. Salt, H. Coetzer, W. Murray, J. Els; B. Deckersen, L. Petersen; P. Bierman, R. McKechnie, L. Stander, N. McIntyre, C. Holtzhausen (*capt.*), K. Fourie, B. Stander, B. Wilkinson.

Substitute: P. Junker for Els.

British Lions:

J. P. R. Williams (*capt.*); A. R. Irvine, R. T. E. Bergiers, I. R. McGeechan, T. O. Grace; C. M. H. Gibson, J. J. Moloney; A. B. Carmichael, K. W. Kennedy, M. A. Burton, C. W. Ralston, R. M. Uttley, T. P. David, S. A. McKinney, A. G. Ripley.

Referee: S. Strydom (*Orange Free State*).

MATCH 22

South Africa 13 pts., British Lions 13

Played at Johannesburg on Saturday, July 27, 1974

SCORERS: SOUTH AFRICA

Try: Cronje.
Penalty goals: Snyman (3).

BRITISH LIONS

Tries: Irvine, Uttley.
Conversion: Bennett.
Penalty goal: Irvine.

South Africa:

O. A. Roux; C. F. Pope, J. J. Schlebusch, P. A. Cronje, G. H. Muller; J. C. P. Snyman, P. C. R. Bayvel; N. S. E. Bezuidenhout, J. F. B. van Wyk, J. F. K. Marais (*capt.*), J. L. van Heerden, J. G. Williams, J. L. Kritzinger, J. H. Ellis, C. J. Grobler.
Substitute: R. Stander for Bezuidenhout.

British Lions:

J. P. R. Williams; A. R. Irvine, R. A. Milliken, I. R. McGeechan, J. J. Williams; P. Bennett, G. O. Edwards; J. McLauchlan, R. W. Windsor, F. E. Cotton, W. J. McBride (*capt.*), C. W. Ralston, R. M. Uttley, J. F. Slattery, T. M. Davies.
Referee: M. Baise (*Cape Town*).

Appendix 2

	Born	*Height ft.*	*ins.*	*Weight st.*	*lb.*	*Club*	*Caps*
MANAGER—							
Alun Gruffydd Thomas	Aged 48					Swansea, Cardiff, Llanelli	13
ASSISTANT MANAGER—							
Sydney Millar	23.5.34					Ballymena	37
CAPTAIN—							
William John McBride	6.6.40	6	3	16	12	Ballymena	57
Phillip Bennett	24.10.48	5	7	11	4	Llanelli	15
Roy Thomas Edmond Bergiers	11.11.50	6	1	13	10	Llanelli	10
Gordon Lamont Brown	1.11.47	6	5	16	10	West of Scotland	21
Michael Alan Burton	18.12.45	6	2	16	4	Gloucester	7
Alexander Bennett Carmichael	2.2.44	6	2	16	3	West of Scotland	35
Frances Edward Cotton	3.1.48	6	2	16	7	Coventry	11
Thomas Patrick David	2.4.48	6	0	15	2	Llanelli	2
Thomas Mervyn Davies	9.12.46	6	4½	14	12	Swansea	29
Gareth Owen Edwards	12.7.47	5	8	12	9	Cardiff	36
Geoffrey William Evans	10.12.50	5	10	13	0	Coventry	9
Cameron Michael Henderson Gibson	3.12.42	5	11	12	10	North of Ireland	47

Thomas Oliver Grace	24.10.48	6	2	13	0	St. Mary's College, Dublin	8
Andrew Robertson Irvine	16.9.51	5	10	12	4	Heriot's F.P.	10
Kenneth William Kennedy	10.5.42	5	11½	13	4	London Irish	41
Ian Robert McGeechan	30.10.46	5	9	11	8	Headingley	10
Stewart Alexander McKinney	20.11.46	6	0	15	0	Dungannon	8
John McLauchlan	14.4.42	5	9	14	2	Jordanhill	22
Richard Alexander Milliken	2.9.50	5	11	13	7	Bangor	8
John Joseph Moloney	27.8.49	5	10	11	5	St. Mary's College, Dublin	12
Alan John Morley	25.6.50	5	10	13	2	Bristol	4
Anthony Neary	25.11.48	6	1	14	6	Broughton Park	22
Alan Gerald Bernard Old	23.9.45	5	11	11	10	Leicester	11
Christopher Wayne Ralston	25.5.44	6	6	16	7	Richmond	18
Clive Frederick William Rees	6.10.51	5	9	11	9	London Welsh	1
Andrew George Ripley	1.12.47	6	5	15	10	Rosslyn Park	16
John Fergus Slattery	12.2.49	6	1	14	0	Blackrock College	21
William Charles Common Steele	18.4.47	5	11	11	10	Bedford	14
Roger Miles Uttley	11.9.49	6	4½	15	7	Gosforth	8
Robert William Windsor	31.1.48	5	9½	14	10	Pontypool	5
John James Williams	1.4.48	5	9½	11	0	Llanelli	6
John Peter Rhys Williams	2.3.49	6	1	14	0	London Welsh	27

Appendix 3

	APPEARANCES			POINTS SCORED			
	Tests	*Provincial*	*Tries*	*Conversions*	*Penalty Goals*	*Dropped Goals*	*Total*
Irvine	2	13(1s)	5	26	27	1	156
Bennett	4	7	1	14	21	2	101
Old	0	4	1	17	7	—	59
Grace	0	11	13	—	—	—	52
Williams, J. J.	4	8	12	—	—	—	48
Brown	3	9	8	—	—	—	32
Edwards	4	11(1s)	7	—	—	1	31
Steele	2	7	7	—	—	—	28
Milliken	4	9	6	—	—	—	24
Slattery	4	8	6	—	—	—	24
David	0	9	5	—	—	—	20
Davies	4	7	5	—	—	—	20
Ripley	0	10	5	—	—	—	20
Evans	0	8	4	—	—	—	16
Moloney	0	8	3	—	—	—	12
Rees	0	6	3	—	—	—	12
Williams, J. P. R.	4	11(3s)	3	—	—	—	12
Gibson	0	7	2	1	—	—	10
Bergiers	0	10(1s)	2	—	—	—	8
Kennedy	0	9	2	—	—	—	8
Neary	0	8	2	—	—	—	8
Uttley	4	12(2s)	2	—	—	—	8
McGeechan	4	10	1	—	—	1	7
McBride	4	9	1	—	—	—	4
Morley	0	2	1	—	—	—	4
McKinney	0	8	—	—	1	—	3
Burton	0	8	—	—	—	—	—
Carmichael	0	10	—	—	—	—	—
Cotton	4	10(1s)	—	—	—	—	—
McLauchlan	4	9	—	—	—	—	—
Ralston	1	12	—	—	—	—	—
Windsor	4	9	—	—	—	—	—

Figures in brackets followed by an "s" indicates the times the player appeared as a substitute in the total of matches.
Played 22, won 21, drew 1. Points for 729, against 207.